Port Pricing and Investment Policy for Developing Countries

A World Bank Research Publication

Port Pricing
and Investment Policy
for Developing Countries

Esra Bennathan and A. A. Walters

Published for the World Bank
Oxford University Press

Oxford University Press

NEW YORK OXFORD LONDON GLASGOW
TORONTO MELBOURNE WELLINGTON HONG KONG
TOKYO KUALA LUMPUR SINGAPORE JAKARTA
DELHI BOMBAY CALCUTTA MADRAS KARACHI
NAIROBI DAR ES SALAAM CAPE TOWN

Library of Congress Cataloging in Publication Data
Bennathan, Esra.
Port pricing and investment policy for developing countries.
Bibliography: p. 220
Includes index.
1. Harbors—Port charges. 2. Underdeveloped areas—
Harbors—Finance. 3. Underdeveloped areas—Investments,
Foreign. I. Walters, A. A., joint author. II. Title.
HE951.B46   387.1   78-26143
ISBN 0-19-520092-6
ISBN 0-19-520093-4 pbk.

Contents

Figures

Tables

Preface

SINCE WORLD WAR II, international trade has expanded at rates of growth never before achieved. The reduction in the relative cost of transport and particularly of ocean shipping has had much to do with this progress. During the past two decades there have been dramatic changes in the technology of shipping and in the associated technologies of ports. Substantial capital expenditure on vessels has been accompanied by large investments in ports. Unlike ocean shipping, the ports of developing countries are usually owned by governments; thus the cost of these large investments is part of government development programs. The surpluses or deficits of port authorities become part of the government's budget, and the financial health of a port is a matter for general concern.

The main instrument by which port authorities can cover their costs—or indeed earn a surplus—is the system of port tariffs. But these prices for port services are not merely instruments for ensuring balanced accounts; the port tariffs have important effects in encouraging or discouraging the use of port services: the occupation of quays and cranes and loading of warehouses and godowns. Variations in port charges can considerably affect the efficiency with which the port is used. And better use of existing assets is a desirable preliminary to any expansion of assets. Similarly, for new ports it is best to ensure that they are used as efficiently as possible.

In its operations in developing countries, the World Bank has encountered a large variety of pricing practices and widely diverse effects on efficient port operation. In the belief that there must be a systematic set of principles that would much improve port pricing, professors Esra Bennathan (of the University of Bristol) and A. A. Walters (then of the London School of Economics) were asked to undertake this study.

The main conclusion of their sometimes involved discussion is that the main basis of port tariffs should be marginal cost. But within this general conclusion, certain rather surprising and unorthodox recommendations emerge, such as the proposal that ports should charge congestion levies. I believe that these investigations represent a substantial contribution to knowledge and have produced ideas that that could have wide practical utility. Thus, the World Bank is making the study available for general circulation. The World Bank is not necessarily endorsing the view of the authors, however, nor is it recommending that such principles be invariably used in port pricing and planning. (Indeed, the authors themselves emphasize that their principles have not been tested adequately in the hard school of experience.) And whatever the reader's final judgment on the issues raised and explored in the following pages, I am sure that this volume will be considered a stimulating contribution to the continuing debate on pricing and investment policy.

CHRISTOPHER R. WILLOUGHBY
Director, Transportation Department
The World Bank

May 1979

Acknowledgments

THE AUTHORS HAVE BENEFITED from criticism and discussion with many colleagues. They would especially like to thank Edward V. K. Jaycox, Anthony A. Churchill, Clell G. Harral, A. J. Carmichael, Miguel E. Martinez, Benjamin B. King, Jenifer A. Wishart, and the many other members of the staff of the World Bank who gave much time and thought to the ideas advanced in this study. Trevor D. Heaver and C. Ruppenthal reviewed some of the ideas at an early stage of the work. Stephen C. Littlechild and B. J. Abrahamsson provided many detailed comments on the manuscript, which have assisted the authors in improving the text. V. Kanapathy and Raja Lope in Kuala Lumpur and Donald Blake and Danko Koludrovic of the United Nations Economic and Social Commission for Asia and the Pacific in Bangkok made most useful contributions to the research program. The research assistants, S. R. Hill, Georgina Brookfield, and Angela Edge, provided untiring support.

In addition, the authors have received the cooperation and assistance of many port authorities in Bangladesh, Seattle (United States), Bristol (England), Vancouver (Canada), India, Malaysia, Philippines, Singapore, and Thailand. Without such assistance, it would have been impossible to complete this study.

Virginia deHaven Orr edited the final manuscript. Brian J. Svikhart directed design and production of the book, Harry Einhorn read and corrected proofs, the Graphics Unit of the World Bank's Art and Design Section prepared the charts, and Joan Culver indexed the text.

Port Pricing
and Investment Policy
for Developing Countries

Introduction and Summary

THE ORIGINS OF THIS STUDY lie in the widespread dissatisfaction with the economics of ports in developing countries. In our first forays into the field, we tried to survey the existing principles of port economics in the hope that we could elucidate the foundations for port investment and tariff policies. We failed, however, to find any coherent and widely accepted doctrine which provided a basis for policy.

Yet there is broadly the same motivation for all policies on ports— the promotion of the national interest. But such a general and amorphous idea has not prevented the development of widely differing principles which underlie the pricing policies and investment programs of ports. Probably the two best-known principles may be conveniently, if inaccurately, called the (continental) European and the Anglo-Saxon doctrines. The European doctrine views the port as part of the social infrastructure of a whole region. The value of a port should be assessed not in the accounts of the facilities but in terms of the progress of industry and trade in the hinterland. Thus, the European doctrine holds that it is certainly not necessary that the port break even, or perhaps earn a profit, either on existing or proposed investment; justification is pursued and usually found well outside the perimeter of the port. The Anglo-Saxon view is that, notwithstanding the benefits to the hinterland, the port, like the tub, should stand on its own bottom. At least it should not incur a loss and at best should earn a reasonable profit.[1] So the main rationale for investment proposals and tariff policy is that they make money.

Whether the European or Anglo-Saxon view is embraced, the policymaker has still little to guide his hand. The national interests which are supposed to motivate the European are elusive and nebulous. Nevertheless, most people would agree that the term somehow expresses the spirit which should guide port policy. Clearly it is necessary to develop and give meaning to the concept of national interests. So, in this study, we normally have defined national interests as the greatest possible benefits accruing to the nationals or residents of the country. To the developing countries this means that the benefits accruing to the foreign shipowners or suppliers should not be considered; only domestic effects matter. This will then give content, form, and substance to the development of pricing and investment policy.

Similarly, the Anglo-Saxon principle of balanced budgets provides little guidance on actual tariff policy. In practice, the gap has been filled by nostrums similar to those hallowed by use in railway freight tariffs. Perhaps the most famous of these is "charging what the traffic will bear" and its various adjuncts such as "pricing to promote traffic." These notions have a firm basis in theory and the valuable characteristic of many years of practical use and success. But it is not clear that they can be made to satisfy a national interest objective. Thus, there appears to be a real conflict between the European and Anglo-Saxon traditions.

But the confusion of principles and conflicts of policy are not the most important reasons for undertaking this study. More persuasive than these inadequacies is the fact that, throughout the developing countries, ports are often either the bottleneck or the white elephant of development programs. The contrast between the three-month queues at Lagos in 1975 and the gaunt underused container berths in many countries should suggest that, at least, all is not well. It would be arrogant and quite wrong to suppose that the only thing amiss with the ports of the world is their economic policies. Yet without the right economics, ports will be plagued by problems of long queues or empty berths. Worse still, benefits will leak away to foreign ship-

1. Over the years the labels European and Anglo-Saxon have been quite discredited by practice, but they are convenient and do reflect underlying attitudes and principles.

owners and traders. Economic analysis is by no means sufficient to solve these problems and plug the leak, but it is a necessary part of the solution.

The Shape of the Study

In the following chapters, we concentrate on one important aspect of port economics—the pricing or tariff policy—and we generally give short shrift to investment problems. The two are closely related, but we have pursued the issues of tariff policy largely because they apply generally to all countries, whereas investment problems are usually more specific and sometimes unique. Furthermore, it may be suggested that a sensible tariff policy is a prerequisite of an appropriate investment program. Thus, we indicate only the outline and general direction of investment plans that would result from our suggested principles of port pricing. The following sections summarize the findings of this study chapter by chapter.

Ports and ships

Since ports are the intermediaries between ships and domestic transport, they take on some of the technological and economic complexion of their customers. The size of ship and the time spent in port are important factors in determining the cost per ton of shipping, and the depth of the dredged channel and the speed of loading and discharging cargo are usually dominant elements in the cost of ports. These relations are at the heart of much shipping and port economics.

Several conclusions are drawn from this analysis, many of which are entirely consistent with common intuition. First, the optimum size of vessel increases with the (square root of the) distance of the voyage. Second, assuming that the port and shipowner fix charges on the basis of the cost of providing services, the port authority can have a dominant influence in securing least-cost shipping—and the greatest national benefit—by an appropriate tariff and investment policy. Port tariffs ought to reflect the relative cost of the services provided so that the appropriate ship technology is chosen. Third, contrary to intuition, it is more efficient to have one capacity-ton of a large ship idle and queueing in the roads than one capacity-ton of a small ship. This implies that an investment that reduces waiting time will tend relatively to benefit the trade carried in the smaller vessels. However, investments that raise the rate of cargo working tend to increase the size of the minimum-cost ship. The important conclusion is that, by its capital program, a port can affect not merely the cost of shipping services but also the competitive conditions they are supplied under.

On the other hand, the main exogenous determinants of the pricing or tariff policy of a port are the conditions of demand. Assuming that there is no competition between ports and that port and ship services are required in fixed proportions, the elasticity of demand for port services will be small—around 0.1 (absolute) is the appropriate order of magnitude.[2] If that were really the case, pricing policy would then be a matter of merely revenue collection. But it is not. There are many opportunities for substitution in the short run and many more in the long run, which increase the elasticity considerably. The fixed proportions assumption is a serious travesty of the facts. And in many cases, there is vigorous competition between one port and another. Thus, there are many advantages to be obtained from appropriate pricing and tariff policies: demand can be induced to shy away from those facilities that are crowded and to settle on those that are under-used.

Marginal cost

The basis of all port tariffs should be short-run marginal cost, which measures the resources used up by supplying a unit of port service. It is the appropriate basis for pricing even when the authorities have made mistakes with their investment policy or where the port has experienced large and unexpected changes in demand. But strictly setting price equal to marginal cost is best only in a perfectly competitive free economy or in an efficient socialist economy. In practice, the port is confronted with organized and largely foreign-owned shipping cartels; thus, there is no reason to suppose that fixing prices at marginal cost would be best for the country. It is at least possible to develop port pricing arrangements that take some, if not all, of the surplus away from the foreigners.

Marginal cost is also required for efficient management. Although there is often considerable and sometimes total ignorance about total cost, the authorities should use marginal cost to set prices (or the

2. Elasticity of demand is the percent change in the quantity demanded in response to a 1 percent charge in the price.

variable charge) so that the facilities are used efficiently. The port authorities probably know the assigned variable cost of providing the service; thus, the tariff should be checked to see that it at least covers this variable cost.

Economies of scale

One of the abiding disadvantages of marginal cost pricing is that the policy will result in a financial deficit where there are economies of scale. For a given country with a specified distribution of resources, economies of scale in ports are likely; the larger the port, the lower the cost. But ultimately the cost of internal transport will ensure that diseconomies become dominant; where the population of a country is sparse and widely dispersed, domestic distribution cost particularly will constrain port size.

The existence of economies of scale in ports suggests that there is indeed substantial, albeit theoretical, support for the European doctrine of subsidized ports. But it is important to examine all the implications of such subsidies including the effects on efficiency and administration as well as on the distribution of resources. Taxes that must be raised to finance the subsidies are usually expensive to collect, involve substantial distortion of effort, and are often imposed on traded goods (in excise and import or export levies)—precisely the commodities whose trade is supposedly promoted by the port subsidy. Such subsidies will tend to politicize the issue of port tariffs, and interest groups will form to compete for and to bid up the subsidy. In particular port labor will be encouraged to exploit its bargaining power on the soft featherbed of a state handout. And there will be no budgetary check, whether weak or strong, to inhibit the growth of the port bureaucracy. The general conclusion is that, despite the theoretical case for subsidies, there are powerful practical arguments against them.

Congestion levies and surcharges

In many developing countries the high demand for very limited port services causes congestion. This suggests that there are good reasons to earn high profits in the ports by raising congestion charges. If the demand for a service is very high, relative to normal conditions, the price of that service should be increased so that users have the incentive to economize on the scarce service. Port authorities rarely, if ever, respond in this way. Normally, they keep prices low. Thus large queues of vessels form in the roads, and shipowners are quick to add their queuing cost to the freight rates. The domestic producer and consumer pay for the real cost caused by scarce port capacity and the fact that the port authority does not raise its tariffs.

The main issue is, however, a positive one: what would be the consequences of the port raising a congestion levy? And more germane still, would the residents of the country be better off than under the low port price and queuing regime? Generally the price of the overall shipping service (freight rates plus port charge) will rise above the value which would apply if the port did not charge a congestion levy. The increase in price, however, is likely to be considerably less then the congestion levy. If the demand for port services is inelastic, the port will increase its revenue—even when shipping is a monopolized service—at the expense of domestic traders. Congestion charges will give the authorities a source of finance to extend port facilities. And they may also increase the throughput of the port considerably if the congestion charges are levied only on those particular facilities (such as transit sheds) that are congested.

From this survey of congestion, it is concluded that there is a powerful case for the ports charging congestion levies. However, the case is based on our general understanding of economic forces and on a close study of the nature of the shipping business and its interaction with the domestic economy; we cannot point to the experience of any port which has introduced such charges. Until such crucial experiments have been made, the case for such charges cannot be substantiated.[3]

Port prices and the national interest

Although, as defined, congestion charges would add considerably to the revenue of a port, they are unlikely to generate the maximum profit that the port could earn. And it is worthwhile to consider the consequences of profit maximization, largely because there are several cases where the ports have overexpanded or where conventional

3. An interesting analogue is the congestion levies for urban areas. The case for such levies, argued in many studies (for example, A. A. Walters, *Economics of Road User Charges*, World Bank Staff Occasional Papers, no. 5 (Baltimore: Johns Hopkins Press, 1968)), remained speculative until the area licensing scheme was introduced in Singapore in 1974. Then, although many mistakes were made, the undoubted success of that scheme showed that the theoretical and empirical studies had predictive relevance. The same may be true of port congestion charges.

facilities are in excess supply and where the port authority, following an Anglo-Saxon policy, might resort to monopolistic restriction to cover its financial obligations. To explore the implications, a simple model of a hinterland to a monopolist port is used. Using profit-maximizing principles, the monopolist port authority would be induced to reduce traffic to a flow equal to four-ninths of its (marginal cost) potential. Although these results are derived from an idealized model, they do suggest that the consequences of an unfettered monopolist port would not be felicitous.

Therefore, the more difficult criterion is pursued—national benefit. Assuming, for simplicity, that all ships are owned by foreigners, prices and tariffs should be set so that the marginal gain to domestic traders and consumers is just equal to the marginal loss of the port. Although easy to state, this is very difficult to put into operation. The main problem is to predict the relation between port tariff and freight rate.

Much depends, of course, on competitive conditions in the shipping industry that supplies the services. As a general rule, it will always be advantageous for a country to be faced by many competitive shipowners rather than by one cartel or monopoly. In the extreme case of a bilateral monopoly where the shipping company pursues complex interaction strategies, there are no rules for the port to follow—except, of course, to abjure policies that get it into such a situation. With a passive shipping monopoly, however, the extent to which a given increase in the port tariff is passed on to the trader depends critically not merely on the elasticity of demand but on the change in the elasticity as the quantity of throughput increases. Both technological and economic conditions suggest powerful reasons for supposing that the elasticity of demand for shipping services declines as the quantity of throughput increases. Intuitively, it is unwise to subsidize port operations if the gain in traffic becomes rapidly smaller as the subsidy grows. In the case of competitive shipping, therefore, the port charge that will maximize the national benefit will exceed the marginal cost of the port. Only if the elasticity of demand is constant (an unlikely case) is the optimum port tariff equal to the marginal port cost.

Strategic pricing

To unravel some of the knotty issues of port pricing it is essential to assume that the port cannot affect the competitive environment of the shipping firms that use its facilities. But such an assumption is often inappropriate. By their investment and pricing arrangements, ports can have a significant effect on the competitive structure of their shipping services. At first sight, the casual evidence of shipping freight rates seems to discredit such a proposition. Certainly for liner conferences it appears that considerable variations in port charges or conditions do not appear in differences in freight rates. This is because conference rates do not reflect the niceties of changes in cost but are determined mainly by the pressure of the competitive shipping sector. The possibility of arranging port tariffs and investments so that they benefit competitive shipping and so bring pressure to bear on the monopoly power of the conference is one that might usefully be remembered in designing port policies; but again too much should not be expected. It is doubtful whether it is possible or, if feasible, whether it is desirable to attempt directly to use port pricing to offset geographical or commodity discrimination by conferences. However, there are good grounds for considering the development of ship charges or cargo levies and other forms of multipart pricing to encourage bulkers and tramps. Thus, port tariff policies may be used strategically for the benefit of nationals.

Competition among ports

Ports often are considered to be simple but formidable monopolies. For many ports in developing countries, this has been and sometimes still is a useful caricature. But increasingly, the monopoly prices which ports once enjoyed are being eroded. In part, this has been caused by the development of internal transport links that enable ports to compete for similar catchment areas that may straddle national boundaries. In recent years, the development of containerization has provided even more interport competition and has reversed the general decline in transshipment business. Main container terminals, which must be very large, will be able to serve efficiently a wide region, such as a region larger than Southeast Asia. Consequently, there is keen competition to be a main terminal and the entrepot of the rapidly expanding container business.

Naturally, the port will be tempted to discriminate in its tariffs against the captive domestic traffic and in favor of boxes transshipped through the main terminal on route to other feeder ports. In Singapore, there is a sharp discrimination between domestic and transshipment traffic. Using certain assumptions about marginal cost for conventional traffic, the implied elasticities of demand for a profit-maximizing port can be calculated. For container traffic, the elasticities are probably much higher. This discrimination in tariffs may enable the large container port to break even or perhaps to earn a profit and provides vigorous competition for shipowners' calls. But correspondingly, container consortia can play off one port against another. Ports that have sunk substantial funds in container facilities are not in a commanding position. In this event, the overbuilding of container facilities and discrimination against domestic shippers and in favor of transshipment traffic may result in subsidization of shipowners by the national exporters and importers and governments of developing countries.

Multipart tariffs

The pattern of port cost as well as strategic reasons suggest that port tariffs would be best developed as two-part or multipart systems of pricing. But there are many obstacles. Perhaps the main impediment is that, unlike electricity supply, ports do not always invest in specific pieces of plant associated exclusively with the supply of services to a particular shipowner. Since much of the business is casual, it is impossible to introduce multipart tariffs for all services. There always must be the option for a one-off call.

Nevertheless, there are many ways of introducing two-part tariffs. Lease-a-quay (LAQ) is perhaps the most obvious form. Although it is clearly efficient and profitable, because of the need for flexibility and for the avoidance of tie-in arrangements, it should be adopted only on a limited range of specialized services. Since services such as bulk carriage and container operation are likely to grow rapidly, however, the LAQ will have expanded applicability eventually. Another possible arrangement is an annual fee to enter (AFTE) the port. The most important purpose of this method of charging is to recover dredging cost in a port where there is little or no congestion. The AFTE should be set so that it encourages the large bulker and the non-conferenceer. Among the many variations of the AFTE is the quantity discount system. This would entail a reduced fee for each visit as the number of calls increases. Thus it would encourage greater efficiency if the price charged for the final visit could be brought nearer to the marginal cost of the ship call. There appears to be considerable scope for various forms of AFTE pricing in developing countries.

Perhaps the most compelling argument for two-part tariffs can be found in container services. Containerization is expanding rapidly in world trade. Yet in many developing countries there is existing or incipient excess capacity. It is also known that striking economies of scale are ubiquitous in container operation. A system whereby a rental charge should be levied for the use of the port by a container ship is suggested; and a low tariff, not much above marginal cost, should be exacted for handling a container. This will encourage containerization to be used instead of conventionally handled traffic, will increase the revenues of the port, and will use the vast sums of capital sunk in container quays more efficiently.

One of the abiding complaints of all tariffs is that they are too complicated. The plea is for simplicity and comprehension. One simple approach that has been used in rail charges is to levy the port tariff as a percentage of the freight charge. The administrative simplicity is not the only attraction of such a system. It would encourage greater frequency and flexible freight rates, and it would discriminate in favor of the short-sea routes where there is least ability to pay. The port charge would vary automatically with the oscillations in freight rates and with the general rate of inflation. There are, however, several side effects that are likely to be undesirable; these would have to be weighed and judged in each case. Generally, there is some considerable scope for the percent-of-freight charge, and it needs further practical exploration.

Port pricing in practice

Recommendations for the various forms of two-part tariffs do not imply that a speedy reorganization of port charges on a grand scale should be pursued. On the contrary, a slow but steady reform is best. To illustrate the state of existing tariffs and to show what might be done, tariffs in certain ports in South and Southeast Asia—Singapore, Kelang (Malaysia), Bangkok, and Chittagong (Bangladesh)—are discussed.

A most important issue in planning port tariffs is to find an appropriate base so that tariffs reflect relative cost. Present practices fix berth hire and channel dues according to the capacity (usually NRT) of the ship, or a berth is rented at a fee which does not vary with the size of the vessel as in Hong Kong and Chittagong. However, the appropriate base is the length of the ship; this measures the amount of quay that is occupied. But it is also important for a port to charge more for the more desirable and convenient berthspace; then the port will appropriate the money value of the benefit conferred by that advantageous location.

Designing charges that encourage a quick turnaround of vessels is particularly important for handling operations. This suggests that handling labor charges should be based not merely on the quantity of tonnage but also on the rate of throughput. Singapore has a dockage remission coefficient that operates successfully along these lines, and it could be applied in other ports.

The application of the principle of marginal cost pricing seems to be particularly appropriate in two cases, namely the charges for use of the dredged channel and for storage. Provided that there is no congestion, once the channel is dredged to any given depth, the passage of a vessel of any draft will impose only the small marginal cost of turbulence erosion. Yet in practice, dredging charges increase dramatically with the draft of the vessel. This penalizes the efficient large ship and inhibits large bulker competition with the conference ring. Although it is assumed generally that warehouse storage should be charged at cost, there is a wide divergence between charge and cost for transit sheds. And there are many cases where the inability to clear transit sheds has determined the throughput of the port. The case for marginal cost pricing is a strong one.

The need for ports to load port tariffs to raise revenue has led to various practices of discrimination with unintended side effects. Discrimination is also practiced in pursuit of wider economic objectives, perhaps the most important of which is to favor export against import cargo. To channel aid to exporters through port tariffs does not seem to be the ideal way to subsidize exports, and in practice such subsidies tend to be offset by commodity export taxes. The result is confounded and confused. In discriminating by commodity, the ports generally tend to reproduce the same differentials as those used by the conference and thus reflect the ability to pay. But containerization is eroding such differentials.

Port facilities that are not allocated by the pricing mechanism will be distributed among competing users by some administrative rule. Although some allocation by rule always will be efficient, there is considerable scope for extending the port price system. Priorities will then have to be paid for, and the port will receive the appropriate reward.

Concluding Comments

The purpose of this study is to elucidate and to criticize principles for guiding policy. The consequences of various forms of port pricing policies and their effects are evaluated. But, of course, the main weakness of this study is the fact that there are few examples where the methods of pricing discussed have been put even partially into operation. What would happen in practice can be inferred only indirectly. Unfortunately, there are no experimental results to provide the acid test of these propositions.

But policy cannot await the long process of scientific methodology. Decisions have to be made on existing evidence, whether fragile or robust. However, there are many aspects of port tariffs that cry out for reform and for which there is no need to seek further justification than that of simple reasoning and, often, common sense. Decisions on these can proceed apace. But many of these proposals do require much further thought and reflection before being inflicted on the practitioner. Many a ghost has been laid to rest, many specters also have been raised.

Chapter 1

Ports and Ships

THE RANGE OF ACTIVITIES in individual ports may differ greatly, but all ports have several activities in common. The basic activity consists of the ownership of land, quays, piers, and port surface. The port either maintains and controls these facilities itself or rents them out to other parties. Many ports are also conservancy authorities, responsible for maintaining and dredging the channel to the harbor and for the control and safety of traffic in those channels, including the provision and maintenance of navigational aids, pilotage, towage, and tugging. The port typically owns and operates or rents mechanical equipment such as cranes, forklifts, and trailers. It owns and operates transit sheds which form part of the standard general cargo berth and also open or sheltered storage areas beyond the sheds. It frequently owns warehouses that it either operates itself as warehouseman or rents to shippers; ports are thus often landlords on a large scale. Finally, most ports employ at least some of the labor required for moving cargo, but the degree of control over cargo operations forms one of the chief differences between ports.

Some ports, for example, those of Singapore or Port Kelang, employ directly all the labor required for moving cargo, whether on board (stevedores) or ashore (wharf labor). Elsewhere, for example, in Chittagong or Bangkok, stevedoring is carried out by licensed contractors, and private labor sometimes is employed for certain shore operations also. Labor in container freight stations may again be either privately employed or port labor. The widespread trend toward decasualization of port labor and the introduction of long-term wage contracts has meant that more and more ports have had to become the direct employers of all the labor normally working for them. In practice, it has also meant that port employment is being extended to all the labor working in the port's confines.

The port, however, may not be free to reduce its labor force at will. Its freedom to adapt its labor force to produce at minimum cost is often circumscribed by law, by contract, or by political conditions. In that case, labor has to be considered an item of fixed cost. Marginal cost of labor operations is zero until the force is employed fully on one shift, and only when overtime rates have to be paid will marginal cost become positive. But all this is merely a crude simplification of a situation which is complicated through specialization, demarcation rules, and union arrangement.

Port Activities

The services produced by these activities fall into three major categories:

Sea-related services: provision of access to the port by buoys and moorings, berths, pilots, and tugs and lighters.

Land-related services: cargo handling by port labor, port's cranes, other equipment and vehicles, and storage (in sheds or open).

Delivery-related services: handling (for example, to customs or consignee's vehicle), container freight station (stuffing/stripping), warehousing, and port's own transport.[1]

The list of services supplied in each category is far from exhaustive, but it indicates some of the main substitution possibilities that exist in ports. Some users demand only the services of one department, such as vessels calling for bunkers or for shelter. The different cargo systems—tankers, dry bulk transport, conventional break-bulk or unitized general cargo or container transport—each impose their own pattern on port use. For most of the users, however, demand for port services is joint, that is to say, most of them require a combination of berth space, tug towing, cargo handling, warehousing, cranage, and so forth. But the proportions that they require the services in are not

---

1. Port and shipping terms used throughout this volume are defined in the Glossary following Chapter 9.

fixed and vary considerably. This characteristic of the demand for port services has great importance for the effectiveness of port pricing and will be discussed later in this chapter.

Ship Size, Port Time, and Cost

In later chapters some of the effects that ports and ships exert on each other through the prices they charge and through variations in the shipowners' demand for port services and in the ports' supply are considered. In this section, the effect of port conditions, investments, and charges on the cost of shipping are analyzed in general terms with the aid of a simple model. Each of the services involved is assumed to be priced at long-run average (equal to marginal) cost. Thus it is assumed that there is perfect competition in the shipping industry and that the price for providing port services is set competitively. This competitive model is not meant to be a realistic representation of reality; in many respects it is not. But some sort of benchmark is needed if the phenomena and the data available are to be disentangled, and the competitive model provides the easiest categories to interpret.

Some choice is available in slanting the analysis; it can be worked either through the cost conditions of the shipowner or through the cost decisions of the port authority. Experience shows that the most interesting problems are those relating to the choice of ship technology, so the former approach has been chosen. The analysis concentrates solely on the cost that is borne by the shipowner and that is passed on to the shipper or customer as a consequence of different technologies and vessel sizes.

To simplify the analysis, also suppose that the ship is full and that the total cargo is loaded or discharged in one operation. Thus, the time that the ship spends in port during each ship call depends on the rate at which it can unload cargo. For the same technology, the daily tons moved for a ship of size C may be approximated as: $L + mC$, where L and m are constants. Thus, the time in port measured in days (T_p) is:

$$(1) \qquad T_p = C(L + mC)^{-1}.$$

The daily cost of operating a ship in port is:

$$(2) \qquad K_p = A + gC \qquad [g \geqq 0; A \geqq 0],$$

where A is the fixed cost and g the variable cost for each ton reflecting daily operating cost of the ship in port as well as the various payments in the port. A difficulty arises because certain costs of calling at ports, such as the cost of steaming into and out of a port, are not affected by the number of days spent in port. But there is a considerable indirect relation between the size of vessel and the cost of a call, which is reflected in the coefficient g. The analysis assumes that the call cost, which is independent of size and length of stay, is small enough to be neglected.

Port charges, as distinct from port costs, are included in both the A and g; again, the linear approximation is taken for simplicity.

The cost of a port call for each ship is then:

$$(3) \qquad T_p K_p = C(L + mC)^{-1}(A + gC).$$

The only other variable needed is the cost of operating a ship for a day at sea. Suppose this can be linearized as: $B + hC$, with B as the fixed cost and h as the variable cost for each ton. Also assume that speed is the same for all vessels so that the distance of the voyage is strictly proportional to the number of days for each voyage, D. The sea cost of a voyage is: $D(B + hC)$. Thus, the cost of a complete voyage, including two port calls, is:

$$(4) \qquad V = D(B + hC) + 2C(L + mC)^{-1}(A + gC).$$

Under competitive conditions, and even under monopoly conditions, if the monopolist is pursuing maximum profits, the technology chosen will be that which minimizes voyage cost per ton: that is, min V/C. Equation (4) is divided by C, differentiated with respect to C, equated to zero, and solved for the minimum-cost size of vessel:

$$(5) \quad C = mLDB \pm L\,[2(gL - mA)DB]^{1/2}$$
$$[2(gL - mA) - m^2DB]^{-1}.$$

Although this result seems rather complicated, several basic conclusions emerge. First, there is a basic tendency to a "square root law," such as appears in the simple models of inventories and other models of economies of scale. The result can be seen most starkly by supposing that $m = 0$ and that L is strictly positive, so that whatever the size of ship, it can unload only L tons a day. Then:

$$(6) \qquad C = \pm \sqrt{(DBL/2g)}$$

(only the positive root is relevant). The greater the distance D, the larger the vessel size.

Second, the critical role played by port cost and by the efficiency with which vessels can be loaded or discharged is shown in the general formula. The size of vessel varies according to the order $(gL - mA)^{-1/2}$. In words the bracketed term is:

$$
\begin{bmatrix} \text{Port} \\ \text{cost} \\ \text{for} \\ \text{each} \\ \text{ton} \end{bmatrix}
\begin{bmatrix} \text{Tons} \\ \text{unloaded} \\ \text{each day,} \\ \text{irrespective} \\ \text{of size} \end{bmatrix}
-
\begin{bmatrix} \text{Increase in} \\ \text{tons unloaded} \\ \text{each day for} \\ \text{additional} \\ \text{DWT of ship} \end{bmatrix}
\begin{bmatrix} \text{Fixed} \\ \text{port} \\ \text{cost} \end{bmatrix}
$$

In this term certain elements are controlled by the port directly; they are contained in ship's cost in port for each ton (which includes the port's charges for each ton) and in its fixed port costs. But certain others are clearly those over which the port authority has only an indirect effect, such as the tons unloaded each day irrespective of size and the fraction of cargo unloaded during an additional day in port. The port controls directly the prices that are levied for its services, but it controls only indirectly the choice of technology of the shipping companies. But, of course, L and m are determined by the shipping companies in association with the port conditions. It may be thought, however, that L is largely under the control of the port authority. The authority can choose the load-per-day (L) value by most of its investment decisions made either in the past or to be made in the future (including general facilities and cargo sheds). Assume that the port's control is greatest over g (which contains the bulk of port charges, including handling cost) and L (which is affected by the port's general efficiency, layout, and equipment). If that is so, the port influences the size of vessels and thus the extent to which its national shippers obtain the economies of shipping in large vessels.[2] One may envision a minimization procedure in which the shipping company chooses a technology, as embodied in L, m, A, g, B, and h, such that V/C is minimized subject to specific re-

2. This conclusion holds for bulk shipments and, to a much lesser extent, for general cargo traffic. An instructive illustration of the effect of port improvement on speed of cargo working and, through it, on vessel size was discovered in the World Bank's study on the port of La Goulette which was improved by the construction of a specialized berth and silo for cereals and by dredging. The speed of unloading rose in consequence from 600 tons/day/ship to 1,300 tons. Before the project, only about 12 percent of arriving ships had a draft of over 8 meters; after it, the share of the larger classes rose to 65 percent. Miguel Martinez, "Distribution of Benefits of Port Improvements: Case Study of the Port of La Goulette (Tunisia)" (study prepared for the World Bank, 1976; processed).

actions on the part of the port authority in terms of the port charge component of g and A and perhaps also of L. Stated as such, that is an intractable problem. It can be simplified by supposing (realistically?) that the port authority's reaction is passive; that is to say, it pursues no deep tactical policy but simply offers its stipulated services at a specified rate. Then the question is what functional interdependencies exist between the L, m, A, g, and B and for different technologies.

In comparing these parameters for the conventional and container conditions much depends on the use of berths and particularly the single common berths. However, as a very rough approximation, it is assumed that the container ship and port technology imply that $m = 0$. Thus the number of containers moved each day does not vary with the size of the ship. For large container ships, additional cranes will be used; but in any case, container throughput is limited largely in the transit storage areas.[8] For container operation, therefore, interest will center primarily on an element in the value of g—the port cost for each ton. This varies enormously with the size of ship. The provision of a short-sea (small ship) or feeder service berth can be operated at about one-third to one-half the cost of a deep-sea large ship berth.[4] A simple application of the formula above can be obtained by writing $C = L$. Suppose that B is constant and does not vary from small ship to large ship; that is, the cost of a ship-day at sea can be linearized as suggested. Then the resulting size of ship depends on port cost and distance. If the long distance voyage is assumed to be ten times the short voyage and the port cost for each ton for small ships to be roughly twice that for large ships, it can be seen that the large ships would be two-and-a-half times the size of the small ships.[5]

An interesting development of this model is possible by introducing idle time (I) to account for queuing or a minimum time in port. Thus, assume that each ship has to spend a full I days in port, but that a fraction α of this time can be used for cargo working. Voyage

3. For accuracy, it should, however, be said that the assumption holds only for relatively small numbers of containers on any one vessel. Thus the port's cost for each container may be assumed to be relatively insensitive to the number of containers aboard for the range of 0 to 350 units which typically move during each vessel call in secondary Asian ports.

4. See H. K. Dally, "Containers—a Note on Berth Throughputs and Terminal Handling," *National Ports Council Bulletin* (London), no. 4, (April 1973), pp. 60–65.

5. $C = DBL/2g$, $D_{long} = 10D_{short}$, $C = L$, $g_{long} = 2g_{short}$.

cost, corresponding to Equation (4) but with the additional assumption of an inescapable minimum stay in port, now becomes:

$$(7) \quad V = D(hC + B) + 2I(A + gC) + \left[\frac{2C}{L + mC} - 2\alpha I\right](A + gC),$$

subject to $[C/(L + mC)] > \alpha I$. Again the shipowner is relied upon to minimize voyage cost for each ton (V/C). After differentiating with respect to C, equating to zero, and solving for the minimum cost C, a moderately complicated result is obtained. This is again amenable to various simplifications. The feature of all solutions is that the minimum cost size of ship increases with the days of idleness. For example, if $m = 0$ and $L > 0$:

$$(8) \qquad C = \sqrt{(L[DB + 2AI(1 - \alpha)]/2g)}.$$

The optimum size of vessel increases with idleness. This result seems against intuition, but a little further thought shows that it is consistent with common sense. Larger ships are cheaper per DWT so it is better to keep a big-ship DWT in idleness than a small-ship DWT. The same result does not follow if the cost of the ship rather than the cost of a DWT is of concern.

Two important conclusions follow when idleness is identified with congestion. First, the cost of shipping into a small congested port that is unsuitable for large ships will be greater than for an equally congested port that does not place the same constraints on ship size. Second, port developments that remove congestion will benefit small vessels particularly. One of the barriers to shipowning is thereby reduced. This is the exact opposite of the result of increasing the speed of cargo working in an uncongested port. Improvements that raise the amount of cargo that can be worked in a day $(L$ or $m)$ act just like lengthening the voyage distance (D). Other things being equal, such improvements in port facilities or ship design will increase the minimum-cost size of ship. By the same token, they will raise a barrier to entry into the shipping industry.

The Structure of Port Prices

The prices charged by ports, however great the differences in detail, fall broadly into two categories: user charges and service charges. User charges include dues levied on the ship for each call, which vary continuously with one or more of the vessel's dimensions and discontinuously with the length of stay; river conservancy dues; dues falling on cargo (for example, wharfage) levied usually on the quantity of cargo moved; and storage fees which cover sheds and warehouses. Service charges include charges for the use of labor and ancillary equipment, which vary with the amount of the service used in moving the cargo; cranage charges, which vary with the amount of crane service consumed; mooring and berthing charges; pilotage, which varies normally with the dimensions of the vessel (such as GRT and draft); and towage and tugging.

For conventional break-bulk cargo, the general rule is that the ship is charged ship dues and stevedoring charges, and the shipper is charged with the rest except for the use of port equipment such as cranes, the charge for which may be distributed between the two parties. Liner terms usually include the entire cost of moving the cargo from the ship to the transit shed or vice versa in the freight rate. Containerization, if it involves through transport, normally changes the system by placing all port charges on the party which controls the movement, usually the sea carrier. In the case of chartered vessels, on the other hand, the charterer (corresponding to the shipper) will normally pay all that is due in the port.

The Cost of Using Ports

The expenses of cargo working form the main item of terminal expenses for ships—some 30 to 36 percent of voyage operating cost for conventional vessels and above 50 percent for a container vessel (Table 1.1). The remainder of port charges, such as port dues, account for another 4 to 9 percent of the voyage cost of conventional liners. These are averages, and they do not strictly reflect the share of port and cargo expenses in the cost of sailing into one particular set of ports. Nevertheless assume that port expenses lie between 5 and 10 percent and cargo expenses between 25 and 40 percent of this specific port voyage cost on long distances, the two parts together varying around 38 percent for conventional liners. This conjecture is founded on scanty evidence; other researchers have suggested significantly lower values, around 25 percent, for conventional liner voyages.[6] For container ships on high density routes, the proportion of

6. United Nations, Conference on Trade and Development, Secretariat. *Port Pricing.* (TD/B/C.4/1110/Rev. 1) (New York, 1975), paragraphs 155 and 156 and sources quoted therein.

TABLE 1.1.   SHARE OF PORT AND CARGO EXPENSES IN VOYAGE COST

Vessel and voyage	Percentage of total cost excluding depreciation	
	Cargo expenses	Other port expenses
a. *Single round voyage*		
Conventional liner, modern 560,000 cubic feet (10,000 DWT); Europe–Far East round voyage; 1971; 143 days (14–30 days in port); utilization: approximately 90 percent	29	7.0
Conventional liner, 10 years old, 6,400 DWT; Bangkok–Japan round voyage; 1970; 56 days (23 days in port); utilization: approximately 80 percent	37	9.5
b. *Annual overall voyage cost, 1969 data*		
Break-bulk, 3 years old, 711,000 cubic feet (12,500 DWT), 20 knots; assumed days at sea, 185; annual output capability, 11.20 × 10⁹ ton miles	36	9.0
Containership, built 1971, 1,210 TEU, 23 knots; assumed days at sea, 253; annual output capability, 27.2 × 10⁹ ton miles	56	8.0

Note: Information in brackets supplied by authors as typical of the route.
Sources:
a. Data outside brackets from B. M. Deakin, *Shipping Conferences*, University of Cambridge, Department of Applied Economics Occasional Papers, no. 37 (Cambridge: Cambridge University Press, 1973), pp. 117–118.
b. Adapted from James R. McCaul, Robert B. Zubaly, and Edward V. Lewis, "Increasing the Productivity of U.S. Shipping" (paper read at the Spring Meeting, Williamsburg, Va., May 24–27, 1972, no. 3. New York: the Society of Naval Architects and Marine Engineers, 1972).

cargo expenses appears to be rather higher (especially if the cost of stuffing and stripping LCL containers is included), and the two categories of ship's port expenses may amount to 60 percent of specific voyage cost.[7]

The share of port expenses in voyage cost is, however, only an incomplete measure of the cost of using ports. First, for the shipowner there is also the cost of keeping the ship in port. Conventional liners on long distance trades may spend approximately one-half of

7. Others have proposed significantly higher values.

their annual voyage time in port.[8] Port expenses plus the cost of time in port may then amount to about 60 percent of annual voyage cost. For container ships this proportion may be higher.

Second, the liner ship is normally charged only part of the port expenses arising during a normal cargo call; the rest is charged to the shipper. From the economic point of view, this division is arbitrary, and it does not of course occur in the usual charter operation. If the cost of using the port is to be accurately established, the shipper's payments should be added to the ship's expenses, and, since they form part and parcel of the cost of transporting the goods, they will also have to be added to the voyage cost. The size of these payments may be deduced from the figures in Table 1.2, which is derived from a medium-sized British port in 1975. If, therefore, it is assumed that the shipper pays to the port roughly as much as the ship and that the ship's port expenses are 38 percent of its voyage cost, then the combined port expenses will be 56 percent of the augmented voyage cost.

So far, the port expenses have been compared with the total operating cost of a voyage. That is the appropriate calculation to determine the effect of changes in cost which affect all ports equally, that is, to determine predominantly the effects of general changes in port technology or in international wage movements. But if the question is narrowed down to the effect of changes in the costs or charges of one port, then the fact that the voyage cost associated with one shipment includes two sets of cargo expenses must be allowed for. This may be dealt with (at the cost of a minor inaccuracy) by halving the ratio of the ship's aggregate port expenses to voyage cost, from 25–38 percent to 13–19 percent.[9] If liner companies used port services and other resources in strictly fixed proportions, it would follow from

8. B. M. Deakin. *Shipping Conferences,* University of Cambridge, Department of Applied Economics Occasional Papers no. 37 (Cambridge: Cambridge University Press, 1973), p. 116 and Producers Boards' Shipping Utilization Committee, New Zealand, *New Zealand's Overseas Trade: Report on Shipping, Ports, Transport, and Other Services* (New Zealand and London, February 1964), pp. 39–41.

9. The higher percentage arises from the earlier conjecture that port expenses form 38 percent of voyage (operating) cost; the lower one corresponds to the lower estimates accepted by United Nations, Conference on Trade and Development, Secretariat. *Port Pricing.* (TD/B/C.4/1110/Rev. 1) (New York, 1975), paragraphs 155 and 156.

TABLE 1.2. THE COMPOSITION OF PAYMENTS IN A BRITISH PORT: CASES I AND II, 1974

	Percentage of total payment in port	
Total payment made in port = 100 percent	I	II
Dues		
Ships dues	18.3	10.3
Import dues (wharfage)	20.2	13.9
Cargo working; cases and bags, ex-ship to truck		
Stevedoring (excluding cranage)	19.1	20.8[a]
	(24.1)[a]	
Port labor (excluding cranage)	32.3	54.9[a]
	(37.3)[a]	
Cranage	10.1	n.a.
Payments by ship = 100 percent		
Dues	43	33
Stevedoring (including cranage)	57	67
Payments by shipper = 100 percent		
Dues	35	20
Labor (including cranage)	65	80

Note: Case I: vessel of 6,400 NRT (1,200 DWT), long distance voyage, staying 1 day, discharging 532 metric tons, mixed cargo. Case II: vessel of 4,359 NRT (10,345 DWT), long distance voyage, staying 1½ days, discharging 545 metric tons, mixed cargo.

a. Including cranage which could not be distinguished in Case II.

n.a. = not available.

the numbers that a 10 percent across-the-board increase in port charges would raise voyage cost by 1.3 to 1.9 percent. Whether freight rates also rise in a similar proportion will depend first on whether depreciation and profit, which was excluded from voyage cost, can thus be neglected and on whether the liner industry is competitive. But if the increase in voyage cost is passed on fully to the shipper, insofar as he makes separate payments to the port, he will have to pay more than this. Assume again that port charges are paid by the ship and the shipper in equal amounts. Then, if liner companies pass on the full increase in port cost, the shipper's total transport cost will rise by 2 to 2.8 percent in response to a 10 percent increase in port charges.[10]

10. The higher percentage arises from the earlier conjecture that port expenses form 38 percent of voyage (operating) cost; the lower one corresponds to the lower estimates accepted by UNCTAD, Port Pricing.

Elasticity of Demand for Port Services:
The Case of the Single Port

The most obvious factor that determines the elasticity of demand for the services of one port is the ease with which another port can be used in its stead. Interport competition raises its own issues of policy and pricing, and these are dealt with separately in Chapter 7. In this section, competition between ports is eliminated altogether. Thus it is assumed that there is no alternative port accessible to the country and that the only alternative to using the port is not to export or import at all. Assume also that:

(a) There is perfect competition in the shipping industry (for example, tramps);

(b) Port charges do not vary with the quantity of throughput;

(c) The country exports a commodity which is a small part of a large world market;

(d) There is a rising supply curve of the export commodity at the port gate (resulting from internal transport cost, limits of cultivation, or some other limiting factor); and

(e) It is not possible to substitute port services for shipping services or vice versa; port services and shipping services must be supplied in fixed proportions.

These conditions are illustrated in Figure 1.1 where the supply c.i.f. includes the steamship (tramp) cost of OS per unit and the port charges of SH per unit. Equilibrium is where the country exports the quantity X.

The elasticity of demand for the services of the port is calculated by making a small proportionate change $\Delta SH/SH$ and calculating the effect on the quantity $\Delta X/X$. With the c.i.f. supply elasticity denoted by ϵ, the elasticity of demand for port services is clearly given by:

(9) (SH/OP) $\times$ ϵ

or in words: $\begin{bmatrix} \text{The fraction of port cost} \\ \text{in the c.i.f. price} \end{bmatrix} \times \begin{bmatrix} \text{Elasticity of supply} \\ \text{with c.i.f. price} \end{bmatrix}$

This is, of course, nothing more than Marshall's old law, and it demonstrates that, in the absence of port competition and by the presumption of fixed proportions, the elasticity of demand for port services is likely to be very low.

FIGURE 1.1.   DERIVED DEMAND FOR SHIPPING
AND FOR PORT SERVICES IN THE CASE OF FIXED PROPORTIONS

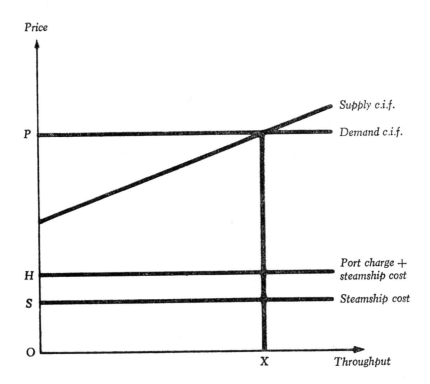

The share of port charges in the c.i.f. price of goods can be estimated either directly from samples of consignments in different ports
or indirectly through the share of port charges in transport cost and
the proportion of freight cost to the c.i.f. price. A few direct estimates
for liner cargo have been published.[11] Those that appear to have been

11. Notably, D. Shoup, *Ports and Economic Development* (Washington, D.C.:
Brookings Institution, 1967). Also, Organization for Economic Cooperation and
Development, "Ocean Freight Rates as Part of Total Transport Costs." (Paris,
1968), pp. 15, 29. A certain amount of evidence can also be derived from United
Nations, Economic and Social Council, Economic Commission for Latin America,
ECLA/OAS Joint Transport Programme, *Maritime Freight Rates in the Foreign
Trade of Latin America*, part I (E/CN.12/812/Rev. 1) and part II (E/CN.12/
812/Add. 1) (New York, 1970; processed), appendixes VI and VII. Shipper's
payments to the port are not, however, included.

made on the inclusive basis which was adopted in the preceding section (including cargo expenses as well as payments by shippers or consignees) show a wide range of values, but most of the observations fall between 1.5 and 3 percent. Our own indirect estimates, using data from a variety of sources,[12] lead to slightly higher estimates. On balance, however, the proportion of total port charges in c.i.f. price will lie below 5 percent of c.i.f. value for most countries and most commodities.

It would be supposed then that the elasticity of demand for the port services is only 5 percent of the elasticity of supply of the commodity. Such elasticities of supply as have been calculated suggest values of no more than five, and usually values of around unity are more appropriate.[13] Thus the elasticity of demand for port services clearly is likely to be less than 0.2 even under the most propitious circumstances, and probably 0.1 is the most sensible lower limit under the assumptions listed above.

The assumption that the demand curve c.i.f. is perfectly elastic can be changed easily. With a downward-sloping demand curve of given elasticity, the increase in the port charge would raise the final price (c.i.f.) and so modify the reduction in throughput as the supply curve is raised. The greater the inelasticity of demand, the greater the inelasticity of demand for port services, and of course this adds even more credibility to the presumption of a highly inelastic demand for port services. In the case of imports, this inelastic demand model may be more useful than the inelastic supply model. It may be supposed that imports are supplied on the world markets in perfectly elastic supply (except for variations in port charges) and that the demand is not perfectly elastic but reflects the availability of possible home substitutes for the imported commodities. In this case, the simple Marshall formula applies; the demand elasticity of the port services is equal to the demand elasticity for imports multiplied by the fraction

---

12. OECD, *Ocean Freight Rates as Part of Total Transport Costs*; ECLA, *Maritime Freight Rates in the Foreign Trade of Latin America*; our own study of the cost of ocean transport in the regional and extra-regional trades of Bangkok (to be published); United States Congress, Subcommittee on Federal Procurement and Regulation of the Joint Economic Committee, *Discriminatory Ocean Freight Rates and the Balance of Payments*, Hearing. 89 Cong., 1st sess., June 30, 1965. (Washington, D.C.: U.S. Government Printing Office, 1965), pp. 414–441.

13. See A. A. Walters. "A Development Model of Transport," *American Economic Review* (Papers and Proceedings), vol. 58, no. 2. (May 1968), pp. 360–377.

of port charges in total c.i.f. price.[14] Again, many econometric studies suggest that the elasticity of demand for imports may be well below two.[15] Even allowing for a considerable downward bias in these estimates, it is clear that the elasticity of demand for port services must be very low, assuming the rigidity of fixed proportions and the absence of competitive ports.

If these low elasticities existed in practice, the issue of pricing the services of the port would be largely irrelevant. Certainly variations in the price of the port service would have little effect on the quantity. Then it would be important to plan the appropriate level of facilities of the port, and, as far as the distribution of resources is concerned, it would matter little what price was levied. However, the port would be a most useful source of revenue for government.

In fact, these calculations of elasticities are entirely misleading. Their main fault is that they ignore the very large opportunities for substitution.

The port produces a wide variety of services, each with its own unique competitive conditions. Consider first, for example, the docking and quay facilities of a port. Clearly the substitutes for such facilities can only be docks and quays elsewhere, that is to say, a competing port. The storage facilities that are provided by the port on the other hand can more or less equally well be provided by private entrepreneurs or truckers. Thus there is great competition in the supply of storage, and the port may be considerably constrained in its charging practices. These constraints operate whether or not the port as a supplier of bonded storage is protected by the existence of customs duties coupled with high interest rates. The elasticity of demand for the services of the transit shed as such may, therefore, be very high indeed. Even for quay occupancy there may be considerable opportunities for substitution. The most dramatic examples of these effects are in the use of palettes or other more advanced unitized methods of cargo handling. There is, furthermore, a high degree of substitutability between ship's gear and port cranes. Similarly, there is the choice between working cargo alongside the quay and loading

14. See E. Bennathan and A. A. Walters, *The Economics of Ocean Freight Rates*, Praeger Special Studies in International Economics and Development (New York: Praeger, 1969), Technical Appendix, note 1.

15. Compare, for example, H. S. Houthakker and S. P. Magee, "Income and Price Elasticities in World Trade," *The Review of Economics and Statistics*, vol. LI, no. 2. (May 1969), pp. 111–125.

or unloading over the side into lighters that have access to shallow berths or that may distribute it directly to private wharves.

The substantive issue is that the port services consist of an à la carte selection rather than a fixed menu. Even though a shipowner is compelled to patronize the port, there are many opportunities for cost-reducing substitutions.[16] These opportunities vary considerably according to the time allowed for adjustments. Some may involve the adaptation of equipment of a vessel, and others may involve building a different type of vessel.

Therefore, the fixed proportions model is unlikely to be appropriate for most ports and leads to a serious underestimation of the long-run elasticity of demand for the services of the seemingly monopolistic port.

16. If all the prices of port services are increased proportionately, the extent of substitution will be different for each type of service.

Chapter 2

Marginal Cost

ONE OF THE MAIN THEMES of this study is that an appropriate basis for pricing port services is the marginal cost of supplying the services. One of the first tasks is to develop the principles of marginal cost pricing in their applications to ports. The background to marginal cost pricing has been described in some detail in its application to highways, and this survey is restricted to the highlights.

Short-run Marginal Cost Pricing and the Consequences

The argument for marginal cost pricing is that, under conditions where the rest of the national economy behaves (or is planned to behave) as if perfect competition existed, the price should be set equal to the cost of the resources absorbed in producing the service. If the price exceeds the cost, too little of the service will be produced, and resources will be used inefficiently to produce other commodities and services. Similarly, if the price is below the cost, too much of the service will be produced relative to the quantity of other goods.

But what marginal cost is appropriate to be considered here—short, long, medium, or some combination? Only a conditional answer can be given to this. If it is assumed that it costs very little to change the price, then the short-run marginal cost is an appropriate basis for pricing. If, however, the price is costly to change (or administratively difficult, which amounts to the same thing), then a somewhat longer-run marginal cost is the proper criterion. The constraints on the movement of prices (or the shadow price of such constraints) should be the only reason to switch from the short-run basis of marginal cost to the longer-run basis.

Whether short-run marginal cost is less than or exceeds the long-run marginal cost depends, among other things, on the existence of returns to scale in the port industry and on whether the capital stock and equipment is adjusted to the level of output to allow production at least cost. First, suppose that the demand conditions for future traffic levels are known exactly and that the port authorities have invested wisely to ensure the best technology for their scale of operations. This means that the port authorities are conducting their business at minimum cost and that the average long-run cost is the same as the average short-run cost.

But short-run and long-run marginal cost (SRMC and LRMC) will be equal only if there are constant returns to scale for the levels of traffic for which the facilities have been built, as can be seen in Figure 2.1. Pricing the services at short-run marginal cost will attract just enough traffic to cover the port's cost. For traffic levels substantially lower, however, the port facilities would be underused and the short-run marginal cost would fall below the long-run marginal cost. For these low levels of tonnage there would be economies of scale. The general result, therefore, is that with no economies of scale, if the port has the optimal level of traffic, the long- and short-run marginal costs are equal. Furthermore, if there are economies of scale, levying a price of SRMC=LRMC will give rise to deficits.

Now assume that the port authorities are not perfect administrators and that, being perhaps human, they make mistakes. Thus the wharves and equipment are not always appropriately adjusted to the level of traffic, perhaps because tonnage grew at an unanticipated high (or low) rate. Suppose, for example, that the demand turned out much larger than the authorities anticipated. Thus the short-run marginal cost will be high, reflecting the scarcity of port capacity, and well above the long-run marginal cost. If the port tariff were fixed near the value of long-run marginal cost, inefficient congestion would result. The tariff should reflect the scarcity value of the port's facilities as measured in the short-run marginal cost; then congestion would be virtually eliminated.

Suppose, on the other hand, that the authorities overbuild their ports. Then the short-run marginal cost is well below the long-run

FIGURE 2.1. COST AND OUTPUT

Cost ($)

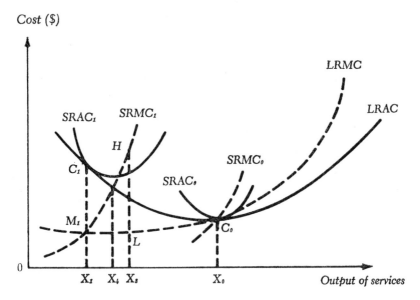

Output of services

Note: $SRMC_i$ = short-run marginal cost associated with the ith plant and technology; $SRAC_i$ = short-run average cost; $LRMC_i$ = long-run marginal cost; $LRAC_i$ = curve associated with the ith plant and technology.

value. But if long-run cost was levied, the use of the underutilized port would be discouraged; thus the short-run is the appropriate value for the tariff.

The overall result, therefore, is that the long-run marginal cost is a suitable basis for pricing only when it happens to be the same as the short-run marginal cost, and this will occur only when the authorities predict their output and capacity correctly. However, the short-run marginal cost is always an appropriate base for pricing, irrespective of the efficacy of the authorities' forecasts and planning and whether or not they make mistakes. This seems to be a good reason to concentrate solely on short-run values. If the tariff is set at short-run marginal cost when there are increasing returns to scale, a deficit is likely; there will be a surplus only when the authorities fail to expand the plant by a fairly large margin and operate the port under highly congested conditions.

So far the assumption has been that the port authorities could make continuous adjustments in the size of plant and that, similarly, labor and other factors may be hired in small numbers. In practice there may be rather large discontinuities in port construction and operations. Such lumpiness does not change the substance of the above conclusions, but they may change the weight which should be accorded to them. For example, the argument that short-run marginal cost is always correct and long-run marginal cost only occasionally correct as a basis for pricing still stands, but when there are large lumps of plant involved and a few discontinuous jumps from one size to another, the long- and short-run marginal costs will coincide for wide ranges of output from the same size of plant. Long-run marginal cost would therefore be an appropriate guide for pricing policy for all outputs if the authorities did not operate too small or too large a plant (Figure 2.2). Consider, for example an authority that produced output X_H with plant 1. Clearly it would be inappropriate to charge

FIGURE 2.2. COST AND OUTPUT WITH DISCONTINUITIES

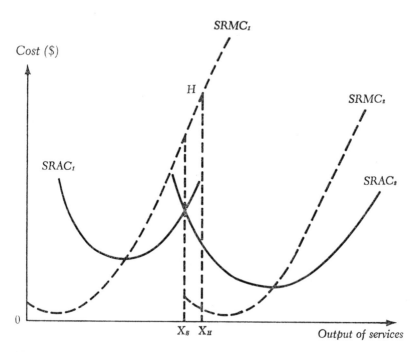

Note: Definitions as in Figure 2.1.

a low price shown by the SRMC$_2$ (LRMC), and the proper price is HX_H. As before, the long-run marginal cost is appropriate only if the size of plant corresponding to the measure of long-run marginal cost has been constructed and is operating. If the value of long-run marginal cost corresponds to a hypothetical correct plant which differs from the actual plant, then the LRMC is irrelevant.

Marginal Cost Pricing Principles in a Noncompetitive Environment

The arguments for marginal cost pricing spring from the assumption that the price of a resource measures its marginal cost. This condition may arise in a capitalist economy if there is perfect competition in other activities. Marginal cost pricing may be obtained in a socialist or dirigiste economy by fiat of the authorities who regulate prices. But both are ideal states—like perfect vacuums or perfectly accurate measures; in fact neither in a socialist nor in a market economy can marginal cost pricing be precise. Mistakes will be made, monopolies will arise, taxation will distort prices, political pressure will be brought to bear, and so on. The question is whether a rule of pricing that is strictly relevant only when ideal marginal-cost-equals-price conditions are present can be used also in the mundane world of mistakes and imperfections.

To answer this question it is necessary to consider some alternative principle. As substitute for marginal cost pricing the only really serious candidate is average cost pricing. (For this discussion the combinations of the two which are characteristic of two-part tariffs are ignored.) It is true that when marginal cost and price differ in the rest of the economy, there is no simple rule for adjusting the marginal price of the port. In particular, even though prices are above marginal cost in the rest of the economy, it is not known whether the port tariff should be above or below marginal cost. Nevertheless, if the competitors for the specific resources used by the port (for example, capital) charge prices that are considerably above marginal cost, then it may be wise to raise tariffs above marginal cost in the port; otherwise the port may expand too much and take too many of these scarce resources from the other industry. (However, this supposes that the resources are not producible, which is not true in the case of capital.)

As far as competition for resources is concerned, decisions can only be made on the evidence presented by the particular circumstances. Much depends on whether the competing demands for the resources used by the port come from commodities or services that are competitive with or complementary to port services. In particular, if the competing buyer of capital produces complements to the port's output (for example, road transport to or from the port), the most advantageous pricing rule would be for the port to set its prices below its marginal cost and vice versa for the case where the competitor for the port's resources is the monopolistic producer of goods or services that are substitutes for the port's output (for example, another national port or import-competing production in general). As a practical matter it seems that the main competitor for resources is probably road transport, including the provision of highways. The output of road services usually complements that of port services—but they are often produced in conditions of energetic competition. Other competitors for resources may be domestic construction industries. Here again competitive conditions are usually observed. Therefore, it is deduced that there are no substantial arguments for pricing below marginal cost.[1]

Whether prices should be levied substantially above marginal cost depends, among other things, on the structure of competition among the customers of the port. The most interesting case here is the liner conference and its relation with the traders who, in turn, comprise its customers. These considerations involve many problems about the reaction of the shipping conferences to changes in their cost and will have to be pursued at length elsewhere.

The alternative principle of average cost pricing is difficult to define in a unique way when there are many services performed by broadly the same activities. The common cost of central activities must be allocated arbitrarily among the different services produced by the port. There is no unique measure of average cost for the multiproduct firm. In many costing studies common cost is allocated according to weight, or some other measure of volume, or perhaps according to some measure of what the traffic will bear, or some combination of the two. But of course the allocations are not of interest for pricing purposes except as approximations of the avoidable cost of providing the services.

---

1. Where highway transport is a substitute for port services—that is to say, where there are land alternatives to sea transit—this follows directly from the rule stated earlier.

Perhaps the most important aspect of noncompetitive behavior in the shipping and port business is the practice of conferences. The port may not compete with monopolies for its resources, but neither does it sell all of its services in a perfectly competitive market. It is often sensible to assume that the traders in a country and the traders of its trading partners are in a competitive environment, although there are exceptions in state trading and marketing organizations. Since the port sells services directly to traders and since traders can decide more or less freely how much they will buy (storage services seem to be a common example), there is no problem of a monopsonistic purchaser. But with the charges levied against the ship for port services, the authorities must deal with the monopsonistic conference.

The confrontation of monopoly and monopsony—the port and the conference—gives rise to many problems, few of which can be solved in a deterministic way. The main issues are whether and to what extent variations in port charges will be passed on by the conference to the competitive traders. This involves not merely questions of analysis but also of strategy, which are discussed in Chapter 6.

To put this discussion into perspective, it is urged that port pricing never be used to right the wrongs or to eliminate the distortions that arise elsewhere in the domestic economy. For example, it would be unwise to try to induce a domestic monopoly that buys port services to expand output by reducing the price of port services below their marginal cost.[2] In economics, as in many aspects of life, two wrongs do not make a right, and the port should not be the main agent used to reform the economy.

Variations in Demand and the Cost of Changing the Tariffs

The cost of changing the price charged for port services varies considerably among ports according to the legal and administrative systems. The supposition that the cost of changing prices is not trivial does mean that the authority should not vary the tariff to follow every little ripple of demand.

2. However, when the port deals with foreign-owned monopolies, such as the shipping conferences, any increase in the net income of the foreign monopoly at the expense of domestic residents is a dead loss. The variations in pricing policy which are designed to deal with these familiar cases are pursued in Chapter 5.

There are two or even three dimensions to the concept of difficulty-of-adjustment-of-price; there is the simple cost in dollar terms of informing buyers, there is the goodwill or diplomatic cost, and there is the fact that the change takes time. The authority must ensure that the price does not follow transitory shifts in demand or cost which are expected to disappear in a few weeks; the authority should be concerned only about more or less permanent shifts which will persist for months or years. It is important to distinguish between those regular, predictable shifts—such as seasonal variation—and those which are generated by unpredictable random forces, such as the weather. It may be sensible to vary the tariff to reflect the known seasonal demand. But changing prices to respond to random effects is likely to be uneconomic.

This suggests that in calculating price, these random variations must be considered when assessing the resources used up to produce the services. To see the problems involved consider a stylized example where there are two demands—a high and a low demand as illustrated by D_h and D_l in Figure 2.3. These demands must be specified for a given quality of service produced by the port; they can be called the no-waiting demand curves, which assume that the ships are serviced immediately (and take one week to clear) by the port authorities. Furthermore, suppose that the high demand curve occurs with probability 0.10 and that the low demand curve has a 0.90 chance of occurring—both independent events in time.[3] The short-run marginal cost is stylized so that it is constant up to capacity (X_c) and then rises vertically.

At price P_o the low demand is for X_2 which means that there is spare capacity of X_2X_c on nine out of ten occasions. On the other hand, when demand is high, X_h ships turn up to be serviced, and there are X_h minus X_c which, chosen randomly from the arrivals, have to wait. If $X_c - X_2 = X_h - X_c$, then the waiting ships can be serviced in a week (on the assumptions made above). But if these demand curves are for a given quality of service—for example, no waiting—then one of the conditions of the demand curve has been violated. Two artifices are possible. First the no-waiting demand curves may be retained, with the port authority compensating the

---

3. The complication that the high demand may occur in successive periods and so produce a queue which cannot be cleared in the following week is ignored; it could be imagined that the demand adjusts on information received of such a contingency.

FIGURE 2.3. VARIATIONS IN DEMAND

Price, cost ($)

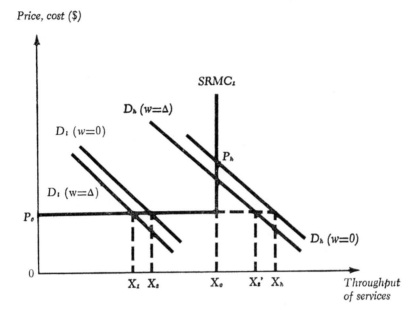

Note: D_h $(w{=}0)$ = high demand curve for port services when there is no
waiting; D_h $(w{=}\Delta)$ = high demand curve for port services when there is a one-
in-ten chance of waiting for one week; D_l $(w{=}0)$ = low demand with no waiting;
D_l $(w{=}\Delta)$ = low demand with a one-in-ten chance of waiting for one week.

steamship owners for waiting; this, however, requires some additional
doctoring of the cost curves, and it is not easy to do on the traditional
figure.[4] A second and more convenient approach considers that steamship owners will know that there is a one-in-ten chance that they
will have to wait one week in the roads, and so the amount that
they are willing to pay for the services of the port is thereby reduced.
This is shown in the figure as the demand curves $D_l(w = \Delta)$ and
$D_h(w = \Delta)$ where w is the week's waiting time, and, of course, no
compensation is paid for waiting.[5] The probability of uncompen-

4. In principle, costs must vary according to the excess of X_h over X_c multiplied
by one-tenth of the cost of one week's wait for a ship in the roads.
5. Although the obvious symbolic representation of one week's waiting is
$w = 1$, the average waiting time is only one-tenth of a week; thus the more
general symbol Δ has been used in the figure.

sated waiting reduces demand below what it would otherwise have been and so reduces the amount of waiting. There is a complex interaction effect in the figure; for any given price there is a quantity of waiting which itself determines simultaneously the position of the demand curve. In other words, the vertical shift in the demand curve from $w = 0$ to $w = \Delta$ must be consistent with the amount of waiting $X_h - X_c$.

The contrast between a probabilistic demand and a known seasonal variation can be illustrated easily. If the high demand curve were a consequence of seasonal factors rather than of random events, the price would be fixed at P_h for the high season and at P_o for the off season. This would ensure that there was no delay in dealing with ships, and the appropriate demands would be those with zero waiting time. But with random demands the position of the demand curves depends on the single price that must be chosen since that price in conjunction with the amount of capacity provided determines the fraction of ships that must wait in the roads.

Pricing in Ignorance of Cost

The final question in this discussion is the issue of imperfect knowledge and marginal cost pricing. One of the recurrent themes of many port studies is that the authorities do not know what their cost is. And if they lack knowledge of their accounting cost, however defined, it seems at least likely that they do not know their marginal cost. This is particularly important since marginal cost is a useful tool for efficient management.

Some knowledge of cost is necessary for a port authority to discharge its most basic obligations. These include the efficient conduct of the business such as buying properly, preventing and rooting out fraud, and adopting the best techniques and administrative practices. Knowledge of marginal cost, both in the short and long run, is very useful for making the appropriate decisions on investment to meet new or growing demands for port services.

In practice many of the components of marginal cost can be adduced from the financial accounts of the port. But the financial accounts of some port authorities contain an assortment of transactions which are difficult to disentangle, and in some cases the port accounts are inextricably mixed up with other agencies. To determine marginal cost it is then necessary to instigate specific surveys of port activities. Only then can the alternative investment programs be judged on their ability to meet future demands.

But the appropriate pricing for port services need not wait for such time-consuming and costly studies; the tariffs can be improved immediately. In practice the first step is to levy charges so that the use of the port is either increased or reduced to what is regarded in port economics as the efficient level. The efficient level of port use can be derived by observing ports, perhaps in other countries, where the management is efficient and where the port is operating at the "best" level. This comparative standard will provide a good enough first approximation for pricing purposes. Then the port authorities need to estimate the reaction of the demand for port services to changes in the price. Essentially, instead of calculating marginal costs, the problem is reduced to estimating the elasticity of demand for port services. The evidence which should be considered in this problem is discussed in Chapter 7, but at this stage it is not necessary to know marginal cost to pursue an appropriate pricing policy for existing port complexes.

This argument applies to the general level of port prices. In addition the structure of port tariffs must be correct so that the price of each service reflects the cost involved in supplying it. This principle should be applied to the separate services and activities of the port. Thus, the price of storage should be fixed so that the facility is used as near to its physical capacity as is efficient, and similarly quay charges should be varied until the utilization of the quay is appropriate. (This may involve very high congestion charges on some facilities.)

Strictly speaking, the method outlined above is only appropriate for pricing facilities whose use does not incur avoidable cost. In that case the rule of pricing for the full use of capacity is appropriate simply because the definition of full capacity is likely to be that volume of output at which marginal cost starts to rise rapidly. By extension, the rule may apply also to pricing facilities which incur little variable cost in their use. The rule is not appropriate, however, for services which have a substantial cost that varies with the amount of the service produced.

But port authorities are never totally ignorant of cost. Usually, they have only hazy or erroneous notions about fixed cost, but they generally can formulate much more accurately the magnitude of variable (or avoidable) cost. If the variable cost of a service can be guessed with some confidence, marginal cost can be derived from it; in that sense, marginal-cost pricing demands less information about cost than does pricing according to average cost. Indeed, since marginal cost can be approximated as the change in variable cost as output changes, a clear idea about absolute variable cost is not required. To ascertain changes in variable cost may require study, but less than a study of the full cost for the port.

Last, and perhaps most realistically, the port authorities may be able to quantify only part of the variable cost of a service. Such a port will then fix its prices substantially above that known element of variable cost to recoup unknown cost elements. If the authority must cover its cost, it will seek a total revenue equal to or above total variable cost plus total assumed amortization of assets. So far as the cost of rendering a particular service is concerned, the port is most likely to know the direct variable cost and to feel ignorant about indirect items. These are frequently the costs of services or supplies used in common by several activities.[6] In that realistic case, again, part of the marginal cost of rendering the service can be estimated from what is known. The marginal-cost pricing rule then yields the important principle that the price charged for the service must not be less than this ascertainable marginal cost.[7]

When investment criteria and the nature of the knowledge of cost required for efficient decisions are examined, it is observed that historical costs are irrelevant. In the case of abandoning a port, an assessment of the value of the assets that would be released by closure is needed; this may exceed or be less than the historical valuation. In the case of expanding port facilities, the cost of the new facilities must be known, and this can be ascertained usually from costing the plans. These considerations, however, should not be construed necessarily as an argument for replacement cost accounting systems for the port. The case for such accounting methods must be founded on demonstrations of the increased efficiency of port management, and that subject lies beyond the scope of this study.

---

6. The port is thus expected to know the wage cost of 1 hour of crane or trucking service but not necessarily the cost of the required petrol and lubricants or maintenance services.

7. Always assuming that short-run marginal cost is not declining.

Chapter 3

Economies of Scale

IN DESIGNING TARIFF SYSTEMS one of the general questions is whether
there are economies of scale in the provision of the services when the
equipment and size of the port are just right for the level of traffic.
If there are economies of scale in the production of a service and if
the appropriate capital stock is available, the marginal cost pricing
of that service will not generate enough revenue to cover the cost.
There will be a deficit that must be financed either by raising tariffs
above marginal cost or by some other means. Similarly if there are
diseconomies of scale, tariffs levied at marginal cost will produce a
surplus over cost.

Theory and Implications of Port Cost

It is first necessary to examine the general conditions—especially
those of geography and indivisibility—that are important in determining the patterns of cost. The hypotheses which arise from these
general reflections have many implications for pricing policy.

Are there economies of scale in ports?

To answer this question, it is convenient to split it into two parts.
First the economies of location of port facilities and then the appropriate size of those facilities must be considered.

At any given time, it is clear that there is an ordered list of preferred sites for a port that reflects not merely the cost of the port but also the demand for its services. For example, there is normally a trade-off between a port with good navigational access but remote from the internal origin or destination of cargoes and another that is near to the center of population but more difficult navigationally or that requires substantial dredging to accommodate vessels. As demand grows, new facilities must be located in less desirable locations. Other things being equal, successive additions to port capacity will, therefore, be associated with rising unit cost.

The presumption of optimal location can be applied only at the planning stage of port construction but not at later dates in the history of an actual port. Most of the world's ports, including those in the developing countries, were built quite a long time ago. Many of them would not be situated in the same location if the decision to build were taken today; the demand for the port's services as well as the technology of port construction or dredging have often changed sufficiently to render old locations inefficient. On the superior site unit cost may well decline, but this does not constitute evidence of increasing returns to scale.[1]

This point can be demonstrated simply. Let demand for the port's services increase so that the port is led to expand from the existing suboptimal to the optimal site. Unit cost will then decline for the port's entire output. Next, let demand fall to its original value. The port will then reduce its output by scrapping and selling off the highest-cost berths which lie in its original location, so that unit cost will once again decline. But this happens because of the resiting of activity. Analytically the port has moved on to lower cost curves which were not available when the port was originally built. What appears to be diminishing cost as output expands is thus merely the result of conventional accounting methods.

Rational choice of location thus implies that unit cost will rise as output expands. Thus, the size effects on the cost of the port capacity must be considered. This location disadvantage will be offset to some

---

1. Exactly similar results would follow from a mistake made at the planning stage of the port. If the planners propose to locate the port in a suboptimal site, expansion from this into a superior location would itself tend to reduce unit cost of port services. If this is discovered in the course of planning, it will signal that a mistake was made and will lead to relocation of the planned port.

FIGURE 3.1. PORT COST WITH DISECONOMIES OF SCALE

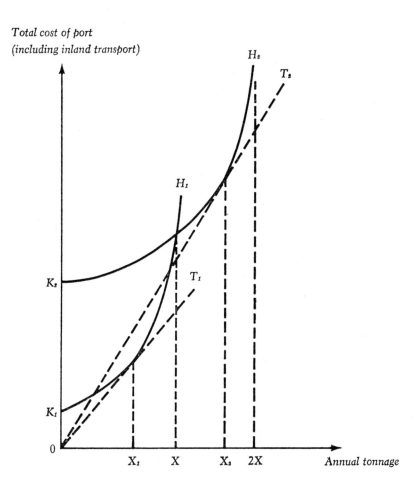

Total cost of port
(including inland transport)

Note: K_1 = annual fixed cost for a small port; K_2 = annual fixed cost for a large port. K_1H_1 = annual total cost for a small port; K_2H_2 = annual total cost for a large port.

extent by economies of scale in the provision of port services.[2] These economies come from the use of large indivisible units of equipment, the provision of deep harbors, large ship facilities, and so on. The operation of more frequent services will make a port more attractive than one that has only infrequent service: demand responds with a finite elasticity to the frequency of service.

The typical cost pattern of port development is illustrated in Figure 3.1. The total cost of the first port is described by the curve H_1. This shows the cost of the most advantageous location and includes not merely the port cost but also the inland transport cost.[3] This gives rise to a low average cost at the volume X_1 where minimum average cost is shown by the ray T_1. To accommodate tonnages larger than X, however, the port must be expanded by increasing quays and drafts and other facilities or by developing another location. Either of these alternatives involves higher capital cost (K_2 compared with K_1 in the figure). The unit variable cost may be less with the larger facility but not low enough to offset the higher capital cost, thus giving decreasing returns to scale from X_1 to X. In Figure 3.1, it has been assumed that there are discontinuities in the provision of port facilities—there can be either a small port or the larger port complex, and there is no in-between. If this is indeed the case, then there will be periods of increasing cost and other periods of excess capacity when average cost falls.

The effects of economies of scale in port and associated inland transport operations would be to ensure that the minimum average cost of the large port complex is lower than that of the small port (the ray T_2 would be below T_1 in Figure 3.1). The larger port can generally use more efficient equipment and deal with larger vessels than the small port. Alternatively the larger port may deal with approximately the same size of vessel but can increase the frequency of services.[4]

Diminishing average cost arises also from the typical pattern of ship

2. Large ports usually have more labor problems, although these are probably mainly pecuniary and redistributional in their effects. The dockers appropriate part of the surplus of the port.

3. It is assumed that inland transport may be bought at a constant price (per ton kilometer); thus capacity constraints are imposed only by port capacity.

4. Again the precise trade-off between frequency and price may be examined in the context of a comparison of rates for regular, frequent services compared with the tramp service.

arrivals and from the associated probability of ships having to wait for berth. Port planners frequently calculate an optimal occupancy rate of berths by a method which involves minimizing the sum of port cost and ship cost.[5] The normal procedure is to approximate ship arrivals by the Poisson frequency distribution where the probability of a ship arrival in a time interval (for example, a day) is constant and is independent of arrivals on previous days. Given the number of channels to the port, the size of the port, the expected annual tonnage of cargo, and the pattern of ship arrivals, the total number of days which ships would spend waiting for berths can be calculated. These ship-days spent in the queue involve costs. Similarly the number of days when the berths are vacant may be estimated. The joint cost of idle berth and ship time is then minimized, and this minimum defines the optimal number of berths and hence also the average annual occupancy rate of those berths. The relation between these two variables can be generalized in the shape of curve G in Figure 3.2.

This curve shows that the minimum cost occupancy rate of berths rises as the number of berths rises and that the optimal excess capacity in each berth falls as the capacity of the port increases. The output of the port can be measured approximately as the product of occupancy rate and number of berths. Thus output rises in greater proportion than port size. Other things being equal and without any offsetting diseconomies in inland transport, for example, a competitive market for shipping and port services would tend to produce large ports. High occupancy rates are therefore to be expected in private berths, financed and managed by shipping companies (as is the case of container berths in some ports), or in a competitive port dealing mainly with bulk carriers and tramps.

An important practical case is where a port expands its capacity by dredging a deeper channel and by providing equipment for dealing with larger ships and bulk carriers. Once the dredging is complete (and assuming a small annual maintenance dredge), these costs are past, and there is no sure way of recovering the investment. The marginal cost (including port operation and ocean freight but excluding, for the time being, inland transportation) per cargo ton will be lower

5. Compare, Carl H. Plumlee, "Optimum Size Seaport," *Journal of the Waterways and Harbors Division* (proceedings of the American Society of Civil Engineers) vol. 92, no. WW3 (August 1966), pp. 1–24.

FIGURE 3.2.   AVERAGE OCCUPANCY RATE AT WHICH
COSTS ARE MINIMIZED FOR A SPECIFIC NUMBER OF BERTHS

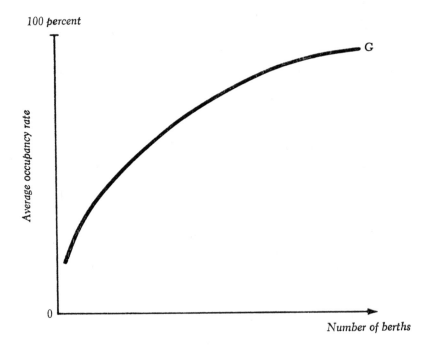

100 percent

Average occupancy rate

0

Number of berths

Note: The curvature and intercept of G vary with the relative daily cost of idle ship time and idle berth time.

than with the small-ship configuration, at least over the medium and higher ranges of tonnage throughput.

The one-large-port solution, however, would normally involve higher internal transport cost than the two-port option, ignoring for now the complicated question of different frequencies. The sample case is illustrated in Figure 3.3. The curve H_1 describes the total cost of a small port, with K_1 measuring the fixed cost (dredging, construction of quays, etc.) as before. The cost curve is stylized by supposing that there are constant average variable and marginal costs up to the level of capacity of the port (X_1). At that point no more traffic can be carried, so the cost curve becomes vertical. Now consider adding another small port to the first; the port may be duplicated at another location, or the capacity of the existing port may be simply increased for the

FIGURE 3.3   TOTAL COST OF TWO IDENTICAL PORTS
AND A ONE-PORT ALTERNATIVE

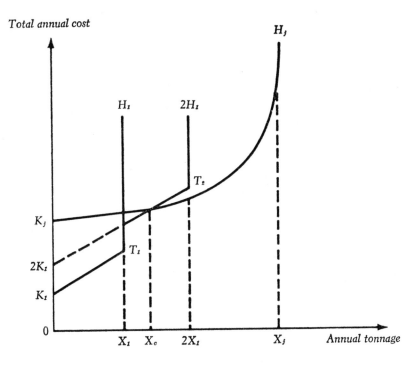

Note: K_i = annual cost of capital for a small port; K_j = annual cost of capital for a large port.

same types of relatively small ships. Then if the new port is simply a replica of the old (at least two equally preferred locations are assumed), twice the capacity will imply double the fixed cost. Thus the points T_1 and T_2 will lie on a ray through the origin (not shown), that is to say, average cost at T_1 and T_2 is the same. Similarly the marginal cost conditions are the same.

The alternative large-scale deep-water port is represented by a much larger fixed cost than the two-port complex (that is, K_j compared with $2K_1$), but at first marginal cost is lower because of the low variable cost of the large port and because of the economies of the large vessel. But the concentration of traffic in one port does increase internal transport cost, and after a certain quantity these may more than offset the economies of the large port and large vessel system. Consequently marginal cost rises until the capacity of the port is reached at X_j.[6] It is not merely internal transport cost that accounts for the rise in the marginal cost. Clearly the adoption of bulk-cargo or unitized techniques with generally larger consignment size will involve costs of distribution such as break-bulk wholesale functions and also the additional cost of inventories.

The main point of this discussion is that, for a given country with a certain specified distribution of resources, there are economies of scale in ports. The larger the port, other things being equal and for certain quantity ranges, the lower the cost. But ultimately the additional cost of internal transport and other distribution costs will ensure that the diseconomies set in, illustrating the truth of the adage that economies of scale are limited by the size of the market. The diseconomies will occur at lower volumes the more dispersed the population and resources of the country and the higher the natural barriers to internal transport.[7]

No doubt it would be possible to develop a theory of port size and location for an idealized population with specified (and very simple) transport requirements that would suggest the appropriate number and distribution of ports. However, since circumstances vary so greatly from one country to another, such a model is unlikely to be of any general use.

Methodology of measuring port costs

It is always good practice to test theories of cost by confronting the hypotheses with the facts. In principle it should be possible to

6. It may be argued that even though the port investment is very large, the marginal cost for small quantities of traffic should be about the same as under the small port conditions since small boats have to be used and since the elaborate equipment is not useful in these circumstances. There is much in this argument, and it should be reflected in a slope of the H_j curve initially equal to that of the H_1 curve but then falling as the quantity increases. This would give the traditional textbook shape for the total cost function for a given plant size.

7. The cost curves of Figures 3.1 and 3.3 (above) have been drawn assuming that internal transport cost has been included in the cost calculations of the port. This is not the traditional costing approach to ports. The additional internal transport cost would normally be treated as the reduction in port charges required to penetrate more distant markets. This is only a matter of convenience of treatment and not of substance.

examine various manifestations of port cost to see whether the theory is relevant to reality. First, a cross section of different port sizes can be examined to see how unit cost varies with the tonnage throughput. Some attempt has been made to carry out such an analysis for certain North American ports, and the general results are reported in the second half of this chapter. Second, the costs of a port could be traced through time as it expands to cater to an increasing volume of traffic. No such time series analysis has been attempted in this study, partly because so many other factors change over time, and it is difficult to distill the effects of increased traffic from all other incidental variables. The third approach is to examine and to cost engineering and manning specifications for typical ports. The disadvantages of such an approach are well known. But there is such a wealth of material on port plans that it is worthwhile to survey it to give a general view on the appropriateness of the proposed cost model. The example of a Central American port is pursued in the second half of this chapter. Here these results of examining cost conditions are summarized.

The general shape of the empirical curves is similar to those derived from theoretical conjecture in Figure 3.3 above. For a particular size port (in terms of facilities) unit cost falls up to full use and then rises quite rapidly as congestion sets in.[8] Fixed costs (such as dredging cost and provision of berths) tend to be relatively low for a small port, but this is compensated for by the high variable cost of operation. Dredging a new channel, building more berths, and installing more moving equipment will increase vastly the fixed cost of the port, but it will also reduce the variable cost per unit as larger ships are used and cheaper handling techniques become feasible.

There are clearly some discontinuities in port construction. For example, it would be inefficient to dredge a channel an inch deeper each month for 5 years to increase the depth of the channel by 5 feet; it is best done in one go. Similarly berths are expanded most efficiently by building in large, more-or-less-standardized units. Consequently in practice the choice may be between the two ports whose cost functions are illustrated in Figure 3.4.

If traffic expands gradually (and for simplicity, if traffic is not affected by port charges), then it becomes efficient to convert the small port into a large one well before the small port has achieved

8. For example, handling costs of containers in one developing country's projections fell from US$25 per movement to US$4 as container movements in-increased from 20,000 to 200,000.

FIGURE 3.4.   COST.AND DISCONTINUITIES OF PORTS

Total cost

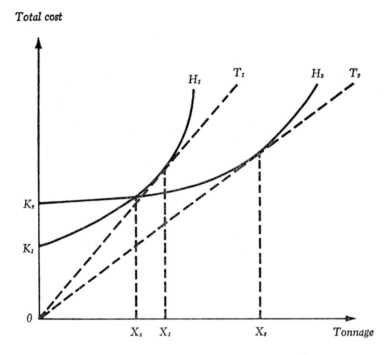

Note: X_1 = tonnage at which average costs are minimized with harbor size represented by K_1H_1; X_2 = minimum cost tonnage with K_2H_2; X_3 = output level at which the authorities will build the large harbor, K_2H_2. Over the range 0 to X_3 average cost for the authority will decrease if the harbor is the appropriate size.

minimum unit cost. Furthermore the large port will continue to exhibit apparent excess capacity for some time as traffic continues to expand. This apparent overbuilding of ports is, however, quite rational in the cost conditions of the figure. That is to say, to get the lower cost, too much capacity must be installed relative to the quantity of present traffic.[9]

9. Many of the complications involved in the dynamics of adjustment have been ignored here; for example, the cost relations should all be in terms of present values of the future discounted cost streams. Such additional embellishments, however, do not affect the substance of the argument.

With a growing level of traffic through time, it may be best to overbuild the port and suffer the excess cost at low traffic volumes to secure the lower cost at later high traffic volumes. For example, suppose that in Figure 3.4 there is a choice between the port characterized by the cost curve K_1H_1 and that by K_2H_2. Furthermore, imagine that the life of these ports is very long, say 50 years, and that it is very expensive to expand capacity once K_1H_1 is built. Then minimizing the discounted future cost streams, it may be best to build the large port even for the initial low traffic volumes—that is to say, for throughputs lower than X_s—to enjoy the low cost on the increased traffic in later years. Of course, the average throughput of the large port throughout its life must be considerably larger than X_s. But this example illustrates that for ports with long lives, the problem is to find the best size and type of equipment that is adaptable to large variations of perhaps rapid growth of traffic.[10]

Pricing implications of economies of scale

With economies of scale and marginal cost below average cost, the usual implication is that the price of the port service should be fixed at marginal cost and that the port should be subsidized. But of course this argument assumes, among other things, that there is always spare capacity in all port activities. Furthermore it assumes that port capacity is always nicely adjusted; in particular there are no lags in port development and no unforeseen bursts of traffic. Perfect port planning and adaptation to traffic flows are theoretical concepts only and are of little relevance for planning port charges systems.[11]

Furthermore there are considerable objections to financing much of the port cost out of the general budgetary revenues. The requirement that the port recover its cost provides a valuable administrative incentive to the port authority to control its cost and expansion plans. Without such discipline the port authorities are likely to overbuild ports on one hand and run a somewhat inefficient port on the other. The open check book of the public authorities is a standing invitation

10. If the small port is built and later a larger port is considered to expand capacity, then the capital cost of the existing port is irrelevant for such decisions.

11. The arguments to be pursued here are exactly analogous to those in A. A. Walters, *Economics of Road User Charges*, World Bank Staff Occasional Papers, no. 5 (Baltimore: Johns Hopkins Press, 1968) and will not be repeated here.

to labor unions and other groups such as traders and shippers to exploit the situation.

This objection does not apply to government undertaking specific and very limited subsidies, such as central government provision of the land for the port, undertaking to keep the channel dredged, providing light services, and so on. These activities can be separated administratively from the port accounts, just as the on-route navigational aides may be separated from the accounts of airport authorities. Whether it is wise to load these items on to the general accounts of the Treasury or to levy specific user fees is another matter.[12] This will depend on the elasticity of demand for the port services with respect to the price, on the cost of raising revenue in terms of the administrative expense of the tax dollar and the inefficiencies caused by such taxes, on the degree of under- or over-valuation of the exchange rate, and on such difficult problems as the distributional effects of the subsidy compared with distributional effects of the marginal taxes.

In this study the broad effects of these considerations are only outlined. It is presumed that, except in the case of competitive ports, the elasticity of demand for port services is rather low on the usual argument that the port charge is a small element of the total transport charge that is itself a small element of the delivered price. With no substitution possibilities, therefore, the elasticity of demand for port services would be expected to be a small fraction of the final elasticity. If the elasticity of demand is very low, then ensuring that the port pays its way will not create substantial inefficiencies.

The cost of raising revenue varies from country to country, but as a general rule the less developed the country, the more inefficient the collection of revenue. Finally there is some distributional presumption that the beneficiaries should pay for the services from which they profit; but the precise incidence of both cost and benefit is impossible to determine with any certainty.

There is, however, one aspect of the distributional problem that is a central focus of this study—the extent to which variation of port charges will be passed on or absorbed by the shipping companies or foreign traders. The question is whether the benefit of port investment or the lowering of port charges is enjoyed by the steamship owners or whether it is largely passed on to the residents of the country. This will be discussed in detail in Chapter 5.

---

12. See, for example, R. H. Coase, "The Economics of the Lighthouse," *Journal of Law and Economics*, vol. XVIII, no. 1 (April 1975), pp. 25–31.

Port Cost in Practice

Large variations in port cost arise because of the different factor proportions used in various cargo systems. But even with similar cargo systems, it is difficult to identify cross-section studies of different ports that give clear evidence on economies of scale. In practice engineering studies of synthesized cost must be relied upon heavily.

Factor proportions and port cost

Major variations in factor proportions are connected with differences in the cargo system. These differences are illustrated in Table 3.1 by the planned costs for three different berths at Port Kelang. In each case the full operating cost for the project has been calculated for the expected annual throughput of the berth, roughly equal to the level of optimal use or full capacity.[13] The range of services provided in each of the three berths is rather different, but these differences can be standardized by comparing the bulk berth with the general cargo berth (omitting back-up facilities) and with the container berth (omitting the container freight station). The cost of land reclamation, which is more a requirement of a particular port expansion scheme than of berth construction as such, is ignored. Comparing rows a, b, and c, a common feature of all three berths emerges: the high share of fixed cost in total annual cost. It ranges from about 50 percent for conventional general cargo berths to some 80 percent for the container berth. The main source of differences in the share of fixed cost, however, is the relative degree of mechanization of the three types of berths. The modern dry-bulk berth shows the largest share of plant and equipment cost on an annual basis, followed by the container berth and by the relatively lightly mechanized general cargo berth. The relative labor intensity of port services, related to delivery is also confirmed; when the CFS is included in the project, the share of fixed cost in the annual cost of the container berth drops by one-eighth.

The fixed cost in Table 3.1 was computed as the replacement cost

13. The consultants' proposal for the construction of the three berths was based in each case on comparisons between the cost of delays to ships arriving according to a Poisson distribution and the cost of providing new berths.

TABLE 3.1. Composition of Annual Port Cost for the Expected Annual Throughput of Three Planned Berths, Port Kelang, 1974

At expected annual throughput[a]	Dry bulk berth (fertilizer) (percent) 1	General cargo berth		Container berth	
		Excluding back-up facility[c] (percent) 2	Including back-up facility (percent) 3	Excluding CFS[a] (percent) 4	Including CFS (percent) 5
Annual cost of fixed assets[b] as percent of total annual cost	78	52	57	82	71
Annual cost of fixed assets[b] as percent of total annual cost, omitting cost of land reclamation	77	52	57	81	70
Annual capital cost of land reclamation, capital dredging, and wharf as percent of total annual cost	43	47	40	59	45
Annual capital cost of plant as percent of total annual cost	35	3	4	23	19

a. Expected throughput per year: dry bulk berth, 215,000 tons; general cargo berth, 200,000 tons; container berth, 100,000 containers (TEU).

b. The components of fixed assets are: for dry bulk berths—land reclamation, wharf, bridge, dolphins, conveyer, steelwork, dredging, cranes, conveyers, electrical works; for the additional general cargo berth—wharf and bridges, transit shed, services, dredging and back-up facilities (land, roads, godown, services), and plant for wharf and back-up facilities; for the container berth—land reclamation, wharf and bridges, roads, stacking area, dredging, wharf cranes, straddle carriers, prime movers and trailers, and CFS (station buildings, services, and forklifts).

c. The back-up facility has not been charged with any part of the annual labor cost of maintaining and operating the berth.

d. The CFS has not been charged with any part of the annual administration cost of the container berth.

Source: Coopers and Lybrand Associates Limited in association with Sir Bruce White, Wolfe Barry, and Partners, and Shankland Cox Partnership, "Lembaga Pelabohan Kelang. Port Development Feasibility Study," Final Report (August 1974), pp. 141, 149, 153, and various parts.

of plant and works. But most ports still compute fixed cost at historical values, and this leads normally (and patently so in times of high inflation) to underestimation. The error introduced into cost estimates by using out-of-date prices poses a particularly serious threat to cost recovery when it affects the fixed cost of the capital-intensive port. It is an open invitation to charge too little and to invest too much.

The chief reason for this brief survey of port cost is to build up a general notion on the relation between cost and output. A high share of fixed cost at full capacity operation does not, of course, constitute hard and fast evidence on the behavior of cost per unit for throughputs below that level. But with the indivisibilities that characterize investment in infrastructure, the presumption is that the average cost of port services will decline noticeably as output is increased toward full capacity and that marginal cost is therefore below average cost. This question is discussed in Chapter 8, but at this stage more direct information on the relation between unit cost and output in container terminals is offered. Port planners assume that the cost of the berth and of operating it stay more or less constant up to high levels of use, and this means that the short-run average cost of container berths declines over wide ranges of output. According to a summary of British container port experience, an increase in berth throughput from 10,000 to 75,000 units (in a berth with maximum annual capacity of 100,000 standard units) may be assumed to be associated with a decline of cost per unit from 7 to 1 in ratio terms.[14] Short-run marginal cost thus lies below short-run average cost. If the size of the berth is itself varied to cope with different volumes of annual throughput, the cost per container will decline from £75 to £16[15] as berth capacity is raised from 10,000 to 100,000 TEU per year. It follows then that long-run marginal cost also lies below long-run average cost.

14. National Ports Council. The estimate is based on 1972 prices and refers to a single-user berth. The decline in unit cost is much less—from 3 to 1 in ratio terms—in common user berths with similar maximum capacity. H. K. Dally, "Containers—a Note on Berth Throughputs and Terminal Handling," National Ports Council Bulletin (London), no. 4, (April 1973), pp. 60–65.

15. Exchange rates in terms of SDRs (special drawing rights) for the currencies of the United Kingdom, Bangladesh, Thailand, Malaysia, Singapore, India, and the United States are given in the Glossary following Chapter 9.

Evidence on port cost and economies of scale

It is extraordinarily difficult to accumulate comparable data on port cost to estimate the appropriate slopes of the cost functions. This arises not merely because of the shortage of statistics, although that is common enough, but from the lack of comparable port situations in respect of both traffic and geography. Cross-sectional analysis can be very misleading and cannot be relied upon.

Consider the example of Seattle and Vancouver with respect to their most standardized product service—the container trade.

TABLE 3.2. TOTAL CONTAINER TRAFFIC
AND FACILITIES, 1973

	Traffic (TEU)[a]	No. of berths	Cranes	Acres
Vancouver	88,000	3	1	15
Seattle	377,000	11	12	161

Source: Trevor D. Heaver, "The Routing of Canadian Container Traffic through Vancouver and Seattle," a study prepared for the Western Transportation Advisory Council and the Centre for Transportation Studies of the University of British Columbia (Vancouver, B.C.: WESTAC, January 1975), pp. 11 and 75.
a. Includes inbound, outbound, loaded, and empty containers.

From the evidence of this table it may seem at first that there are economies of scale in container operations. With less than a four-fold increase in the number of berths, Seattle carries more than four times as many containers as Vancouver. But Seattle has much more equipment and greater acreage than Vancouver. Furthermore the traffic at Vancouver is much more balanced than that through Seattle, and the containers are treated differently at the two ports.[16] Little or nothing about the existence of economies of scale can be adduced from such statistics.

However, some light might be shed on the issue by the charges for container traffic through the two ports. If it is assumed that normal profits are being earned in the two ports, then the port charges per container might approximate the average cost. Table 3.3 illustrates the charges that accrue to port operations in Seattle and Vancouver.

16. *See:* "The Routing of Container Traffic Through Vancouver and Seattle" (WESTMAC: Vancouver, 1975).

TABLE 3.3. PORT CHARGES TO THE CONSIGNEE
ON CONTAINER TRAFFIC

	Vancouver ($)	Seattle ($)
Wharfage	23.63	33.75
Handling and through port charge	81.27	40.00
Vessel service and facilities charge	0	21.60
Tailgate loading	22.28	0
Total of port charges per container	127.18	95.35

This suggests that there are indeed economies of scale in the container business—approximately a fourfold increase in size reduces cost by about one quarter. However, with this comparison even more caveats apply. One of the most important is the problem of accounts reflecting historical cost and not the replacement cost of assets; similarly there are various arbitrary allocations of cost in the determination of charges. The price charged for handling a container is determined largely by the competitive conditions of alternative handling arrangements and not by the cost. It would be necessary to assume that the markup of handling charge over cost was equal in both Seattle and Vancouver, and there is no reason to suppose that is the case. Another difficulty is that the services performed for the charge set out in Table 3.3 are not identical in the two cases, and it is difficult to standardize the figures for this effect.

Somewhat older Canadian data (1971–72) give no clear lead on the question of economies of scale (Table 3.4). A comparison of Quebec with Halifax points to the number of cranes (and perhaps also to the amount of storage area) as the limiting factor in Quebec. But in comparing Vancouver and Halifax, output and capacity (in terms of berths and cranes) seem to rise in the same proportion although there may be a saving in land area for storage as size and throughput grow. Charges were somewhat higher per container (account being taken of different charging systems) in the smaller facility. If forces were at work to bring charges down to the level of cost—as would be ensured by competition—a mild tendency to economies of scale in container terminals could be inferred from the difference in charges and perhaps also from the difference in storage capacity. But the presumption of enough competition to make charges equal to cost would be difficult to reconcile with marked discrepancies in charges for similar services. It may be concluded that it is impossible to obtain reliable indications of the cost functions for ports from cross-section studies of different sized ports.

TABLE 3.4.   CANADIAN CONTAINER PORT CAPACITY, ANNUAL
CONTAINER HANDLING, AND CHARGES

	Halifax (Chalterm)	Quebec (Wolfe's Cove)	Vancouver (Centennial "6")
Capacity			
Number of berths	2	2	1
Depth (feet)	40	37	40
Cranes and capacity (tons)	1–40 / 1–45	1–35	1–40
Storage[a] (TEU)	3,100	2,000	2,000
1972 capacity (containers)[b]	100,000	50,000	50,000
Output (1972)			
Container handlings 1972	97,453	51,990	48,294
Handling charges (1971) (Canadian $ per container)			
Inward	59.00	n.a.	60.00[c]–77.50[d]
Outward	59.00	n.a.	58.75[c]–66.875[d]

n.a. = not available.

a. Total storage based on 20-foot container equivalents stacked two high.

b. Assuming a capacity of 100,000 20-foot containers per year for a single berth/two-crane facility. For a single-crane facility, it is assumed that the throughput is limited to a crane capacity of 50,000 20-foot containers per year.

c. Weight tons, 12.5; density, 40 cubic feet/ton (12.5 measurement tons).

d. Weight tons, 12.5; density, 80 cubic feet/ton (25 measurement tons).

Source: Canadian Transport Commission, Systems Analysis Branch, *The Container Study in Summary.* Report 70 (principal authors, P. M. Bunting and L. M. O'Connell) (Ottawa, November 1973), pp. 42, 43, 71.

Planning and engineering studies

The other source of material about the cost functions of ports are the engineering studies of port development. These are difficult to interpret quantitatively in cost terms on a standardized basis. However, certain general points emerge.

The most interesting study for the purposes of this discussion was the World Bank investigation into the investment programs of Central America[17] which explored the cost which would emerge if certain Central American ports were expanded and if traffic were

17. Anandarup Ray and James W. Loudon, "Central American Ports Study," World Bank Economic Staff Working Paper, no. 117 (Washington, D.C.: The World Bank, October 1971).

concentrated at these ports. The methodology forecasts the probable structure of port investment and port cost for different levels of traffic. Generally these showed that unit cost diminished as the capacity throughput of the port was increased. Exceptions to this general rule occurred where there were expensive natural obstacles to be overcome. These were usually specific to the site, as suggested above. In general there were substantial economies in port size for conventional general cargo operations. However, the study noted that although these gains were real, they were not large enough to offset the increase in inland transport cost which a concentration on a few ports would entail.

For the purposes of this study, it is sufficient to illustrate the phenomenon of economies of scale in a conventional port. Table 3.5 shows the calculated costs in 1971 U.S. dollars per metric ton of a two, three, four, and five berth port at Henecon in Central America. The economies of scale are reflected clearly in the marked reduction in capital and maintenance cost per metric ton as the size of port increases. The cost per ton for administration and for cargo handling was thought to be constant and so not affected by the size of the port. Operating the port below capacity, however, will cause unit cost to increase above that at capacity throughput. Thus the cost developed by port planners conforms to the pattern shown in Figure 3.4 and exhibits increasing returns to scale.[18]

18. Additional examples of this typical shape of the cost curves are given in Ray and Loudon, *Central American Ports Study.*

TABLE 3.5.   COST PER METRIC TON OF MULTIBERTH PORT (ALONGSIDE) BERTHS AT HENECON (1971 US$)

Berths used to capacity	Metric tons per year	Capital cost	Mainte-nance cost	Adminis-trative cost	Cargo handling cost	Total cost
2	200,000	4.96	4.56	0.70	1.64	11.86
3	340,000	3.91	2.81	0.70	1.64	9.06
4	460,000	2.99	2.14	0.70	1.64	7.47
5	580,000	3.00	1.74	0.70	1.64	7.08

Source: Anandarup Ray and James W. Loudon, "Central American Ports Study," World Bank Economic Staff Working Paper, no. 117 (Washington, D.C.: World Bank, October 1971), Appendix 3.

The conclusion of this section, therefore, is that the evidence seems to be consistent with the suggested pattern of cost curves and that marked economies of scale exist for most port locations. Only where there are severe natural constraints would decreasing returns be found.

Chapter 4

Congestion Levies and Surcharges

CONGESTION IS A MARKED FEATURE of many transport facilities. On land it takes the form of crawling traffic and occasional jams; in ports it is manifest in long queues of vessels waiting in the roads for berth space or in transit sheds clogged with merchandise. The considerable cost involved suggests that some changes in the system might reduce these wastes and increase efficiency.

The existence of congestion indicates that the port authority possesses a valuable scarce resource. If the port were owned by a private party unconstrained by government and custom, it would raise port charges and profit from the scarcity. The long line of ships in the roads would be reduced to a few vessels as shipowners and shippers switched to alternative facilities.

In practice, the port authority does not usually respond by raising the level of port tariffs, perhaps because the tariffs are regulated by

Note: After completing this study the authors became aware of an article by A. H. Vanags, first published in 1973 in the *Proceedings of a Conference on Marine Traffic Engineering* and recently republished under the title of "Maritime Congestion, an Economic Analysis," in *Advances in Maritime Economics*, ed. R. O. Goss (Cambridge: Cambridge University Press, 1977). Standard congestion theory is applied to marine facilities, and the results are formally identical to those of the present study. Vanags developed the case where ships arrive at the port following a Poisson distribution, whereas in this study the less formal substitution effects and their interaction with congestion levies have been developed. Vanags' prior claim to this extension of congestion analysis is acknowledged.

government or ossified by long custom. Tariffs are kept low in a congested port because of the belief—right or wrong—that a rise in port prices would be reflected, and perhaps even magnified, in increased domestic prices of imported and lowered domestic prices for exported goods. Higher port tariffs, it may be thought, would merely take money from the pockets of domestic producers and consumers and transfer it to the coffers of the port authority.

The absence of high tariffs for congested ports, however, has not saved domestic traders and consumers from the high cost of congestion. Both competitive tramp owner and cartelized liner operator will charge at least for the time that their ships spend in the queue; the former in the freight charges or charter contract and the latter in the form of congestion surcharges. Domestic prices and quantities must reflect these congestion costs.

But suppose that the port authority were to impose its own congestion levy at a level which reduced the length of the queue to a normal length. What would be the consequences? This is the main question of policy which is examined in this and the following chapters.

In discussing the policy of a port authority, an old problem prominent in international trade policy is encountered—what should be the objective of policy? This aspect of the analysis is discussed in the following chapter, but the main outlines are reviewed here so that the contribution of congestion charges can be seen in its proper context.

First, the best congestion charges to be levied by the port can be considered from the point of view of all trading nations in the world. A system of port charges can be devised so that the world as a whole is better off. For a particular port in a country, however, the port authority can make the country better off by exploiting whatever monopoly power it may have, thus raising port charges above the marginal cost (including the value of the scarce port resources) and increasing the profit of the port. Some part of this additional revenue —but not normally all of it—will accrue to the port as a mere transfer from other residents; higher port charges will raise freight rates, increase the domestic price of imports, and reduce the domestic price of exports. Clearly, the rule is to find the port tariff (including congestion levies) that causes the marginal profit of the port to be just equal to the additional money required to compensate domestic traders and consumers for the increase in port charges (the compensating variation).

Although simple to state, this policy objective is difficult to achieve.

In part, this is because the reaction of the shipping cartels to different levels of port charges must be analyzed. Little is known in practice about the bargaining strategies of conferences and how they would respond to congestion prices levied by the port.

This chapter is concerned primarily with the analysis of the broad effects of port congestion levies. This description of the consequences of the port levying congestion charges can be carried out largely without resorting to mathematics; simple diagrams (or figures) will carry the argument. However, the literary or diagrammatic account is deficient in two respects. First the detailed response of steamship owners—in particular, the extent to which they pass on the port congestion levy—will be determined by the elasticity of demand for shipping services. Indeed, much will depend on the change in the elasticity as the quantity of traffic increases. Second, the detailed redistribution of profits and other incomes cannot be analyzed.

The analytical framework of this chapter will not, therefore, allow firm conclusions to be reached about passing-on of congestion levies and distributional consequences. Nevertheless, it reveals issues and problems which are explored in considerable detail, although with some mathematics, in Chapters 5 and 6.

Theory of Congestion

It is best to begin with a fiction. Suppose that the shipping industry is owned entirely by many domestic nationals who compete vigorously to provide shipping services. No monopoly or cartel exists, and no foreigners intrude in this scenario. Consequently, the welfare of shipowners is part and parcel of the welfare of the country or of the national interest, as defined in the Introduction. Similarly, assume that the state is but a small part of the international market for both the commodities which are exported and those which are imported; the price of exports and imports in foreign markets can be taken as given and are independent of the country's behavior. However, the port is assumed to have monopoly power since, for simplicity but not from necessity, it is designated to be the only port in the country, and alternative transport arrangements that use other ports or modes will involve considerably greater cost. The port is owned by nationals, perhaps even by the government, but whatever its equity structure, it is certainly publicly controlled.

FIGURE 4.1.   PORT CONGESTION WITH COMPETITIVE SHIPPING

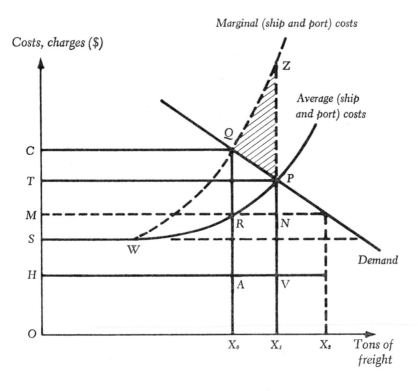

Note: Cost: OH = port variable cost and overhead = port charge (here
                assumed constant);
        HS = ship cost when there is no congestion;
        HM = ship cost when there is normal congestion;
        TM = NP = the congestion levy charged by shipowners over the
                normal freight rate.
     Revenue: OHVX$_1$ = revenue accruing to the port authority;
        HMNV = normal revenue to shipowners;
        MTPN = congestion levy revenue to shipowners.
     Traffic: X$_0$ = optimum traffic;
        X$_1$ = traffic with shipowners' congestion levy;
        X$_2$ = traffic with no congestion levy.

The consequences of different policies on port tariffs can be explored using Figure 4.1. The horizontal axis measures the total traffic, both exports and imports, of the port in tons. But since all exports and imports have to pass through the port and since, by assumption, each ton requires a fixed amount of port service, the horizontal axis also measures total trade flows. The demand for port services is derived in two stages—from the demand and supply conditions of export and import markets (which are assumed to remain constant), and from the all-in price (port charge and freight rate) of transport. This all-in price is the value recorded on the vertical axis of Figure 4.1, and the derived demand for shipping as a function of the all-in price is labeled demand. This demand curve represents the demand for shipping, and, by earlier assumptions, the demand for port services is proportional to it.

To see the consequences of port policies, it is imagined that the port pursues a normal Anglo-Saxon policy and charges the variable cost per ton together with a markup for overheads as shown by OH per ton.[1] This tariff of OH is levied whatever the conditions in the port, whether it be underused or congested.[2]

The cost of the ship operation is shown as HS for low levels of traffic where there is virtually no waiting for berths at all; but as traffic increases, this cost rises to R (at X_0) and P (at X_1) for each shipowner.[3] For convenience, assume that the shipowner supposes that there will be a normal amount of congestion at any port and fixes his charge accordingly. Further, normal congestion is assumed to be that which would prevail if, with the demand curve as drawn,

1. Although this analysis is given in terms of cargo tons rather than of ships, many of the port charges relate to vessels rather than tons. This is unlikely to be a crucial factor here and is taken up in a later discussion of practical problems.

2. If the objective is merely to cover cost or to earn some predetermined percentage of profit on capital, port tariffs will be higher for an underused port than for a congested one. The perverseness of such a policy is obvious. For an exposition of this argument, see A. A. Walters, *Economics of Road User Charges*, World Bank Staff Occasional Papers, no. 5 (Baltimore: Johns Hopkins Press, 1968), pp. 18, 146.

3. For convenience here, the inventory costs of cargo in transit are included in the shipping costs. This could have been taken into account by reducing the demand curve for shipping services. It is simpler, however, to treat inventory cost, which is related to the time in transit, as part of the cost of shipping. Thus by including inventory cost, just as congestion effects were included, on the cost side, the demand price can be treated as though it refers to a uniform quality of service.

services were sold at marginal cost (OC per ton). This will again simplify the exposition.

With the demand in Figure 4.1, congestion is greater than normal, and there is considerable queuing in the roads. Each competitive shipowner will add these additional expenses to the freight charge, and the average ship and port cost will be equal to the appropriate demand price (intersection P in Figure 4.1). Each shipowner will be levying a congestion surcharge of TM (or PN) a ton.

But this surcharge does not measure the true cost of increasing traffic through the port by an additional ton. This is traced by the marginal cost curve $SWQZ$. Thus at the traffic level X_1 tons, an additional ton of cargo would cost ZX_1, not PX_1. This is because an additional ship service provided by a competitive owner takes into account only the waiting time that his ship spends in the roads; this is the cost incurred in his accounts. But by joining the queue, he delays all the ships that come after him. Their cost is increased, but these additional expenses are not reflected in his accounts. This true cost (or marginal cost) exceeds the value of the service to the users for all traffic in excess of X_0.

Clearly the congestion charge which is levied by competitive shipping is too low. The all-in price at P is less than the marginal cost ZX_1 of providing the shipping service. Too many ships join the queue, and it would be better to reduce traffic to X_0. It might be supposed that, if there is an orderly queuing system, any entrant who causes a permanent lengthening of the queue (for example, by operating an additional weekly service) bears all the cost of his decision. He will take account of the additional queuing time when he calculates the expected profitability of the service. But he does not take account of the additional queuing cost (PZ in Figure 4.1) caused to all other vessels supplying services to the port.

This analysis corresponds precisely to the theory of highway congestion. The policy of charging conventional prices for the services of the port generates the same sort of congestion that arises on urban streets and some intercity highways. And, of course, the solution is the same. The port should raise its charges from OH per ton by RQ per ton, where the RQ per ton represents the congestion levy of the port. Clearly if the port levies RQ per ton, the shipowners will not exact the congestion surcharge PN that they imposed under the congested conditions at X_1 and price P. With traffic at X_0 tons, shipowners' average cost (excluding the port congestion levy) will be OM per ton, and competition in the shipping industry will ensure that they charge no more than this for their freight services. By levying the congestion toll of RQ per ton, the port authority will avoid the waste of providing services at a price less than the cost of producing them; this waste of congestion at X_1 is shown by the shaded area QPZ in Figure 4.1.

It might be thought that the port authority was behaving like a monopolistic exploiter of the domestic shippers and consumers. But such an interpretation would be a travesty. For the port is not maximizing its profits by charging RQ per ton for congestion. Indeed, a port authority that wished to capitalize on its monopoly would charge much higher tariffs and would reduce traffic well below X_0.[4] In fact, levying a congestion fee of RQ per ton simulates what would occur if the port services were produced by a competitive process. The optimum port charge is simply the value that would emerge in a competitive market—if it were possible to organize one.

The price of the overall shipping service (freight rate and port charge) will normally rise above that which would exist if the port authority did not charge a congestion levy.[5] But the increase in price will never be more than the port congestion levy, and it might be expected to be considerably less. Figure 4.1 shows that when a congestion levy is imposed, the greater the elasticity of demand for the services of the port, the smaller the rise in price and the larger the reduction in the quantity shipped through the port. Similarly, if a relatively small reduction in the quantity of tonnage causes a large fall in the cost of ship operations, then again, even though the elasticity of demand is not high, the increase in the overall charge for freight (including the port tariff) will be small.

The revenue accruing to the port authority will include its normal charges $OHAX_0$ and the revenue from the congestion levy $MCQR$

---

4. The port authority would take into account the marginal revenue curve (not shown in Figure 4.1) for its services in deciding its most profitable throughput. And for a given demand curve, profit-maximizing behavior would give results opposite from the optimizing policy; for example, the greater the (absolute) elasticity of demand, the larger the reduction of traffic from optimizing, but the smaller the reduction from monopolistic exploitation.

5. The exception is where the congestion is so heavy that throughput actually is reduced. This is the familiar backward-bending case in highway congestion. See A. A. Walters, "The Theory and Measurement of the Private and Social Costs of Highway Congestion," *Econometrica*, vol. 29 (1961), reprinted in *Readings in Economics of Transport*, ed. Dennis Munby (Penguin, 1969).

(Figure 4.1). The total revenue from both normal charges and congestion levy probably will increase. Only a highly elastic market demand combined with a low congestion levy could possibly cause port revenues to fall when a congestion levy is imposed. This is a most unlikely set of circumstances which, in any case, would not be propitious for imposing such a levy.

In this exposition so far certain important assumptions have been made. The transport process has been assumed to be rigidly prescribed, that is to say, the techniques are fixed and unalterable; there is a fixed load per vessel; the vessels are all homogeneous; the composition of cargo does not change; and port services per ship (and per ton of cargo) are rigidly fixed. This implies that there is no possibility of substitution between cargoes, between vessel and cargo (such as varying the load per ship), between vessel and port (such as port cranes and ship derricks), between one vessel and another, and between one part of the port and another (such as between berths and moorings). Later this chapter explores the effects of these important opportunities of making more efficient use of resources. On the present assumptions, however, the only possible adjustment is in the quantity of cargo (and so ships). If the port imposes the appropriate congestion surcharge RQ, the quantity of cargo will shrink from X_1 to X_0, and the queue of vessels contracts to its normal level.

With fixed proportions the difference between the marginal (ship and port) cost and the associated average cost can be measured. For simplicity, continue to assume that the port marginal cost is equal to its average cost (OH in Figure 4.1 and c_p hereafter). The ship cost includes two parts: the inventory cost of the goods in the waiting ships and the daily cost of the idle ships in the queue. Both of these can be measured by a constant single daily amount c per shipload. The length of the queue in terms of vessels (q) is an increasing function of the throughput of the port (X), where X is measured in terms of shiploads per day. This can be interpreted in terms of the fact that the occupancy rates of berths can be increased only by having a longer queue of vessels. Total cost (K) then consists of two elements:

$$\begin{bmatrix} \text{Port cost} \\ \text{per} \\ \text{shipload} \end{bmatrix} \begin{bmatrix} \text{Port throughput:} \\ \text{shiploads} \\ \text{per day} \end{bmatrix} + \begin{bmatrix} \text{Daily} \\ \text{ship} \\ \text{costs} \end{bmatrix} \begin{bmatrix} \text{Length of queue} \\ \text{and number of} \\ \text{vessels in port} \end{bmatrix}$$

or in symbols:

$$(1) \qquad\qquad K(X) = c_p X + c q(X).$$

The total cost associated with a daily throughput of X shiploads thus is composed of the port's cost of handling these shiploads and the day's cost of the queue. Now it is clear that the delay per ship (D) or number of days the ship spends waiting or in port is then a function of X and is related to q and X as:

(2) $$X = q(X)/D(X).$$

Thus:

$$K(X) = c_pX + cXD(X).$$

The total cost of a particular daily level of throughput is now expressed as the sum of the associated port cost and the cost of the time which those shiploads had to wait before being discharged from the port.

To find the marginal cost of throughput, differentiate the last expression with respect to shiploads:

(3) $$\frac{dK(X)}{dX} = c_p + c\left[D(X) + X\frac{dD(X)}{dX}\right]$$

$$= c_p + cD(X)\left[1 + \frac{X}{D(X)}\frac{dD(X)}{dX}\right].$$

Thus the marginal cost of shiploads of cargo consists of the port cost (constant), plus the cost of time spent by an additional ship $[cD(X)]$, plus the delay cost which that additional shipload imposes on all other users of the port (the last term in the brackets). Or in words:

$$\begin{bmatrix} Marginal \\ cost \\ (per \\ vessel \\ load) \end{bmatrix} = \begin{bmatrix} Port \\ cost \end{bmatrix} + \begin{bmatrix} Own \\ delay \\ cost \end{bmatrix} + \begin{bmatrix} Additional \\ delay\ costs \\ caused\ to \\ all\ other \\ vessels \end{bmatrix}$$

The last term is of particular interest since it measures the difference between SWQZ and SWRP in Figure 4.1. Thus for any particular value of X, the required congestion surcharge can be calculated. It consists of two components: the delay cost per ship (or per shipload), multiplied by the elasticity of delay with respect to the throughput of the port.

The elasticity of delay—the percentage increase in ship delay which would have to be incurred to increase throughput (and so berth use) by 1 percent—is the only unusual element in this formula. It corresponds closely, however, to a concept widely used in planning ports and in calculating the optimal number of berths; an example was shown in Chapter 3.

In any congested port, it should be possible to calculate the congestion surcharge appropriate for the tons of throughput (X) actually observed. In the simplest case, the elements would consist of the daily cost of operating a typical vessel in port or in the line, the daily inventory cost of a shipload of typical cargo, and the elasticity of delay with respect to throughput. In a heavily congested port, the value of this surcharge might be very large because another ship joining the line will lengthen significantly the average waiting time suffered by all the vessels in the circular flow of vessels through this port. The surcharge may then amount to two or three (or more) times the new entrant's own cost of incremental delay. But this surcharge would not be the right level for policy because as the surcharge is imposed, the queue of ships (and shiploads) will contract and, as set out in the example, the total tonnage presented to the port must shrink. The surcharge calculated for the level of throughput under heavy congestion would accordingly cause too great a contraction of the number of vessels sailing to the port; if it were levied, it would have to be lowered again. The surcharge that will lead to the desired level of port use (or the target length of queue) can be calculated only if the elasticity of demand for the port is known. This can be calculated occasionally (Chapter 7 below presents an estimate for a particular port), but more often it will have to be guessed at.

Ownership and the competitive structure of steamship services

For the purpose of exposition, it was supposed that the steamship owners were highly competitive. This may approximate closely conditions in some ports of the world. For example, a port catering more or less exclusively to bulk transport of a standardized commodity, such as La Goulette, will find that there are many ships that compete vigorously for the traffic. But for general cargo conveyed in conventional or unitized vessels, the shipping conferences probably will play an important role in providing services. Thus the next problem is to examine the effects of such conferences on the consequences of the port levying a congestion charge. This carries the model one step nearer reality, but nevertheless one important fiction is retained—

namely that the vessels are all domestically owned. However, the ownership of vessels as distinct from the degree of competition is not relevant for the problem of forecasting what is likely to happen if congestion levies are imposed by the port. This is a question of positive economics concerned with merely the consequences of a specified policy. However, there are also questions of whether the policy is good or bad, and these are issues of normative economics. In judging the desirability of a policy of congestion levies, the nationality of the owner of the ships is most important. Clearly, apart from considerations of domestic distribution, it is important whether the profits of a foreign-owned shipping cartel are increased or decreased at the expense of national residents.

In this chapter, however, even for normative purposes of judging policies, the monopolist or cartel is considered to be domestically owned; this restriction will be removed in the next chapter. But the assumption is still useful for two reasons—one minor and the other important. One reason is that the results will then approximate those for ports where there is a strict and dominant law whereby all traded goods must be carried by domestically owned ships. The main reason, however, is convenience; the problems of the distribution of income can be largely ignored, invoking the usual excuse that government can, if it so wishes, redistribute income away from the monopoly shipping lines.[6]

The form of competition in the shipping industry and the effect on the behavior of the firms must be considered next. There is little doubt that the most common market structure of the shipping industry serving developing countries is that of a number of conferences supplying most of the services for a medium-sized port. (In Bangkok, for example, most general cargo is dominated by four or five conferences.) Each of these conferences will normally behave almost entirely independently of the others, although there may be transitory combinations of port users committees to deal with any common threat to

6. As discussed in the introduction to this chapter, there is one other reason for ignoring the ownership of ships. This is the internationalist or one-world attitude to economic policies. Essentially, this suggests that, for the average human being, the world would be materially better off if all government policy treated foreigners as if they were nationals. This is the argument for universal free trade, and its analogous argument applies in all commercial policies. Although such international idealism undoubtedly is praiseworthy, it will appear to be merely a fable to a poor developing country.

their profits from the port. Thus the port's proposal to levy congestion charges may generate a collusion of conferences to deal with the
menace. Since the interests of each conference will be to secure the
best deal for its members, however, such collusions are likely to be
ephemeral and transitory. Nevertheless, this suggests that it is useful
to analyze the pure monopoly case in some detail before turning to
the normal case of a group of cartels.

A monopolist steamship service

If there were just one shipowner (or one buying cartel) using the
port, then more than the appropriate congestion charge of RQ would
be levied. The shipowner would charge the shippers at least a price
of OC, of which OH would go to the port authority, and HM would
comprise their average cost of operation. The balance of the charge
MC (RQ) represents the surplus which is appropriated by the monopolist cartel. In other words the value RQ measures the rent per
ton which should properly accrue to the port because of the scarce
capacity of the port relative to the high demand for its services. But
since the port is assumed to act passively in its pricing policy, the
surplus is extracted by the monopolist shipping line. Furthermore,
with a monopoly shipping line, there will be another restriction of
throughput since the monopolist will take account of the marginal
revenue curve of the demand from shippers. In other words, the
monopolist conference or steamship company will extract not merely
the port surplus but also a monopoly rent from its exclusive position
as supplier of ocean services.

The implications of a high demand and the consequent congestion
in the case of a monopoly or single cartel should be explored further.
In Figure 4.2 a normal demand and high demand situation with associated marginal revenue curves are shown.

If the monopolist steamship owner produces more output in the
high demand conditions, he will incur a higher marginal cost, and
this difference in cost will be in the form of increased congestion.
The total price charged by the conference is higher in the high
demand situation. The conference would thus claim $p_h - p_n$ as the
pseudo-congestion surcharge in that port. This conference congestion
surcharge can be separated into two parts: the change in marginal
cost (which is truly the increase in congestion cost) and the markup
of price over marginal cost (which depends on the elasticity of demand). The whole of the price increase ($p_h - p_n$) will be attributable

FIGURE 4.2. PORT CONGESTION
WITH MONOPOLIZED SHIPOWNER (OR CARTEL)

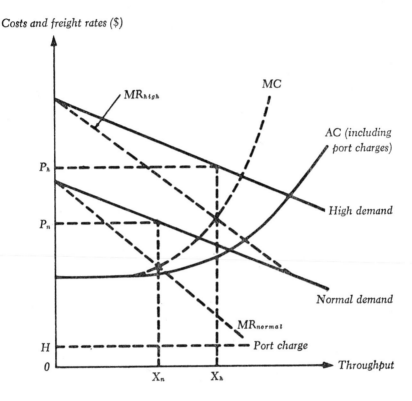

Costs and freight rates ($)

Note: MC = marginal cost; MR_{high}, MR_{normal} = marginal revenues corresponding to high and normal demand, respectively; X_h, X_n = profit-maximizing
throughputs when demand is high and low, respectively; P_h, P_n = freight rate for
X_h and X_n throughputs, respectively. Conference congestion surcharge = $P_h - P_n$.

to the increase in cost (that is to say, true congestion) if, for both
high and low demand curves, the elasticity of demand bears the same
constant proportion to cost.[7] In general, however, it is expected that
the greater the demand, the greater the inelasticity of demand for a
given price and so the greater the markup over marginal cost; the

7. Since $c' = p [(\epsilon + 1)/\epsilon]$, $p - c' = (-c')/(\epsilon + 1)$. Thus, if $(p - c')$
is constant, $c' = $ (constant) $(\epsilon + 1)$.

monopolistic power of the shipowner will be the greater under congested conditions.[8]

It is important to realize that in the monopolist shipowner case, the port is being underused both under conditions of high and low demand; congestion is too little, not too much. The value of port services still exceeds the marginal cost of supplying them, and it would be better if there was additional congestion in the port.

This problem can be illuminated by considering the demand curve for the services of the port (Figure 4.3). This can be derived by taking the difference between the marginal revenue and the marginal cost of the monopolistic conference as the price which the monopolist is just willing to pay for an additional unit of port service over and above the constant port charge actually levied (granted that he has already bought a specified quantity of port services). The equilibrium output of port services (assuming fixed proportions) is shown at X with the port charge of OH. But this is obviously less than optimal. The monopoly steamship owner should be induced to reduce freight rates and to expand his services and extend production to X_1 where marginal cost is equal to price. One way of doing this would be to subsidize port services per unit so that the new lower marginal cost curve for the monopolist shipowner intersects the marginal revenue curve at the output level X_1.[9] This is, of course, the opposite of a congestion levy on the port services. Such cases are examined in Chapter 5, but the implicit argument for subsidies must be treated with great caution because subsidies are likely to become the object of strategic bargaining; if monopolies are being subsidized, monopolies will be formed.

Independent competing steamship owners

The empirically more relevant case is where there are many groups of independent shipowners using the port facilities. These groups

8. It is conceivable that, if the elasticity of demand increases sufficiently when demand increases and when the rise in marginal costs is small, p_h may be below p_n, and the conference may more than absorb the increased congestion cost. This raises interesting theoretical issues, but they are not important in the present context; if congestion cost is small, why worry about it? It is the existence of congestion and the surcharges that constitute the problem for policy.

9. The assumption of fixed proportions is most crucial here, and it may not be possible to lower the cost curve sufficiently by cutting port charges; shipowners may actually have to be paid to use the port.

FIGURE 4.3.   DEMAND FOR OCEAN TRANSPORT
AND DERIVED DEMAND FOR PORT SERVICES

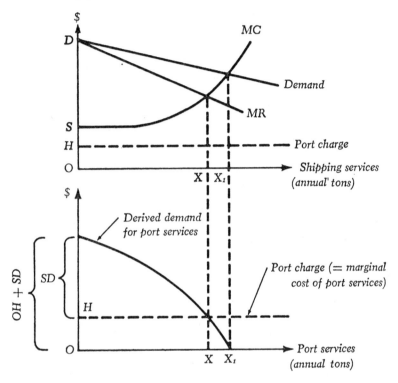

(A) Demand for Ocean Transport

(B) Derived Demand for Port Services

Note: OH = port variable cost and overhead = port charge (here assumed constant); HS = ship cost per ton where there is no congestion.

may take the form of a number of conferences, each one of which takes into account only the rise in congestion caused to its ships by adding another port call. Thus, if a particular conference accounts for 10 percent of the port calls, then it will only reckon 10 percent of the total marginal congestion cost of an additional call. Clearly as far as port behavior is concerned, this approximates the conditions of a perfectly competitive industry.[10] Consequently, in ports where there is no dominant conference (that is to say, the largest conference takes only about 15 to 20 percent of the total traffic), it is sensible to use the competitive model developed in Chapter 1 to forecast the consequences of different port policies.

Reflecting back to Figure 4.1, it will be observed that under congested conditions at traffic level X_1, shipowners levy a congestion surcharge of NP (MT) per ton to cover their cost. There will still be too much congestion at the port, and it would be better to switch traffic to other ports. Although the shipowners raise a total revenue of $MTPN$ in congestion surcharges, this no more than compensates for the additional waiting time cost incurred. This cost of congestion NP (MT) per ton is simply passed along to the consignees. There is no way to avoid this cost being incurred by the cargo owners provided that attempts are made to ship OX_1 through the port. A social loss measured by the shaded triangle is the minimum that will be incurred. Attempts to constrain demand by quotas, administrative edicts, or nonprice rules for priorities will only worsen the loss.[11] The inefficiencies of the nonprice allocation system would have to be taken into account.

Now consider the policy of the port charging congestion levies of RQ per ton.[12] Steamship owners will not now find it possible to levy a congestion charge since congestion will drop back to normal, as shown by the cost OM. If any particular competitive steamship owner tried to charge a congestion surcharge, his freight tariff would rise above cost, and other steamship companies would find it profitable to undercut him. Similarly, with a sufficiently large number of con-

---

10. The conditional clause is important. The conference may exert considerable monopoly power over a particular trade, but that trade is merely one of many that the port caters to.

11. Such nonprice methods of restricting traffic are taken usually either for political reasons to protect certain groups or because of the mistaken belief that increases in the cost of imports will generate domestic inflation. It is important to emphasize that inflation is not controlled by attempting to distort the symptoms. Inflation is generated by excess demand in relation to the quantity of real output. First the nonprice controls will distort demand, not reduce it, and second, they will be likely to reduce useful output (as distinct from the use of additional regulators) below the value it would otherwise have been.

12. The RQ would apply to cargo or to ships depending on where the congestion is located.

ferences, each would experience reduced cost (excluding the port's new congestion levy) as traffic falls from X_1 to X_0. Thus marginal cost, including the port's congestion levy, will rise by less than the new congestion levy.

The crucial question is how much of this rise in the marginal cost is passed on to cargo owners. A critical role is played by the elasticity of demand and particularly by the change in the elasticity as traffic declines. The elasticity of demand that is relevant for this analysis is that for the individual conference, and not the total demand for the services of the port. It has been argued elsewhere that the primary determinant of the long-term elasticity of demand for the traffic of an individual conference is the presence of tramp and bulk-carrier competition.[13]

In the present context, the important issue is to determine what happens to the demand curve and, in particular, to the elasticity of demand for the conference traffic when the port increases its tariffs. Of course, the main influence will be, as always, the cost of tramp and bulk-carrier competition. Later in this chapter, it is shown that, by the usual conference policy of adhering strictly to scheduled sailings, congestion will increase the cost of liners more than the cost of unscheduled tramp and bulker services. Furthermore, if it can be shown that port cost is a smaller fraction of total cost for tramps and bulkers than for conventional liner operations, then the cost and so the freight rates of competitive tramps will rise proportionately less than the cost of liners.[14] Thus a congestion levy imposed by the port will be absolutely and relatively injurious to the liner conference. It will increase the effective competition to the liner conference and will generally increase the elasticity of demand facing the conference. As a corollary, the monopolistic profit of the conference will be reduced.

This account of the effects on the conferences of congestion levy in the port tariff suggests that there will be a more efficient use of resources and a favorable effect on the distribution of income. If the cartels are owned by foreigners, the argument is reinforced. But clearly the quantitative effects depend on the precise elasticities and cost conditions involved, which are dealt with in Chapter 5.

13. E. Bennathan and A. A. Walters, *The Economics of Ocean Freight Rates*, Praeger Special Studies in International Economics and Development (New York: Praeger, 1969).

14. Evidence for the relative importance of port costs is given in Chapter 1.

Units and internal substitution

So far, the argument has been couched in terms of tons of cargo generating the congestion. This may well be true in practice, for example, if the congestion is primarily on the wharves and in the transit sheds. But also congestion may result from lack of quay space to accommodate the ships that attempt to call, and there may be ample shed space and wharf capacity. This suggests that while in the first case the congestion charge should be levied against the use of wharves or transit sheds, in the second case the congestion charge should be levied against the occupancy of the quay. In the latter case, if the occupancy of a narrow channel causes the congestion, then the appropriate charge will be on the ship call and not on the occupancy of the quays.

It is important to ensure that the congestion levy is raised in the appropriate units and on the particularly congested facilities. This will then permit the substitution of noncongested for congested facilities. Thus, if the wharves are overcrowded, the charge should be on the tons crossing the wharves, not on the ship occupancy or call. The extent of substitution between various activities in the port operation and the extent to which use of congested particular facilities can be economized can be revealed only by detailed examination.

The importance of finding the proper unit and base for the congestion surcharge is related to the considerable scope that normally exists for changing the structure of the transport process. The same tonnage of cargo may thus be carried to or from the port by different numbers of vessels; small loads per vessel may be converted into large ones. Some vessels will work cargo faster than others, either as a consequence of different ship design and equipment or because of different stowage arrangements. The packaging of the cargo can be adapted to different handling techniques. In all these cases, a congestion surcharge of appropriate magnitude, levied by the port on the use of its berths, should induce adaptations in the transport process which will lead to a more efficient use of the port's resources. Where such adaptations are undertaken, the congestion surcharge may eliminate the abnormal queues of vessels without reducing the tonnage of cargo passing through the port.

The possibilities are considerable. Consider, for example, a case where the transit sheds are jammed full of merchandise. It is the transit shed throughput that determines the turn-around of vessels and the length of the queue waiting to discharge and load cargo. It is not merely conceivable, but may even be likely, that a charge levied against occupancy of the transit shed would cause a much greater throughput. Thus the total traffic of the port would increase. There would be some cost to such a solution. Those cargo owners and agents who had used the transit sheds as a relatively cheap form of storage until they could dispose of the goods would find that it was not worthwhile because they had to pay now for the true cost of the scarce transit facilities. But the policy would reduce the diversion of traffic to other ports and may even generate new traffic.[15]

Advantages of congestion pricing

One main advantage of congestion pricing is that the port authority appropriates the surplus caused by the demand for its facilities. It is not uncommon for ports, particularly in developing countries, to be congested and simultaneously to show large losses even on operating account; levying congestion charges would avoid this undesirable state of affairs. Secondly, the levies would provide funds to expand port services. This automatic financing arrangement would make it more likely that the port, like the tub, could stand on its own bottom.[16] If, on the other hand, the port is subsidized, then such funds must be raised by taxation; this not only incurs an administrative cost of collection (probably at least 5 percent), but also distorts other decisions on the allocation of resources and effort.

A third advantage is that congestion levies will encourage efficient use of the port facilities. If the congestion charges are raised on the appropriate facilities, this may be associated with a larger throughput of traffic. Even if port throughput is reduced, however, the diversion to other ports or to other uses will be an efficient use of resources.

A fourth advantage of congestion pricing, as distinct from nonprice allocative systems, is that the port authority receives the rent rather than the lucky recipient of the priority or other licensing authorization. Such distributions of wealth among agents, importers, and steamship owners is unlikely to be consistent with the normal canons of equity.

---

15. This policy can be pursued only when the transit shed occupancy is separately controlled and costed. A port authority which operates an all-in charges scheme would find it difficult or impossible to operate such a scheme. They might then have to resort to some administered rationing devices for the transit sheds.

16. For the tale of the tub, see A. A. Walters, *Economics of Road User Charges*, World Bank Staff Occasional Papers, no. 5 (Baltimore: Johns Hopkins Press, 1968).

Disadvantages of Congestion Pricing

Probably the main disadvantage is the administrative difficulty of imposing the levy. In some cases, the handling and wharfage charges (and perhaps quay charges) are combined into one package. But even if they are charged separately in the invoice, it is not easy to organize the congestion levy. For example, demand may be largely seasonal, perhaps with a big random component determined by weather, size of crop, state of the world markets, or other factors. It may be difficult to put on the congestion charge and then take it off again at the appropriate time. Clearly these levies are appropriate only if the congestion is expected to persist for some time.

The second disadvantage is often alleged to be that the congestion charge will be passed on and perhaps even marked up at some percentage rate by the steamship companies. Although this possibility cannot be shown to be analytically incorrect, it does depend either on an unusual combination of elasticities, which will be explored in Chapter 5, or on the intractable strategic bargaining of bilateral monopolists.[17]

Congestion in Practice

Congestion in ports arises from a variety of causes. These must be identified if pricing is to contribute fully to the efficient allocation of resources. Some of the causes are under the control of the parties involved in the transport operations: bunching of ship arrivals which can be alleviated by scheduling voyages or by varying speeds, delays in removing cargo which are partly the responsibility of cargo owners and inland transport operators, and, similarly, the delays in presenting cargo for export. Even breakdowns in port facilities can be forestalled by inspection, maintenance, and stocking of spares. Other causes result from forces outside the control of those in the transport process: storms and heavy rains which delay vessel movements, cargo working and strikes, or procedural delays.

Congestion may affect only a part of a port such as a specialized berth or storage facility. In Chittagong, for example, grain deliveries

17. See the Appendix.

FIGURE 4.4. SHIP DELAY VERSUS BERTH OCCUPANCY,
PORT OF CHITTAGONG, 1972–1973

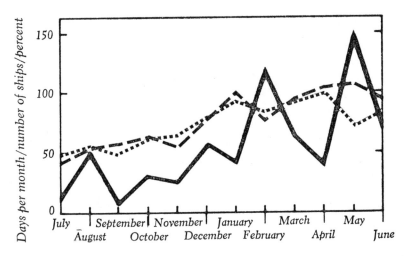

Note: (▬▬▬) = days of waiting for berth; (▬ ▬ ▬) = percent occupancy of berth; (••••••••) = number of ships at jetties 1–17.

Source: Louis Berger International, Inc., "Feasibility Study, Port of Chittagong Expansion, Bangladesh" (study prepared for the Asian Development Bank and Chittagong Port Trust, vol. 1, December 1974; processed), p. vii–9.

to the silo may be held up because of inadequate inland transport. But even if initially localized, congestion, like the plague, tends to spread. Grain may get bagged in the holds and be transferred to lighters or unloaded directly in other (general) berths. But this raises the cost of cargo transfer (although by less than the cost of idle ship time which would be incurred if no such alternatives existed), and it slows down the rest of the port.

Congestion at the wharf is illustrated in its classic form by the records of the number of ships on the berth, percentage berth occupancy, and ship-days of waiting for berth in the port of Chittagong in 1972–73 (Figure 4.4). If ship-days lost in waiting for berth are considered the index of congestion and if the actual number of vessels at the jetties can be considered a measure of monthly output,[18] it

18. This would only be true if the ships are all of similar size, had similar loads for Chittagong, and worked at an equal rate per day. None of these are unreasonable assumptions for the time reviewed in the diagram.

follows that output actually declined as congestion reached its high peaks (February and May 1973). This corresponds to the backward-bending section of the average cost curve in the classical congestion diagram.[19]

There are two measures of congestion. The first focuses on cost, notably the time that ships spend waiting for berth. This delay, when valued in money, forms the upper limit of one major item of congestion cost.[20] The shipper's cost of congestion is more difficult to measure since much of it is internal to his firm. This measure of congestion cost falling on both shipowners and shippers is concerned with the money cost of delay. Alternatively, congestion is measured by the degree of capacity use, in other words, the occupancy rates of berths or sheds. The interpretation of both measures, however, requires knowledge of what is the port's normal level of congestion.

Normal congestion

When a port has the appropriate number of berths and other facilities for the expected traffic, a vessel is likely to experience some delay in its visits to the port, just as a customer in the supermarket expects to wait a few minutes in line before being served. It is efficient for the vessel to wait a few hours or even a day or so on the average before proceeding alongside. The port charge to the ship will reflect the fact that there is this normal delay on the average.

Of course, the delay could be reduced below the normal level—perhaps even eliminated if additional berths and other equipment were built. But the additional cost of this superior no-waiting service will not be worthwhile; the shipowner would rather suffer the average normal delay than pay for the additional cost of immediate service. A balance between the incremental cost of providing more capacity and the consequential reduction in the cost of ship delays is the criterion for defining normal congestion.

The operating techniques of ships and shippers are adapted to this normal level of congestion. This adaptation extends to such matters

19. See A. A. Walters, "The Theory and Measurement of Private and Social Costs of Highway Congestion," *Econometrica*, vol. 29 (1961).

20. Ships can sometimes load or discharge while waiting for berth. If this shortens their subsequent stay at the wharf, the saving has to be offset against the full cost of days the ship is idle, taking account also of the excess cost of working cargo overside.

as the number and functions of shippers' and ships' agents in the port, the amount of transshipment, the distribution of cargoes between alternative ports, inventory policy, and the choice between road and rail, barges and lighters. With a normal level of port congestion, shipowners determine the size of vessel, transshipment patterns, the extent of overside operations, and the cargo handling equipment on board. Alternative techniques have different costs; lightering, for instance, tends to be more expensive than discharge at the wharf.

What matters to the ship is the total cost and time to move a given quantity of cargo. This normal time cost is absorbed into the freight rate. The contrast between normal and abnormal congestion is illustrated by data for two important Indian ports in Table 4.1.

TABLE 4.1.   INDICATORS OF CONGESTION AT TWO MAJOR INDIAN PORTS, 1969–70

Vessel class: "all others"[a]	Port I	Port II
Ship delayed because berths unavailable (percentage of all ships calling)	12.5	8.6
Average delay (days)	5.2	1.7
Expected delay to any ship entering port (days)	0.65	0.15
Ships days lost per berth-day of port[b]	0.16	0.01
Cargo worked per berth-day (tons)[b]	600–700	325
Average turn-round (days)	5.4	8

a. Steamers, excluding tankers, bulkers, and tramps.
b. Berth-day is the day in which the berth is occupied by a vessel.
Source: Computed from Directorate of Transport Research, Ministry of Shipping and Transport, Government of India, *Port Transport Statistics of India* (New Delhi, March 1971), Tables 5.3 and 12.1–12.7.

Port I had queues of waiting ships and longer expected entry delays than did Port II. But cargo was being worked appreciably faster in Port I so that the average turn-around was lower there than in Port II. Port II had markedly higher liner freight rates, whereas Port I had congestion surcharges imposed by liner conferences on its lower rates.

Liner tariffs allow for normal delays, and abnormal congestion is an argument frequently advanced in proposals to increase freight rates. When planning ports that have no close substitutes it is sensible, therefore, to measure the cost of not expanding the port beyond a certain scale by the cost of idle ship time caused by a general excess of demand for berths over available capacity. As used by port planners, the method yields an acceptable approximation.[21] But such a criterion is appropriate only if the freight rates reflect fully the cost of abnormal delays.

Liner conference freight tariffs tend to have uniform rates for ranges of ports. The liner conference covering the trades from Europe to the Bay of Bengal thus sets identical rates for shipments to Calcutta, Chittagong, and Chalna. The Thailand–Europe Conference, again, has a wide range of uniform rating; the same rates apply to cargo carried to Aden and Gulf ports (4,475 to 5,772 nautical miles from Bangkok) and to cargo destined to Narvik (10,425 nautical miles). There are various technical justifications for this method of pricing, including the need to adapt the shipping operation to the slowest moving port in a region. On the whole, however, the explanation has to be sought in the nature of shipping cartels; the practice reflects a rough compromise between different members of the cartels.[22] Its effect, however, is to introduce price discrimination between ports and to blunt the price mechanism. In particular the uniform rates may not reflect the variety of normal congestion at different ports. The distortion is only avoided in those cases where conferences impose quasi-permanent congestion surcharges on particular ports.[23] Unlike the normal congestion element in freight rates, surcharges are specific to individual ports.

Abnormal congestion

Ports use various working rules to diagnose the onset of congestion beyond the normal level. A port authority sometimes defines congestion as the situation where a ship actually leaves the queue and sails to another port. A shipowner, on the other hand, is likely to define abnormal congestion as an excessive waiting time that he can avoid only in the short run by incurring additional steaming and transship-

21. It is less acceptable if applied to special berths within a port. The range of possible substitutes for shipments through a particular berth or by specialized vessels requiring such a berth is necessarily much greater than for an entire port. See Coopers and Lybrand Associates Limited in association with Sir Bruce White, Wolfe Barry and Partners, and Shankland Cox Partnership. "Lembaga Pelabohan Kelang. Port Development Feasibility Study." Final Report, 2 vols. (August 1974).

22. See E. Bennathan and A. A. Walters, *The Economics of Ocean Freight Rates*, chapter 5.

23. An example is the surcharge on Haifa and Ashdod.

ment cost. Other rules of thumb are in terms of critical levels of available capacity use. In the port of Chittagong, congestion is signaled when the volume of general cargo lying in the closed and open storage areas reaches 100,000 to 120,000 tons. This level was exceeded frequently in 1973. But even 70,000 tons of cargo in storage increases the cost to cargo owners and their agents. Berth occupancy is another criterion adopted by port experts. For conventional general cargo berths it is considered to reach its critical level at 70 to 80 percent, depending on the number of the berths. The critical level for container ships is much lower; nearer 30 percent occupancy for a single common user container berth or 60 percent for two. Container ships will not wait.

The cost of congestion (including costs incurred by shippers, ports, and ships in their attempts to escape the consequences of congestion) are not reflected necessarily in prices charged by the port. Ports generally maintain their charges at the normal level even though congestion affects their cost. The response to heightened congestion is frequently faster working which entails higher cost per unit of output but is usually uncompensated by an increase in the tariff.[24] In times of high congestion caused by heavier arrivals more stringent (and costly) maneuvering may give a faster turnaround of vessels.[25]

Revenues respond to congestion delays in that some port rates are charged per unit of time. This is indeed the rule for rental charges for the use of fixed facilities; for example, charges for berth occupancy; for the use of tugs, cranes, and slings; and for the occupancy of sheds or warehouses. Revenues from such charges thus may rise with berth occupancy, and, similarly, congestion may raise the port's income from storage rent. Chittagong, with its chronically congested sheds, thus estimates 1975–76 income from wharf rent at Taka 2.75 crores against only Taka 1.98 crores from cargo handling. In 1973 the port derived 41 percent of its total revenue from storage charges— twice as much as from cargo handling charges, berth hire, and port dues on vessels.[26]

But revenues from charges related not to time but to throughput may decline. The importance of this class of charges varies from port

24. Overtime working is often not charged to the port users. The port's cargo handling charges are typically just based on the tonnage of cargo worked.
25. This may explain the lengthening of ships' average stay in the Port of Chittagong between 1973, a year of high congestion, and 1974.
26. Chittagong Port Trust, *Budget Estimates of Income and Expenditure for 1975–76*, with revised estimates for 1974–75 (Chittagong, 1975).

TABLE 4.2.   MAIN CHARGES TO A SIMULATED STANDARD SHIP AND
CARGO AT THE WHARF, PORT AUTHORITY OF THAILAND, PORT OF
BANGKOK, 1974 RATES[a]

Revenues varying with time		Charges not varying with time	
Source of revenue	Baht	Source of charge	Baht
Berth occupany	4,070	Channel dues	11,100
Towage	2,400	Cargo dues[c]	109,820
Storage (sheds and warehouse)[b]	39,000	Cargo handling	56,250
Total	45,470	Total	177,170

a. Assumptions on cargo: 2,550 metric tons discharged, of which 1,500 tons landed to sheds (40 tons loaded); dimensions, 2 cubic meters per metric ton. Assumptions on vessel and operation: one vessel of 6,550 GRT; berthed for 65 hours; tug time, 60 minutes. Major exclusion: hire of port's mechanical equipment.

b. Assumptions: 600 tons removed within free time. A further 600 tons removed from sheds after average stay of 2.5 days beyond end of free time. A further 300 tons removed from transit sheds after an average of 6 days' stay beyond end of free time, for a full 2 weeks' stay in bonded warehouse.

c. Landing charges and overside charges for imports; quay dues for exports.

Sources: Data except for "storage" and "cargo handling" from Coopers and Lybrand Associates Limited, Report on the Tariff Review (prepared for the Port Authority of Thailand) (London, January 8, 1975). Data for "storage" and "cargo handling" from Port Authority of Thailand, Tariff of Port Charges, Port of Bangkok, 4th ed. (Klongtoi, Bangkok, 1974).

to port, but since they include cargo handling charges as well as cargo dues (or wharfage) and port (or channel) dues, they will form normally the larger part of the payments to the port. This is shown by the calculation of the chief items of payment to the Port Authority of Thailand for a simulated ship call at Bangkok in 1974 (Table 4.2).

The cost to cargo owners consists not just of the increased inventory cost, contractual fines, lost sales, or higher insurance premiums, but also of the cost incurred in attempts to contain those losses by diverting shipments or, in the case of shed congestion, by searching for cargo in various sheds and by incurring the expense of having cargo carried to whichever shed has spare capacity. Frequently this results in additional inland transport and distribution cost.[27]

27. An interesting example of appropriation of scarcity rents appears in Bangkok. The Port of Bangkok consists of the Port Authority of Thailand (PAT) wharves (Klong Toi) and the private wharves on the river. The private wharves are considered part of the port. When there is congestion in the PAT wharves, waiting ships will try to obtain a higher place in the queue by moving into a private wharf, because they are then considered to be already in the port. For this, shipowners pay fees fixed by the owners of the private wharves.

To limit the cost of delays the shipowners increase the amount of cargo working in mid-stream which releases the ship but which may increase congestion in the port through a denser movement of lighters. Shippers may re-route and transship either to cheaper vessels or for inland transport, and, in the longer run, they may vary the technique of shipping. The heavy congestion in Persian Gulf and Arabian ports in 1974 and 1975 thus led to a highly competitive rush of roll-on/roll-off services to these ports to circumvent conventional handling delays and of transshipment services combining sea transport to less congested ports with overland transport into the hinterland of congested ones.[28]

Shippers will try to pass on their congestion cost. The demand for many export products of developing countries is highly elastic with respect to price, and the exporters will normally bear the cost. But importers will more often be able, in those countries, to raise prices throughout at least part of their market area; their position will be the stronger, in this respect, the stronger is the port's monopoly.

In the charter market, many contracts impose the cost of delay on the shipowner. Competition, however, will ensure that charter rates are marked up to include the cost of delay. Pronounced congestion in an important trading area may thus prop up the demand for ships even in a time of general international trade recession.[29]

Congestion surcharges

Liners and liner conferences, which fix their freight rates for a period and publish them in their tariffs, seek to pass on the cost of abnormal congestion by congestion surcharges. Some fifty ports were surcharged in early 1975. The surcharges are expressed normally as a percentage of the freight rate and are not subject to the various forms of loyalty rebate by which conferences seek to tie shippers. The range of surcharges reported in early 1975 was from 5 to 10 percent in

28. For instance, Europe to Iraq (with a heavily congested port at Basrah) through Aqaba.

29. The general firmness of the charter market and of prices for vessels of 3,000 to 12,000 DWT in 1975, in a period of a general decline of demand for shipping space, is thus difficult to explain except by reference to the heavy congestion in Middle East and Arabian ports. Congestion in these and certain other ports may have tied down some 1,500 ships of that size class. Compare, Israel Shipping Research Institute, Freight Research Division, *Information Paper*, no. 46 (Haifa: Israel Shipping Research Institute, April 1975).

Bombay to 130 percent in Tripoli or in Lattakia, where over ninety ships were waiting for berth and where the average delay was 40 days.

Conferences set uniform surcharges for all their members. Since the cost of normal congestion is absorbed in the freight rate and since the normal level is not a precise concept, conferences seem to think of a threshold of congestion. Some U.S. conferences operating in southeast Asia define this threshold as 10 days' berthing delay; where reached, this will provoke a 10 percent surcharge, rising by 1 percent per additional day's delay in steps of 5 percent. Typically, surcharges are applied after abnormal congestion has been experienced and then only after warnings and notifications. Attempts to impose surcharges on expected delays—for example, a surcharge conditional on a threatened strike—are rare.

Short and long abnormal delays

Liner congestion surcharges are usually imposed some time after the onset of abnormal congestion because of the organization of the liner business and the nature of liner cartels. Shippers and conferences in a port are tied by contractual relations which may specify that warnings and notifications precede the actual imposition of the surcharge. The decision to impose a surcharge must be agreed between operators who differ in their interests, their costs, and their competitive positions within the cartel. This takes time. Another explanation, however, is current among shipping experts. According to this view, the cost of short delays (that is to say, congestion which does not last long) is less per unit of time than the cost of prolonged congestion. The reason given is that short delays on a multiport voyage can be made up by faster working in other ports on the voyage at a lesser cost than the cost of ship-days lost through delays when calculated at the daily cost of running the vessel. In a study of Port Swettenham (Kelang) in 1967,[30] shipowners were reported as valuing a day's delay to their ships at M$5,000–M$8,500, this being the sum of operating cost, depreciation allowance, and interest charge attributable (in an accounting sense) to the vessel. Delays of two days could be coped with by working overtime in the next port of call,

---

30. Coode and Partners, Economist Intelligence Unit, and L. E. Taylor, *Port Swettenham Improvement Scheme. 1968 Pre-Investment Feasibility Study*, prepared for the Honourable Minister of Transport, Government of Malaysia (London, 1968), vol. 2, pp. 272–74.

by working weekends if possible, by cutting several days off the ship's maintenance period and servicing it at overtime rates, by rescheduling ports of call, or even by missing out a port of call. The cost of these compensating actions was M$850 to M$2,550 per day's delay, depending on whether the corrective action had to be taken in Far Eastern, European, or Australian ports. Delays beyond a certain duration—perhaps 3 days on a round voyage of 30 days—could not be made up by accelerating at other points of the voyage. Within that limit, the cost of a day's delay was less than the cost of a ship's day, the difference being 50 percent or more according to the figures in the Port Swettenham study.

But if such savings are possible through tighter operations at different points of a voyage or at the time of maintenance or of servicing, why should they be realized only as a result of abnormal congestion? If this is indeed the case, it points to inefficiency in the shipowner's operations which competition would eliminate quickly. In the absence of competitive pressure, a shipowner, of course, can dissipate monopoly profits in unnecessarily high cost. The more competitive the shipowner or the liner conference, the less inefficiency will be tolerated in their operations and the closer should be the daily cost of short delays to the normal cost of delay (that is, to the cost of a ship-day). Therefore, if the operator's private cost of a day's delay rises with the length of the delay, this is sufficient evidence of monopoly and moreover of inefficient monopoly. It should not persist in the long run because even the tightest conference cannot suppress some forms of competition among its members.

Surcharges and the type of service

The private cost of congestion will differ according to the type of vessel used and the contractual stipulations between operators and shippers. Since liner conferences include many types of vessels, the uniform surcharge will reflect some kind of average of congestion costs to different operators in the cartel, weighted presumably by their individual bargaining strength. But will the cost of delay and hence also the surcharge (or its equivalent in charter rates) differ also according to the type of service?

Liners, unlike tramps, work on sailing schedules. Since the dominant conference organization of liners suppresses price competition, operators have to compete by other methods. Frequency of service and reliability are probably the most important forms of this nonprice competition; while some shippers would prefer less regular sailings at lower freight rates, such alternatives are not offered in a cartelized service. The cost of delay can be illustrated again by the Port Swettenham study of 1967. This considers the case of a 4-day delay affecting a liner company operating a 30-day round trip with calls at eight or nine ports. If the normal turnaround time in each of those ports is 2 days, a 4-day delay in one port requires that one of the remaining eight ports on the itinerary be omitted, always assuming that the vessel has to be positioned on time at the terminal port. If four vessels in the company or the conference experience this delay, it accumulates to 16 ship-days. This amounts to a full round of eight port calls missed out on the service which can only be recovered by commissioning a fifth ship and putting it on this service. Assuming the policy of strict scheduling, the entire cost of the additional round trip should be attributed to the congestion.

The Swettenham report illustrates the additional cost of congestion to liners if the conference observes strict scheduling. The cheapest suitable vessel which the conference could charter in 1967 for the additional trip cost M$3,460 per day. The interpolated round trip takes 30 days, each to be valued at the daily cost of the additional ship. Since the additional ship was brought in to compensate for 16 ship-days lost through delay in the congested port, the daily cost of congestion is M$6,500 $[= (30/16) \times$ M$3,460]$—roughly twice the daily cost of the actual ship. For longer round trips the daily cost of congestion thus computed would be greater and so, other things being equal, would be the amount of the surcharge (although not the percentage surcharge[31]). The corresponding percentage surcharge will vary according to the level of the average freight rate and the amount of cargo each ship normally carried to the congested port. The Swettenham report of 1967 did not consider that the rate of vessel use would be affected by the additional voyage and suggested that the surcharge for a 4-day delay should be about 20 percent of the freight rate for scheduled services to Port Swettenham. (The effect of the same delay on the unscheduled carrier could increase the rate per ton only about 10 percent.) The cost differential arises from the liners' strict adherence to schedule. If this cost is charged to the congested port's cargo, the unscheduled tramps and bulk carriers will have a price advantage. Furthermore, the longer the abnormal delay, the wider the gap be-

31. The freight rates which bear the surcharge vary with distance or duration of transit.

tween the cost of shipping on liners and on tramps—provided that the liners continue to cling to their policy of strict scheduling and of charging the resulting cost to the congested port.[32] Since the tramps and bulk carriers would be in a better position to compete away the conference traffic, it is unlikely that the conference freight rates will rise to reflect the full cost of congestion.

Surcharges and the degree of monopoly

If conferences or ships compete, the theory of congestion indicates that the congestion levies will be too low. But conferences would be expected also to use their monopolistic power so that the actual surcharge will be lower as competition increases.

The effect of monopoly on liner conference congestion surcharges can be seen in the relative level of surcharges imposed by conferences serving the same port over different distances (Table 4.3). Intuitively

TABLE 4.3.   CONGESTION SURCHARGES ON SHIPMENTS TO BOMBAY AND KARACHI, 1973

Port	Conference	Route	Effective from	Rate (%)
Bombay	India/Pakistan	UK/India, Pakistan	3.12.73	30
	West coast of India, Pakistan/U.S.	India, Pakistan–U.S. Atlantic and Gulf ports	10.12.73	30
	Japan/India, Persian Gulf/Japan	both ways: Japan– India, Pakistan, Persian Gulf	1.12.73	15
	Gulf, Arabian Sea/ Orient rate agreement	Persian Gulf, Arabian Sea, Southeast Asia, Taiwan, Korea, Philippines	1.12.73	15
Karachi	India/Pakistan		3.12.73	20
	West coast of India, Pakistan/U.S.		10.12.73	20
	Thailand/west coast of India, Pakistan, Persian Gulf	Southeast and South Asia	1.12.73	15

32. In the unnecessarily discrete units of the Swettenham example, a further service may have to be added if delay in the congested port lengthens to 8 days per ship.

it is clear that the shorter the sea distance, the greater the percentage added to normal freight cost by abnormal congestion. Similarly, for ships in direct service to a particular port, the greater the cost per ton of a day's delay in port, the larger the percentage rise in the voyage cost per ton caused by increased congestion.[33] It was shown in Chapter 1, however, that the longer routes will tend to have the larger vessels and that the cost per ton of idling in port is less for those larger vessels. On these grounds, the percentage by which congestion raises the freight charge per ton should be less on the longer routes. These predictions, of course, derive from a competitive model of shipping, and such a pattern would not necessarily be expected to emerge on cartelized routes. Indeed, the dominant feature on long sea routes may be the power of the cartel; as shown in an earlier study, there is a general rule that short routes are competitive and long routes tightly cartelized.[34] The experience of additional demand leading to congestion will tend to add to the monopoly power exercised by the conference as demonstrated in Figure 4.2 (above), and so the conference would be expected to exploit its control of the scarcity.

Table 4.3 shows that in two random instances, surcharges were smaller on the shorter routes than on the long routes to Europe or the United States. Some of the difference may be explained by differences in the percentages of cargo destined for Bombay or Karachi on the intercontinental and the intra-Asian voyages, but the importance of the two ports on these routes makes this an unlikely explanation of the full discrepancy. In this case the lower surcharges seem to give the truer indication of the cost of congestion to the ships.

33. Using the notation of Chapter 1, let the ship's idle time in port rise by ΔI. Voyage cost per ton will then increase by:

$$\Delta I \frac{\partial(V/C)}{\partial I} = \frac{2}{C}(A+gC)(1-\alpha)\Delta I,$$

and so, for the proportional effect of idle time on unit cost:

$$\frac{\Delta I}{V/C} \frac{\partial(V/C)}{\partial I} = \frac{(1-\alpha)\Delta I}{0.5DK+I(1-\alpha)+C/(L+mC)}$$

where $K = (h + B/C)/(g+A/C)$, the ratio of the daily cost per ton of the ship at sea and in port.

The proportional increase in unit cost for another hour's congestion rises with the daily cost of waiting in port, but it declines with the distance of the voyage.

34. E. Bennathan, A. A. Walters, and others, *The Cost of Ocean Transport in the Foreign Trade of Asia* (processed).

Further evidence for a monopolistic element in some surcharges is found in the fact that they are frequently maintained after abnormal congestion has ceased. The explanation lies in the carrier's wish to recoup losses sustained because of the delayed imposition of the levy. This would be impossible in a competitive market. The same port may also be surcharged by one conference but not by others.[35] This would be consistent with variations of the extent of competition on different routes.

To the extent that differences in the size of surcharges reflect the competition faced by conferences, it will be the lower surcharges that represent the better estimates of the congestion cost suffered by ships. The higher surcharges contain a share in the scarcity rent which congestion creates and which conferences appropriate according to the strength of their market position.

This raises a general question: should the port authority not merely take on the job of congestion pricing but also the task of raising revenue for the economy as a whole? Clearly there is the possibility of using the port monopoly as a source of finance for government or as an instrument of the national interest. This is discussed in the next chapter.

Appendix. Bilateral Monopoly and Strategic Behavior

Essentially there is a confrontation of two monopolists: the port and the shipowner. The steamship owner will know the minimum net return (that is to say, net of port charges) which he will require if he is to continue to call in the port, but he is not likely to reveal that value to the port authority or to the owners of cargo. This minimum net return will depend on the alternative use of the ships—perhaps avoiding the call at the port entirely and so being able to use the ships serving the trade elsewhere. Similarly the monopolist steamship owner may know that the extent to which he can raise prices is not merely limited by the availability of other transport services (including steamship and air services), but also by the elasticity of supply and demand of the commodity.

The port authority again will know the minimum price at which it is willing to provide port services. Between the maximum that the

35. All India Shippers Council, *Fourth Annual Report for the Year 1970* (New Delhi, 1971), pp. xxix and following.

steamship company is willing to pay and the minimum at which the port authority is willing to supply, there would normally be a considerable gap.

So far the port authority has been assumed to charge a specific fee (per ton) for its services (as in Figure 4.1, above) and not to charge a congestion levy nor, further, to extract a monopoly profit by charging high tariffs. In other words, the port authority, perhaps realistically, has been assumed to behave in a passive manner. But suppose that the port authority does not adopt a supine stance. Suppose that the authority takes into account the effects of its tariff policy on the behavior of the conference and so, with consummate cunning, calculates the effect on its own accounts.

There is an infinite number of strategies that the port authority could pursue. There is the use of bluff, concealing information, and all the other familiar features of bargaining. Unfortunately, it is impossible to give any precise rules about the outcome of such a process. The monopolist steamship owner is likely to have many port authorities to contend with in other countries, however, and therefore is likely to be quite experienced in the bargaining process; the port authority is likely to lose out.

In general these reflections suggest that the port authority, even when faced with a monopolist steamship owner, should price the facilities of the port according to scarcity in relation to the demand for them. In what follows the problems of strategy, bluff, and counterbid are ignored. Strategic behavior and bargaining nevertheless may be very important for providing special facilities such as exclusive use container terminals or bulk cargo wharves. These are in the nature of once-and-for-all deals for a certain contractual period (say, 5 years). The port authority would be wise to get specialist advice on negotiating such arrangements.

Chapter 5

Port Prices
and the National Interest

THE OBJECT OF MARGINAL COST PRICING is to allocate resources so that
the relative values which users place on another unit of different
goods and services corresponds to the economy's relative cost of
supplying them. In the preceding chapters the conditions under which
marginal cost pricing can achieve that objective were discussed. Economic policy, however, may pursue other objectives. In practice, the
two major alternatives are profit maximization and the maximization
of the national benefit which underlies much foreign trade policy. In
this chapter, both of these alternatives are discussed in relation to
ports.

Port Profit Maximization Compared
with Marginal Cost Pricing

Ports which lack monopoly power have little choice in the way
they set their charges. But most ports have some monopoly power
and thus also some choice between setting prices approximately equal
to marginal cost and pricing their services to maximize profits.

The effects of profit maximization on prices and output depend on
the circumstances of the case and are usually difficult to ascertain even
in specific cases. The difficulty is naturally greatest in enterprises like
ports which are usually multiproduct firms selling each type of service
in a variety of markets, each with its own demand conditions. To

advance beyond the broadest generalities and, in particular, to obtain an idea of the size of the effects of pricing to maximize profits, it is necessary to work with a model. This section explores the effects of profit-maximizing pricing in a port that is a perfect monopoly in relation to the shippers of its hinterland. This is admittedly a limiting case. Only a few ports conform to this type. In most ports, the shippers can either ship overland or by another port.[1] But while the model has no great descriptive value, it contains some realistic features. Thus ports should be expected to be in a stronger position in relation to shippers than ships; and other aspects of the model capture some of the characteristic demand conditions of areas depending chiefly on gathering activities or forestry.

Imagine a port on a northern coast, as shown in Figure 5.1, and suppose that it is an export port only. Traffic originates along the straight road PR, where R is the limit of cultivation of the export product along the highway. The f.o.b. price offered for the export crop at the port is constant, whereas the price that the farmer receives at the farm gate excludes transport cost to the port and the port charge.

The internal transport cost is assumed to remain constant. The only variable considered is the price levied by the port for its services, which are assumed to be homogeneous and are required in identical form for each identical ton of output exported. Even if the basic activity of producing the output crop is subject to conditions of constant return to scale, the increased transport cost, as distance away from the port increases, yields increasing marginal cost for the total production of the commodity. Imagine that land is homogeneous (for example, a 100-square meter plot when cultivated will produce 1 ton) and that the product has to be transported in an east→west or west→east direction to the road at a constant cost of $1 per 100 meters.[2] The area of cultivation will then be RQQ'.

When the price charged by the port for its services is varied there

1. Ports in southern Thailand, western Malaysia, and Singapore are rather far from the situation of this monopolistic port. Chittagong and Bangkok are in an intermediate position, but Manila or Tanjong Priok may be as adequately described by this model as they would be by any other.

2. The assumption corresponds to that made in the Ellet model described in A. A. Walters, *Economics of Road User Charges*, World Bank Staff Occasional Papers, no. 5 (Baltimore: Johns Hopkins Press, 1968). The ton-mile cost of transport along the road is also assumed to be constant and independent of distance.

FIGURE 5.1.   A PORT AND ITS HINTERLAND

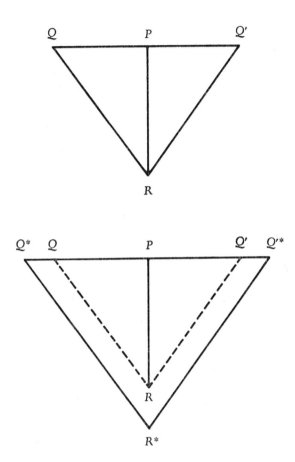

are several consequences. A reduction in the port prices will extend production along the road and also will increase the boundary of cultivation in the east→west direction (Figure 5.1) to the asterisked values. The marginal revenue obtained by the port for a small reduction of port charges would contain the quantity increase represented by the arrow-shaped area Q*QRQ′Q′*R* as one of its components.

The main purpose in developing this model was to explore something like the upper limit of the absolute value of the elasticity of demand that may be expected in port economics. The model incorporates an infinitely elastic demand for the commodity at the port.

Furthermore, in this model all that is required to bring land into production—with the consequent increase in demand for port services—is that it pay for the transport cost to the port and for port charges. Yet the main conclusion that emerges from the formal investigation of this case is that the demand curve is inelastic for monopoly port services. In particular, the elasticity of the demand curve declines rapidly as port prices are reduced.[3]

In these circumstances the port's profit-maximizing price will always exceed marginal cost, provided only that marginal cost is less than the price at which demand for port services would dwindle to nothing:

$$
(1) \quad
\left\{
\begin{bmatrix}
Port's\ profit \\
maximizing \\
price\ for\ its \\
monopoly \\
services
\end{bmatrix}
= \tfrac{2}{3}
\begin{bmatrix}
Port's \\
marginal \\
cost
\end{bmatrix}
+ \tfrac{1}{3}
\begin{bmatrix}
Port's \\
zero- \\
demand \\
price
\end{bmatrix}
\right.
$$

The excess of the profit-maximizing price over marginal cost can also be expressed in terms of internal transport cost to the port: when the port has maximized its profits, its price will be above marginal cost by an amount equal to half the transport cost to the most distant point (in terms of transport cost) in its catchment area.[4]

The effect of profit maximization on output of port services in this model is to reduce it to four-ninths of the level that would be achieved under marginal-cost pricing conditions.[5] This result is illustrated by the demand curve in Figure 5.2, drawn, for convenience, assuming zero marginal cost. The profit-maximizing price is then simply one-third of the zero-demand price for port services.

The most general lesson that may be drawn from this case is that where the monopoly power of the port is considerable, even if it had overinvested considerably, it could usually cover its cost by raising prices and restricting exports. There are then good reasons to expand the output of the port up to somewhere near capacity by using multi-part tariffs or some form of spatial or commodity discrimination. When marginal cost is near zero and considerable capacity is standing empty, it would be wasteful to operate the port at four-ninths of its potential either for reasons of profit maximization or to enable the authority to cover its cost.

3. Appendix A.
4. Appendix A.
5. Appendix A.

FIGURE 5.2.   DEMAND CURVE FOR PORT SERVICES

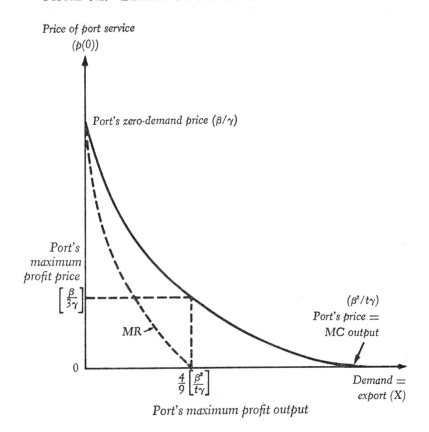

Note: Marginal revenue $= \frac{3}{2}p(0) - \frac{\beta}{2\gamma}$; for monopolist policy of maximum profit,

$p(0) > \beta/3\gamma$; maximum gross revenue $= \frac{4}{27}\left[\frac{\beta^3}{\gamma^2 t}\right]$

Nationally Optimal Pricing and Incidence

National port policy requires a study of the relation between the port price, the freight rate, port profit, and the benefits to traders and domestic consumers. Therefore, the question of how port pricing might serve the general national interest must be considered. The rest of this chapter discusses how port prices must be fixed if the external conditions which face port and national port users are taken as unalterably given.

The distributional aspects of international transport differ in one major respect from those of predominantly national projects. In the normal case of a public utility, for instance, suppliers and consumers are mainly nationals. In that case, marginal cost pricing itself, supplemented where necessary by the computation of shadow prices, performs a major distributional function. Standard fiscal methods can then at least regulate the distribution of any monopolistic surpluses that remain in the economy. In international transport services, however, some, if not actually all, of the suppliers are foreigners. Thus the problem of distribution between foreigners and nationals arises. This is greatly complicated by the fact that nationals, such as national shipowners or airlines, also help to supply the services. This is becoming increasingly characteristic in at least some of the developing countries; ever more of them try to reach the politically accepted target of 40 percent participation of national shipowners in the national sea trades.[6] In this chapter, nevertheless, it is assumed first that shipowners are foreigners and that the port, inland transport operators, traders, and the consumers of imports and producers of export commodities are nationals. This is a most helpful simplification in what is already a far-from-simple problem. This analysis thus presumes that the distribution of income or benefit to and from national shipowners can be taken care of by internal fiscal arrangements.

It is not unusual for ports to seek to control the distribution of costs and benefits between nationals and foreigners through differential increases in charges payable by ships and other charges payable by the shipper. The distinction between charges on the basis of who normally pays them is a common feature of port tariffs. The classification reflects roughly the way in which decisions on the use of port services are taken in a conventional transport operation.[7] It is thus

6. Compare, United Nations, Conference on Trade and Development, *United Nations Conference of Plenipotentiaries on a Code of Conduct for Liner Conferences*, vols. 1 and 2 (New York, 1975) and B. M. Deakin, "Shipping Conferences: Some Economic Aspects of International Regulation," *Maritime Studies and Management*, vol. 2, no. 1 (July 1974), pp. 5–31. See also, A. H. Vanags, "Flag Discrimination: an Economic Analysis," [*Advances in Maritime Economics*, ed. R. O. Goss. (Cambridge: Cambridge University Press, 1977)] and A. A. Walters, review of *Advances in Maritime Economics* [*Journal of Political Economy*. April 1979].

7. The division of actual payment differs according to the terms of carriage. When cargo is carried on liner terms, the shipowner covers the expense of moving the cargo from and to the sheds and includes at least this cost in the freight rate.

in accordance with the principle that the party which causes the port to incur particular costs should both know the price and pay it. When decisions on how the port is to be used tend to be concentrated in one hand, it will be both convenient and efficient that the charges should be levied on that single party, and this is accordingly the principle of many container tariffs. The separation of charges paid by the ship from those paid by shippers is thus functionally efficient and administratively convenient. But it would be a mistake to think that it also can affect the distribution of income or of cost between ships and shippers. A given increase in port charges will have the same effect on the ship and the shippers, whether it is loaded on the charges claimed from the ship or on those claimed from the shipper. Whether the given increase in port revenue is obtained in one way or the other, the effect on freight rates and the ship's revenue will be the same. The port is unable to control the incidence of its charges on ship and shipper. The distribution of the burden is determined exactly as in the case of a commodity tax: by the elasticities of demand and supply of shipping.[8]

Barring strictly short-run effects, it is thus futile for ports to attempt to protect national shippers by raising revenue mainly from the vessels. But the attempt is frequently made.[9] It has also been suggested that dues on foreign shipping are met primarily from external sources whereas dues on cargo are internal revenue and that the country's foreign exchange receipts will, therefore, benefit from raising charges on the ships rather than on the shippers.[10] Excepting again strictly short-run effects, this is another example of the same fallacy.

It may seem that even though ports cannot protect their national shippers by tilting the balance of charges against the vessel, at least nothing will be lost by trying except some wasted ingenuity. But this can obviously not be guaranteed. The efficient use of port resources

8. The time lag between the initial change of port charge and the final state of the distribution of the cost between the parties is ignored. In the case of liner conferences, this lag may be as long as 1 year because conference tariffs are not being changed continuously.

9. Compare, Coopers and Lybrand Associates Limited in association with Sir Bruce White, Wolfe Barry and Partners, and Shankland Cox Partnership. "Lembaga Pelabohan Kelang. Port Development Feasibility Study." Final Report, 2 vols. (August 1974), p. 5.

10. *Feasibility Study, Port of Chittagong Expansion, Bangladesh*, prepared for the Asian Development Bank (Louis Berger International Inc.), vol. II (December 1974).

requires that separate services should be priced according to their cost. If cost rises for services which are paid normally by the shipper, any prior decision to raise revenue to cover cost by increasing the charge to vessels will prejudice the efficiency of port pricing. It will distort the relation between price and cost across the port's operations.

As a start of this analysis, consider the general pattern of port investment and pricing and the effect on nationals according to the following layout.

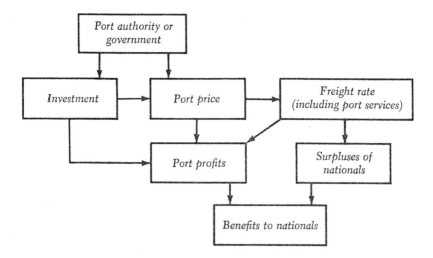

This schematic arrangement ignores the surplus that may accrue to monopolistic labor unions that may control the port; both investment and current cost incurred in running the port are reckoned as opportunity cost.

To simplify matters without doing violence to reality, suppose that the commodities are supplied and demanded at a constant price in world markets which are located a constant distance from the port. Thus variations in the freight rate have their entire effects on domestic residents—traders and consumers—and, of course, on the port.

The criterion for optimum port pricing emerges easily from this scheme. The total benefit is the profit to the port and the surplus earned by traders or enjoyed by domestic consumers. In principle, a reduced charge for port services will be reflected in a reduced freight rate (discussed in more detail in Appendix B), and the reduced freight rate is an advantage to the traders and to the consumers.

The marginal conditions for maximum national benefit also emerge readily from this scheme. The port should fix its price so that the additional loss entailed by a small reduction in this price is just offset by the additional advantage accruing to traders from the resulting reduction in the freight rate. In other words, the marginal loss to the port should be balanced by the marginal gain to the customers of the shipping lines.

One of the main problems is to find the relation between the port price and the freight rate. At the simplest level, it has been suggested that changes in port prices do not have an effect on freight rates.[11] This would eliminate two of the relations in the above figure. Unfortunately, the shipping companies will not absorb variation in port charge unless they are restricted to certain small variations.[12] Some passing on and perhaps multiplication or markup is bound to take place.

Bilateral Monopoly: Ships and Ports

The difficulty with this port–charge/freight-rate relation turns on the competitive structure of the shipping industry. If the country is served by one monopolist firm and if the port industry is organized also as a state monopoly, a bilateral monopoly emerges.

The natural outcome of bilateral monopoly, according to a standard theorem of economics, is the production of that volume of output of the intermediate good or service that maximizes the joint profit of buyer and seller.[13] This result is reached by an all-or-nothing deal (or simply, discriminating monopoly): the stronger party maximizing its own profit while reducing the profits of the weaker party to nothing. An all-or-nothing bargain forced by, say, the strong port on the weak shipping monopoly would dictate that the ships must buy that volume of port services (X_m) for which the port's marginal cost equals the ships' marginal revenue product (Figure 5.3).

11. See, for example, Ian Heggie, "Charging for Port Facilities," *Journal of Transport Economics and Policy*, vol. 8, no. 1 (1972), pp. 15–16.

12. It is clear that the problem would be simple and the solution silly, since the port could simply raise prices and increase its profits endlessly without incurring any penalty of an increase of freight rates.

13. W. Fellner, "Prices and Wages under Bilateral Monopoly," *Quarterly Journal of Economics*, vol. LXI (August 1947), pp. 503–532.

FIGURE 5.3.   BILATERAL MONOPOLY

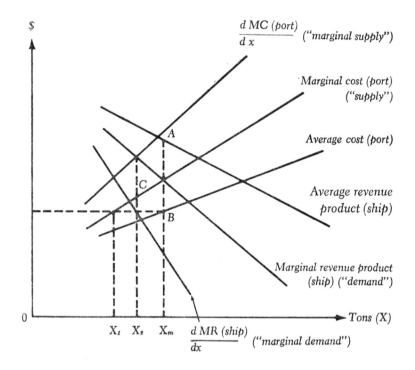

This same transaction would come about between the departments of a profit-maximizing enterprise consisting of a port-plus-shipping company. But the price paid by the ship would be fixed by the strong port at \$A per ton, equal to the ship's average revenue product which excludes profits. Alternatively, a strong ship confronting a weak port would offer a price of only \$B per ton for the same quantity of X_m tons annually and would enforce this deal (and a price at which the port would normally only wish to supply X_1 tons of service annually) by the threat of not calling at this port at all.

This solution, implying the output X_m and an indeterminacy of price between \$A and \$B per ton, is only feasible to the extent that all-or-nothing deals are feasible in the market for port services. The most obvious opportunities for this type of bargain exist in the dealings between ports and container consortia. Consortia bargain for separate terminals in the ports and will seek to obtain this at a profit-maximizing price under threat of omitting the port. The port, on the other hand, may insist on a certain number of annual calls which are paid for whether or not performed.

Large-scale containerization is usually acknowledged to be a matter of national policy and not just of concern to the ports. The deals offered by container operators, therefore, are often addressed to governments rather than to ports, and the question of the incidence of particular proposals is often obscured further by the participation of a national line in the consortium.

A proposal of this kind was made to a southeast Asian government by a domestically owned shipping company on behalf of itself and a major foreign operator from the most important trading partner. The proposal was that two of the country's scarce deep-water berths should be franchised to the national operator to develop into container berths, that the leasees should also be given exclusive rights to the inland transport of containers, and that container traffic in the country's deep-water port should be confined to national carriers and to their foreign associates. In addition, freight rates should not be reduced until the licensees had recovered their outlay, and the port should not exact rent for leasing berths since the expected rate of return (which on closer analysis seemed to be about 16 percent annually) was low. In return, the leasees would both develop the container berths and provide a certain number of container sailings per month on the route to the major trading partner. The proposal was regarded as an all-or-nothing offer by the government and ultimately was rejected.

Where no all-or-nothing deal is technically possible, the solution to the bilateral monopoly situation will be less efficient and will restrict output more. Thus Figure 5.3 shows the case where the monopolist ship confronts the competitive port. The best it can do is to demand X_2 tons of service annually, which the port will supply at $C per ton. With this quantity the ship maximizes its profit, as shown by the fact that the marginal cost of the port service to the ship $[(d(mc)_p)/dx]$ equals the ship's own marginal revenue product.

The difficulty with bilateral monopoly situations is that there is no general rule for the port to follow once it is in such a situation—except the obvious rule that it should avoid getting into the situation by its long-run policy. It is always better for the port to be faced by competitive shipping enterprises than by a monopoly, weak or strong.

But varying the competitive mix of the shipping interests confronting the port, if this is at all practicable, requires a long-run strategy.[14]

Optimal Pricing with Passive Shipowners

The problems of bilateral monopoly can be avoided only by assuming that the steamship monopoly reacts passively to the pricing policy of the port. This assumption gives the maximum leverage to the port authority; this must be remembered in interpreting the results. But even in practice, a port authority is confronted rarely by a single monopolist steamship owner or even by a single conference. The typical case is that of several conferences and a few miscellaneous tramps and bulkers. Again it is difficult to analyze the reactions of such a mixed bag of customers, but this analysis covers the extremes of this case—passive monopoly and perfect competition.

The market price for a quantity X of the port's services will be determined by the demand for the services from the steamship owners. If the steamship owner is a monopoly in relation to the shippers on a route, then he will be willing to buy an additional unit of port services at a maximum price equal to the difference between his marginal revenue and his marginal costs, that is to say:

$$(2) \quad \left[\text{Port price} \right] = \left[\begin{array}{c} \textit{Marginal} \\ \textit{revenue} \\ \textit{of ship} \end{array} \right] - \left[\begin{array}{c} \textit{Marginal ship} \\ \textit{cost (net of} \\ \textit{port charge)} \end{array} \right].$$

Thus, if the marginal cost for ship operation is constant:

$$(3) \quad \left[\begin{array}{c} \textit{Change in port price} \\ \textit{as X increases} \end{array} \right] = \left[\begin{array}{c} \textit{Change in marginal revenue} \\ \textit{as X increases} \end{array} \right].$$

If there is a constant elasticity of demand for shipping:

$$(4) \quad \left[\begin{array}{c} \textit{Change in} \\ \textit{port price} \end{array} \right] = \left[\frac{\epsilon + 1}{\epsilon} \right] \left[\begin{array}{c} \textit{Change in} \\ \textit{freight rate} \end{array} \right].$$

where ϵ is the elasticity of demand which is assumed to be constant.[15]

---

14. However, some pricing policies may, in fact, be inconsistent with that objective, as shown in Chapter 8.

15. $\Delta MR = \Delta \left[p \left(1 + \frac{1}{\epsilon} \right) \right] = \left(1 + \frac{1}{\epsilon} \right) \Delta p + p \Delta \left(\frac{1}{\epsilon} \right)$

$$= \Delta p \left(1 + \frac{1}{\epsilon} \right) \text{ if } \Delta \left(\frac{1}{\epsilon} \right) = 0$$

where ϵ has the range $\infty \leqq \epsilon < -1$.

With a constant elasticity of demand, therefore, any given change in the port price will be magnified by the factor $\epsilon/(\epsilon + 1)$ and will be reflected in the freight rate. Consider, for example, a constant elasticity of minus three; an increase of $0.10 in the port charge per ton will be reflected in a $0.15 rise in the freight rate if marginal cost is constant.

In this special case, any change in port charge is fully, or more than fully, passed on to the shippers. In particular, the monopolistic shipping firm always raises the freight rate by more than the increase in the port charge and lowers the freight rate by more than the decrease in port charge. But the validity of this conclusion requires that the elasticity of demand for shipping be constant. If it is variable and declines in absolute value as quantity increases, then the monopolist's response to variations in his marginal cost will be to pass on less than the full change in port charges. The linear demand curve provides an example. Its elasticity declines as quantity increases, and its slope is numerically equal to one-half of the slope of the marginal revenue curve. In this case[16]:

$$(5) \quad \begin{bmatrix} \textit{Increase in} \\ \textit{freight rate} \end{bmatrix} = \tfrac{1}{2} \begin{bmatrix} \textit{Increase in} \\ \textit{port charge} \end{bmatrix} - \tfrac{1}{2} \begin{bmatrix} \textit{Change in marginal cost} \\ \textit{with reduction in} \\ \textit{quantity supplied} \end{bmatrix}$$

In Figure 5.4, marginal cost is constant with respect to quantity supplied so that the freight rate increases by one-half of the increase in port price. If marginal cost rises as quantity increases, even less of the rise in port charges will be passed on by the shipping monopoly.

The degree of variability of the elasticity of demand for shipping thus is critical for the leverage of ports on freight rates and thus indirectly on the shipper who pays the freight rates. In economic analysis and econometric estimation, models embodying constant elasticities of demand frequently are used. Although this is done for convenience rather than for plausibility, variable elasticity is regarded to be much the more plausible assumption in the economics of shipping and ports. The kinked (concave) demand curve which is used later to explain the pricing decisions of shipping conferences thus has

16. $\dfrac{dp}{dX} = \dfrac{1}{2}\dfrac{d}{dX}$ MR; with ΔMC as a shift in the marginal cost schedule.

$\Delta MC = \dfrac{d}{dX} MR + \dfrac{d}{dX}\dfrac{dC}{dX} dX$ (if C stands for total cost);

Hence, $\dfrac{dp}{dX} dX = \dfrac{1}{2}[\Delta MC - \dfrac{d}{dX}\dfrac{dC}{dX} dX]$.

FIGURE 5.4. LINEAR DEMAND CURVES: THE PROFIT-MAXIMIZING
MONOPOLIST ABSORBS PART OF THE COST CHANGE

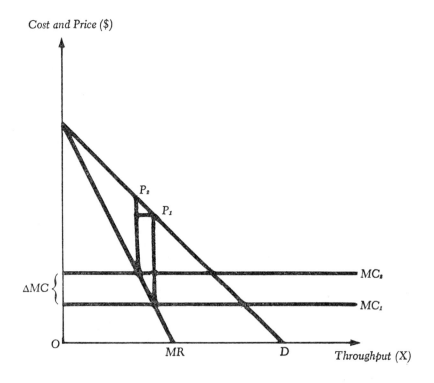

Note: Increase in marginal cost = ΔMC; slope of linear demand curve $D =$ ½ (slope of MR curve); increase in price = $(P_2 - P_1) = $½$\Delta MC$.

elasticity declining with quantity of cargo shipped and forms a limiting case where cost changes over a certain range are wholly absorbed
by the supplier.

Nevertheless, the initial assumption of constant elasticity of demand is held here for a while. This is done not only because of the
great convenience of eliminating one variation from the analysis, but
also because some of those results that are especially interesting are
not discredited in any essential way by the assumption.[17]

17. The relative harmlessness of the implausible assumption is confirmed by
the similarity of the main results under either assumption in the algebraic Appendix B to the chapter.

FIGURE 5.5. INTERACTION OF PORT PRICE AND FREIGHT:
THE CASE OF CONSTANT ELASTICITY OF DEMAND FOR SHIPPING

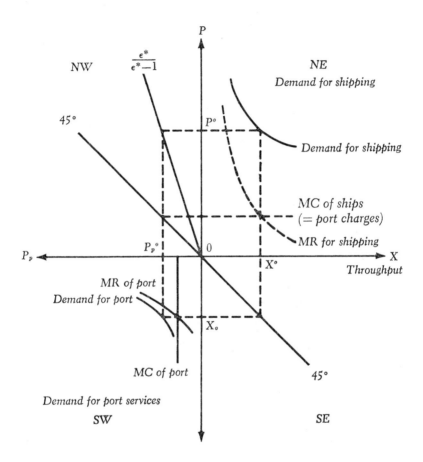

Note: P = freight rate; P_p = port price; ϵ^* = absolute value of the elasticity of demand. The assumptions in this figure are: constant elasticity of demand for freight; zero marginal cost of ship operation; constant marginal cost of port; passive reaction of monopolist shipowners to port pricing policies and profit-maximizing policy of port.

The consistency of port and freight charges, under the assumption of constant elasticity of demand for shipping, may be examined in Figure 5.5. The SW segment shows the demand for the services of the port. Marginal cost is constant in both shipping and port operations, and in shipping it is taken to be zero. The demand curve for shipping is assumed to have a constant elasticity of absolute value greater than unity. Beginning in the SW quadrant, the profit-maximizing port output and price at p_p^0 can be established. This is reflected through the NW quadrant first, at the ratio of unity to give the marginal cost of shipping (equals port charge) and, second, at the ratio $\epsilon^*/(\epsilon^* - 1)$, where ϵ^* is now defined as the absolute value of the demand elasticity, to find the consistent freight rate p^0.[18] Any variation in the port price will be reflected through the transformations in the NW quadrant into the freight rate.

The Incidence of Port Charges on Traders and Consumers

If the port reduces the price of its services below the value that maximizes the port profit, the consequences on the freight rate can be traced easily. If elasticity of demand for shipping is constant:

(6)   *Fall in freight rate* $= [\epsilon^*/(\epsilon^* - 1)]$ [*fall in port price*].

Now the value of the fall in the freight rate to traders and consumers can be measured by the maximum amount they are willing to pay for the rate reduction, which is (*Quantity of freight*) $\times$ (*Fall in freight rate*). For the traders, this is shown as the positively hatched area in Figure 5.6(a), that is to say, $\Delta p^0 X^0$. Since Δp^0 is negative, the gain to traders is minus this value.

Now this gain is compared with the loss to the port. This is shown by the vertically hatched area in Figure 5.6(b) and is simply the difference between the marginal cost and the marginal revenue for an increase of throughput generated by the reduction in the port price (and so the consequential reduction in freight rates) and the expansion of traffic. If the loss to the port is less than the gain to traders,

---

18. It is easy to incorporate constant nonzero marginal cost of shipping operations; then the transformation line is still a line but does not pass as a ray through the origin.

FIGURE 5.6.   DEMAND FOR SHIPPING AND DEMAND FOR PORT

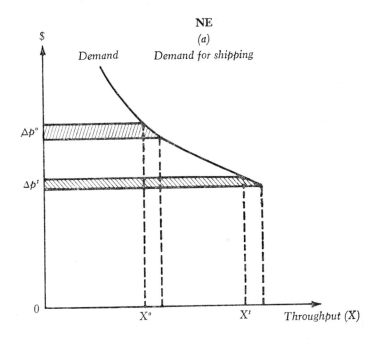

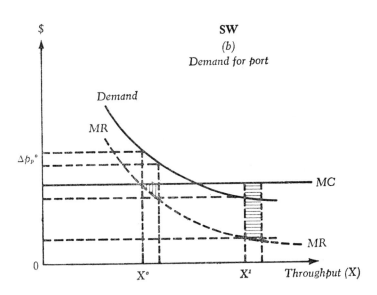

then the port should cut its tariffs and induce the expansion of services. Clearly it is possible that, if the port price has sufficient leverage on the freight rate, it may be best for the port not merely to run at a loss, but also to charge prices for port services which are below the marginal cost of the ports. This possibility is illustrated in the circumstances of X^1 in Figure 5.6(a) and (b). If the negatively hatched area in (a) still exceeds the horizontally hatched area in (b), then it is nationally advantageous for the port to price its services below marginal cost.

In the case of constant elasticity much hinges on the multiplier $\epsilon^*/(\epsilon^* - 1)$ which gives the port price its clout. The lower the absolute value of the elasticity of demand, the greater the multiplicative effect of a given change in the port tariff on the freight rate. This is, of course, a traditional result.[19]

Perfect Competition in Shipping

The case of perfect competition can be analyzed in this framework. Then the change in the port price is reflected in a one-for-one transform to the freight rate. In Figure 5.5 the reflection is effected through the 45° line in the NW quadrant. In the shipping business the freight rate is equal to marginal cost including the price of the services of the port. Clearly the port would best charge the marginal cost for its services since it is tantamount to selling them directly to traders and consumers. The reduced profits that the port suffers from expanding its services from the maximum-profit to the marginal-cost equals-price-output is more than offset by the value of the reduction in freight rates to traders and consumers.[20] But this rule only holds if the elasticity of demand for shipping is constant. If the elasticity declines absolutely as the quantity shipped increases, then the nationally optimal port charge will exceed marginal port cost; the de-

---

19. The limiting case of ϵ approaching infinity is not the case of perfect competition in shipping, however, since ϵ refers to the market elasticity of demand. The case of $\epsilon \to \infty$ is when the price of shipping is essentially fixed irrespective of the domestic demand conditions, and so the quantity of services is determined entirely by the (rising) marginal cost curve.

20. This is presuming that the price of factors of production measures their opportunity cost in alternative employments.

clining elasticity of demand for shipping now acts much like a low elasticity of demand for port services and raises the optimal port price above marginal cost.[21] This is the analogue to the classical optimum tariff of international trade theory.

Shipping Monopoly

The case of the steamship monopoly is not simplified so easily, even with constant elasticity of demand. But it is of central importance to the policy of ports in many developing countries. Therefore the results obtained by rather technical treatment are reported in Appendix B adding some numerical examples below.[22] No special assumption is made about the elasticity of demand for shipping although normally demand curves are considered that exhibit decreasing (absolute) elasticity as the quantity shipped rises.[23]

Marginal profit and profit-maximizing charge of a port

For simplicity assume that the marginal cost of ship operations is constant. Then the increased profit from the expansion of the port's output by 1 ton is:

$$(7) \qquad p_s R - C_s' - C_p' + p_s R_\omega$$

where p_s is the freight rate per ton; R is the ratio of the ship's marginal revenue (MR) to the freight rate, or $1 + (1/\epsilon)$ where ϵ stands for the elasticity of demand for shipping and is less than zero; C_s' is the marginal cost (MC) of ship operations (excluding port charges); C_p' is the marginal cost of port operation; and ω is a term which depends on the rate at which R declines as the quantity of shipping output increases, so that it will, for example, be the larger the faster

21. Appendix B, "Equalizing the Marginal Gain of Traders with the Marginal Loss of the Port."

22. Appendix B, "Maximizing the Benefits to Nationals," which contains the proofs of the propositions and some further analytical development, all unfortunately requiring some mathematical formulations.

23. If the elasticity of demand varies in this way, the absolute leverage of the port on the freight rates is lower than when elasticity is constant; less than the full change in the cost of shipping caused by a change in port charges is passed on to the traders.

R declines with increasing shipping output. If the elasticity of demand ϵ is constant, ω vanishes.[24]

For slightly easier interpretation the above equation may be re-written as the port's marginal profit equal to:

(8) $$[p_s R\,(R + \omega) - C_s'] - C_p'$$

or: $$[MR_{ship}\,(R + \omega) - MC_{ship,\ value\ added}] - MC_{port,}$$

the whole being interpretable as the difference between the port's marginal revenue and its marginal cost, marginal revenue (in brackets) being the difference between a multiple of ship's marginal revenue and ship's marginal cost.

Consider now a port which acts as a profit maximizer in its dealings with a shipping industry (or conference or owner) which is monopolized and yet reacts passively to the port's policy. In these circumstances the port will seek to set the profit-maximizing charge equal to:

(9) $$\left[\frac{1}{R}\,C_p' + \left(\frac{1}{R} - 1\right)C_s'\right] + p_s\omega.$$

The first two terms are a sort of weighted sum of the marginal costs. The third term adds to the port's optimal price according to the rate at which elasticity declines with rising shipping tonnage; for example, the more rapidly elasticity drops off, the more the port will profit from higher charges.

The nationally optimal port charge

The gain to traders from the reduced freight rate associated with expanded output by 1 ton is:

(10) $$-X\Delta p_s = -p_s\,\Delta X \cdot \frac{\Delta p_s}{\Delta X} \cdot \frac{X}{p_s}$$

or: $$-(p_s\Delta X)/\epsilon.$$

which, since $\epsilon < 0$, is positive. The object of a nationally optimal pricing policy will now be to fix the level of port charges so that a slight reduction will cause a gain to the traders which just offsets the

---

24. In this summary of the argument presented in Appendix B, the elasticity is defined as negative.

loss caused to port profit. This nationally optimal price $(p_p{}^n)$ turns out to be[25]:

(11)
$$\frac{1}{R}\left[\frac{1}{\epsilon}(p_s - C_s') + C_p' + p_s R_\omega\right].$$

The nearer R is to 1 (that is to say, the greater the elasticity of demand for shipping), the closer the approximation to marginal cost pricing; except that with variable elasticity of demand (for example, elasticity decreasing as quantity rises) the optimal price will always lie above marginal cost:

(12)
$$p_p{}^n = (C_p' + p_s\omega) \qquad \text{for } R = 1.$$

Next, the port's profit-maximizing price is compared with the nationally optimal price:

(13)
$$\begin{bmatrix} \textit{Profit-maximizing} \\ \textit{port charge} \end{bmatrix} - \begin{bmatrix} \textit{Nationally optimal} \\ \textit{port charge} \end{bmatrix}$$

$$= \frac{1}{R}\frac{p_s}{\epsilon} = \frac{-p_s}{MR_s}\frac{p_s}{\epsilon}$$

where ϵ is less than zero. This can be interpreted as follows: when the port has set the nationally optimal price, this nationally optimal price equals

(14)
$$\begin{bmatrix} \textit{Port's profit-} \\ \textit{maximizing} \\ \textit{price} \end{bmatrix} - \begin{bmatrix} \textit{Degree of} \\ \textit{monopoly} \\ \textit{in shipping} \end{bmatrix} \times \begin{bmatrix} \textit{Marginal gain} \\ \textit{to nationals from} \\ \textit{reduction in freight rate} \end{bmatrix}.$$

The use of the term degree of monopoly is not wholly accurate. Its standard meaning is the ratio of price to marginal cost, but here it is applied to the ratio of price to marginal revenue; but it still serves as an index of monopoly.[26] The implication is clear: the higher this degree of monopoly in shipping, the lower the nationally optimal price relative to the port's profit-maximizing price.

The optimal charge and marginal port cost

If shipping is monopolistic, the port's profit-maximizing charge will always exceed the nationally optimal charge. For example, if the elasticity of demand for shipping, $\epsilon = -2$ (so that $R = 1/2$) and if

25. Equation 8 in Appendix B, after transformation.
26. The ratio of price to marginal revenue should be described as gross degree of monopoly.

the factor representing the variability of the elasticity of demand, $\omega = -.25$, the port's profit-maximizing charge can be calculated as being equal to[27]:

$$(15) \qquad\qquad 4\,C_p' + C_s'$$

but the nationally optimal port charge equals:

$$(16) \qquad\qquad 4/5\,C_p' - 1/5\,C_s'.$$

Maximizing the gain of nationals thus requires a sharp cut in the port's profit-maximizing price. Moreover, in this case the resulting optimal charge fails to cover the marginal cost of port operations even if that is zero. Port operations will therefore require subsidizing. In Appendix B further numerical examples where the optimal port charge falls short of marginal cost are presented, including cases where optimal pricing demands a subsidy that is greater than the port's marginal cost itself.

There may be strong strategic reasons against allowing such indirect subsidies to monopolistic shipowners, but the proposition by itself is in no sense eccentric. The standard prescription for national policy toward monopolies that cannot be broken up is that they should be subsidized through reductions in their input prices. The object is to overcome the monopolistic restriction of output or the price-raising effect of the operation of monopolies. The required size of such an input subsidy is not related to the cost of producing the input (for example, the marginal cost of port operations per ton of throughput) but rather to the strength and responses of the monopoly. This matter is pursued in Appendix B. Here it is only added that input subsidies to monopolies are normally combined with at least the proposal of a lump-sum tax or at least a tax that is independent of the level of output. This suggests that what is really needed is a form of charging for the services of the port similar to two-part tariffs. This subject is discussed in Chapter 8.

National and Foreign Shipping Lines

So far in this chapter, the argument has been pursued on the assumption that the shipping services are all rendered by firms which are owned by foreigners. In practice, however, many developing coun-

---

27. Assume that the marginal cost of shipping operations is constant. For the full equations on which these calculations are based, see Appendix B.

tries have their own shipping industry, and these national companies must be counted as part of the national interest just as much as traders or ports.

The national shipping companies will use domestic resources, such as labor and capital, that will have an opportunity cost elsewhere in the economy. And if successful, such companies will earn a surplus over and above the prices that they pay for their inputs and that are assumed to be approximately equal to their opportunity cost. This surplus is the value of the national merchant marine to the country.

In calculating the effects of variations in port prices, the effects on the surpluses of national shipping companies have been ignored. It is clear, however, that if a reduction in port charge causes an increase in the surplus of the national shipping enterprise, then this ought to be included with the gain of domestic traders.

In many countries, these economic surpluses are negative, representing a misallocation of domestic resources. However, it is still possible for a reduction in port tariff to reduce the loss. While this should be counted as part of the benefit, the policy is very much second best. Rather than pursue any more detailed analyses of this issue, the all-foreign-shipping case is used to investigate the relevance of the model.

Relevance of the Model

As shown in Appendix B, the optimum price for the port may be expressed by the rather fearsome formula:

(17)
$$P_p{}^n = [1/(1 + R^2 - R + R\omega)] \ [(2R - R^2 - 1 - R\omega)C_s{}' + RC_p{}']$$

where $1 + R^2 - R + R\omega \neq 0$. And in the Appendix, values for the port price for various combinations of the parameters are shown.

This formula needs to be used with considerable caution. It should be regarded as a general guide which should be borne in mind when setting tariffs, and it should not be used mechanically nor applied without considerable reflection. Clearly this formula has been derived without considering a large number of constraints and limitations that must apply in the real world.[28] If these constraints were

28. For example, there is an asymptote when the denominator is zero and when the optimum price swings wildly from plus infinity to minus infinity! The reasons for such results are discussed in Appendix B.

included formally, then what is already rather complex would become hopelessly complicated.

There is, however, another approach. The general recommendation is one of marginal cost pricing, and marginal cost is still the basis even when the reaction effects are taken into account as in the formula above. But only relatively small deviations from marginal cost should be considered as feasible. The formula may, with discretion, be used to show the direction of the deviation, and this should be borne in mind in fixing the tariff schedules.

It is important to realize that the pricing policies of ports cannot correct many of the significant distortions in competition in the shipping industry. The amount of leverage is small. However, one of the common (European) propositions—the subsidization of ports—is so important that it deserves a critical review of the basis of the argument.

The assumptions behind the case for subsidy cannot be claimed to be characteristic of many port and shipping conditions. First, the exclusion of strategic and tactical behavior on the part of the port and monopolist conference is a serious omission since some such behavior is apparent in the real world. Second, it has been assumed that there are no possibilities of substitution of different amounts of port service with a given amount of ocean freight carriage. Obviously there are considerable possibilities here, and the assumption of fixed proportions is too stringent. Lastly, increasing marginal cost of shipping operations is likely as the port becomes congested, and the assumption that C'' equals zero is clearly invalid; in fact C'' is greater than zero and may be very large indeed in a highly congested port.

All these reasons suggest that any case for pricing below marginal cost must be modified considerably. For example, it clearly would be wrong to subsidize steamship owners to cover their congestion cost. Nevertheless for throughputs which are considerably below the capacity of the port, the case for a low variable charge and a high fixed levy seems to be good.

A general caveat therefore must be attached to these conclusions, and particularly to the case for subsidies that may arise. This caveat is that none of the conditions under which these conclusions would hold can be presumed to be general; their existence has to be proved in each case. Nor must it be thought that these possible cases for subsidy have anything in common with the standard cases on which claims for subsidies tend to be based in practice. In particular, the view that increased charges would harm nationals is as likely as not to be based on an erroneous understanding of the incidence of port charges.

Appendix A. A Model of the Profit-maximizing Port

The basic equations of the model which was described informally in "Port Profit Maximization Compared with Marginal Cost Pricing." (*above*) and in Figure 5.1 are now set out. The first equation describes the amount of output originating m (100 meters) from the port. This is shown as a linear function of the price levied by the port plus the internal transport cost. Thus:

$$x(m) = \beta - \gamma p(m)$$

where

$$p(m) = p(0) + tm,$$

$2x(m)$ is the quantity offered for export at a distance m (100 meters) down the road, $p(m)$ is the price of transport along the road plus the port charge $p(0)$, and t is the transport cost, constant per ton per 100 meters, along the road. For simplicity, suppose that there are no variable factor inputs into production other than those of transport.

$C(X)$ is the port cost function, where X is the total traffic shipped through the port:

$$X = \int_0^R 2x(m)\, dm.$$

Thus the profit of the port authority is given by:

$$\pi = p(0) \cdot X - C(X)$$

and the marginal profit is

$$\frac{d\pi}{dX} = \frac{dp(0) \cdot X}{dX} + p(0) - C'$$

where C' is marginal cost.

Owing to the choice of units for t and $x(m)$, the total output X can be represented as the product of the distance R and value of $x(0)$.[29]

29. The assumptions imply that the transport costs of a ton on the east → west trails is $1 per ton per 100 meters. Thus, t will generally be less than unity. For the Ellet model, the extent of cultivation is determined by this absolute transport cost, but for the purpose of calculating the elasticities and the effects of different price policies, only the ratio of the two transport costs is relevant.

(That is the base of the triangle QP multiplied by the height PR, see Figure 5.1.) Solving for $x(0)$:

$$x(0) = \beta - \gamma p(0).$$

At R it is clear that:

$$x(R) = 0,$$

and so:

$$x(R) = 0 = \beta - \gamma p(R)$$
$$= \beta - \gamma[p(0) + Rt].$$

Thus:

$$R = \frac{1}{t\gamma}[\beta - \gamma p(0)].$$

Total output is therefore:

$$X = \frac{1}{t\gamma}[\beta - \gamma p(0)]^2.$$

Then:

$$\frac{dX}{dp(0)} = \frac{-2}{t}[\beta - \gamma p(0)].$$

From the first-order condition for profit maximization:

$$\frac{d\pi}{dX} = 0 = -\frac{1}{2\gamma}[\beta - \gamma p(0)] + p(0) - C' = 0$$
$$= -\frac{\beta}{2\gamma} + (p(0)/2 + p(0)) - C' = 0.$$

So that:

$$p(0) = \frac{2}{3}C' + \frac{1}{3}\frac{\beta}{\gamma}.$$

This can be expressed alternatively in terms of R.

Since:

$$p(R) = p(0) + Rt$$

and:

$$p(R) = \beta/\gamma,$$

$$p(0) = \frac{2}{3}C' + \frac{1}{3}p(R)$$

$$= \frac{2}{3}C' + \left[\frac{p(0) + Rt}{3}\right]$$

$$p(0) = C' + \frac{Rt}{2},$$

which gives the markup of price above marginal cost.[30]

If the two price rules are substituted into the output formula, profit maximization reduces output of the exported good to four-ninths of the level that would be achieved under marginal cost pricing conditions (Figure 5.2).

The ratio of the total revenues is given by the more complicated equation:

$$\frac{\text{Maximum } \pi \text{ revenue}}{\text{MC revenue}} = \frac{4}{27}\left[\frac{2\gamma C' + \beta}{C'}\right] \qquad C' > 0,$$

and the profit-maximizing revenue will exceed marginal cost pricing revenue if γ and C' are sufficiently small relative to β so that $\beta > 19/4$ $\gamma C'$. Thus, if marginal cost is very low and if the triangle is not very elongated (that is to say, if R is small relative to the width), then it is very likely that the profit-maximizing revenue will be much greater than the marginal cost revenue. In the limiting case of near-zero marginal cost and capacity in excess of $(4/9)\beta(t\gamma)^{-1}$ the port will charge a price $\beta/(3\gamma)$ to maximize gross and net revenue at $(4/27)[\beta^2/(\gamma^2 t)]$ which will be available for the fixed cost of the port.

The elasticity of demand for the port's services with respect to its own price $p(0)$ can be put in various forms. All, however, involve either the value of $x(0)$ or the value of $p(0)$. With the linear system the elasticities are not independent of the absolute values; the smaller the output the larger the (absolute value of the) elasticity of demand. Thus:

$$\text{elasticity} = \frac{p(0)}{X}\frac{dX}{dp(0)}$$

$$= -2\gamma p(0)/[\beta - \gamma p(0)]$$

30. To avoid error in applying this formula, however, note that R is a function of $p(0)$ and of course a function of marginal cost since $Rt = (2/3t)$ $(-C' + \beta/\gamma)$, and so the expansion of the distance of cultivation along the road is given by dR/dC' which is $-2/3t$.

or

$$= 2 - \frac{2\beta}{x(0)} \qquad 0 < x(0) < \beta.$$

Appendix B. Maximizing the Benefits to Nationals

Let p_p = the price per unit of the port service; p_s = the freight rate; C_p = the cost of port service, and hence, C_p' = the marginal cost of the port service; C_s = the cost of shipping (excluding port charge), and hence, C_s' = the marginal cost of shipping (excluding port charge), and so forth for higher derivatives, C_s'' etc.; X = tonnage of ship cargo = port throughput; ϵ = elasticity of demand for shipping; $R = (1 + (1/\epsilon))$, the ratio of marginal revenue in shipping to the freight rate. Other symbols will be introduced and explained as the need arises.

Monopolist shipowners

The price which the monopolistic shipping conference would be prepared to pay for the port's service is the difference between their marginal revenue (MR_s) and marginal cost. Thus, with fixed proportions:

(1) $$p_p = MR_s - C_s' = p_s R - C_s'.$$

The profits of the port (π) are then:

$$\pi = X p_p - \text{port cost for } X = X p_p - C_p.$$

From this the marginal profit of port throughput is:

$$\frac{d\pi}{dX} = \frac{d(X p_p)}{dX} - C_p'$$

$$= \frac{d}{dX}[X(p_s R - C_s')] - C_p'$$

$$= X \frac{d}{dX}(p_s R - C_s') + (p_s R - C_s') - C_p'$$

$$= p_s \left[X \frac{dR}{dX} \right] + XR \frac{dp_s}{dX} - XC_s'' + (p_s R - C_s') - C_p'.$$

$X(dR/dX)$ can be written as $R\omega$ where ω is the elasticity of R with respect to changes in ship or port throughput, X. If the elasticity of demand for shipping (ϵ) is constant, $dR/dX = 0$, and hence also $\omega = 0$. If the elasticity of demand for shipping decreases in absolute value as X increases, dR/dX and ω will both be negative; but both will be positive if the absolute value of the elasticity of demand for shipping increases as X increases.[31] Thus the last expression for marginal port profit can be rewritten:

(2) $\quad \dfrac{d\pi}{dX} = p_s R\omega + XR\dfrac{dp_s}{dX} - XC_s'' + p_s R - C_s' - C_p'.$

Next:

$$ XR\frac{dp_s}{dX} = X\left[1 + \frac{1}{\epsilon}\right]\frac{dp_s}{dX} = \frac{p_s}{\epsilon}\left[1 + \frac{1}{\epsilon}\right]. $$

Therefore:

$$ \frac{d\pi}{dX} = p_s R\omega + \frac{p_s}{\epsilon}\left[1 + \frac{1}{\epsilon}\right] - C_s''X + p_s\left[1 + \frac{1}{\epsilon}\right] - C_s' - C_p' $$

$$ = p_s R\omega + p_s\left[1 + \frac{1}{\epsilon}\right]^2 - C_s''X - C_s' - C_p' $$

or

(3) $\quad \dfrac{d\pi}{dX} = p_s R\omega + p_s R^2 - C_s''X - C_s' - C_p'.$

Finally, since $p_p = p_s R - C_s'$:

(4) $\quad \dfrac{d\pi}{dX} = p_s R\omega + p_p R + C_s'R + C_s''X - C_s' - C_p'.$

The profit-maximizing port will fix its price so that $d\pi/dX = 0$. After introducing this marginal condition into Equation (4), the maximum profit price is:

(5) $\quad p_p = \dfrac{1}{R}\,[C_s' + C_s''X + C_p' - C_s'R - p_s R\omega]$

$$ = \frac{1}{R}\,[C_p' + C_s'(1 - R) + C_s''X - p_s R\omega]. $$

---

31. With certain special forms of demand function there is a unique functional relation between R and ω. One example is the linear demand curve. For most other demand curves, however, there is no simple functional relation between R and ω.

This general equation can now be applied to a number of special cases.

The simplification of constant marginal cost of ship operations $(C_s'' = 0)$ merely removes one term from Equation (5). As $R \to 1$, $p_p \to (C_p' - p_s\omega)$.

THE CASE WHEN ϵ IS CONSTANT. In this case, $\omega = 0$, and a further term is removed from Equation (5). The port's profit-maximizing price is now:

$$(6.1) \qquad p_p = \frac{1}{R} [C_p' + (1 - R)C_s'] \qquad 0 < R \leqslant 1.$$

Hence, as $R \to 1$, $p_p \to C_p'$. As R decreases there is a double kick to the price of the port since it marks up on its own (port) marginal cost by $1/R$ and adds on the steamship owner's marginal costs marked up by $(1 - R)/R = -1/(1+\epsilon)$.

THE CASE WHEN $|\epsilon|$ IS NOT CONSTANT AND DECREASES AS X INCREASES. This is the most plausible situation. It embraces the cases of linear demand curves for shipping and of demand curves which are kinked concave to the origin.

In this case dR/dX is negative and so, therefore, is ω. The profit-maximizing price of port services now becomes (from Equation 5):

$$(6.2) \qquad p_p = \frac{1}{R} [C_p' + C_s'(1 - R) - p_s R\omega].$$

The last term in the brackets is negative, and it is thus an addition to p_p whenever the elasticity of demand for shipping is not constant but decreases (absolutely) as quantity shipped rises. This addition will be the greater the more rapidly the elasticity of demand declines and the higher is the shipping freight rate.

As $R \to 1$, $p_p \to (C_p' - p_s\omega)$, which means that the port's profit-maximizing price will stay above marginal port cost according to the speed at which elasticity of demand for shipping declines as throughput rises.

THE CASE WHEN $|\epsilon|$ IS NOT CONSTANT BUT INCREASES AS X INCREASES $(\omega > 0)$. This will give a modifying influence to the markup of the port price above cost since the port will be encouraged to charge lower prices to exploit the much larger quantity generated at high throughput volumes.

Competitive steamship owners

This can be derived easily from the monopolistic case (Equation 2) by writing $R = 1$. Thus:

$$\frac{d\pi}{dx} = [X \frac{dp_s}{dX} - C_s''X + p_s - C_s' - C_p'] + p_{s\omega}$$

$$= [p_s [1 + \frac{1}{\epsilon}] - C_s' - C_s''X - C_p'] + p_{s\omega}$$

(7) $$= [p_sR - C_s' - C_s''X - C_p'] + p_{s\omega}.$$

Consider first the terms in square brackets. The first term is the market marginal revenue curve of the freight market. The last term is the marginal cost of the port services. The middle two terms of Equation (7) $(C_s' - C_s''X)$ describe the marginal change in total freight cost as output is increased; that is:

$$C_s' - C_s''X = C_s' \left[1 - \frac{dC_s'}{dX} \cdot \frac{X}{C_s'} \right]$$

$$= C_s' \left[1 - \left(\frac{C_s'}{X} \frac{dX}{dC_s'} \right)^{-1} \right]$$

which looks like the familiar marginal revenue elasticity formula.

If the marginal cost is plotted (Figure 5.7), the shaded area can be deducted from the value of C_s'.
Now $p_p = p_s - C_s'$ for a competitive shipping industry, so $p_s = p_p + C_s'$. Substituting into Equation 7:

$$\frac{d\pi}{dX} = [(p_p + C_s')R - C_s' - C_s''X - C_p'] + p_{s\omega}.$$

If the port was a profit maximizer:

$$p_p = \frac{1}{R} [C_p' + (1 - R) C_s' + C_s''X - p_{s\omega}].$$

Or if C'' is assumed to be zero (constant marginal cost of shipping):

$$p_p = \frac{1}{R} [C_p' + (1 - R)C_s' - p_{s\omega}],$$

and if the elasticity of demand for shipping is assumed to be constant ($\omega = 0$), then this is the same as Equation (6.1) above: the profit maximizing port charges the same price whether it is confronted

FIGURE 5.7.   INCREASING MARGINAL SHIPPING COST
AND INCREMENTAL LOSS

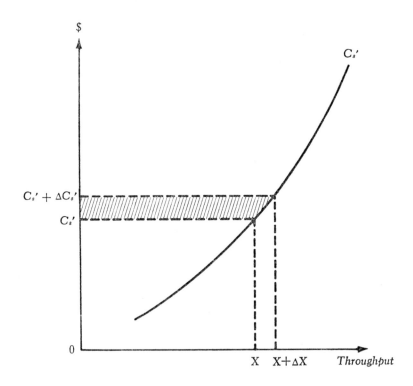

by competitive shipowners or by monopolists. For example, if $R = \frac{1}{2}$ (elasticity of minus 2), then the profit-maximizing port price is given by:

$$p_p = 2C_p' + C_s'.$$

But the output is lower in the monopolist case than under competitive conditions. Consequently, the port profit (when maximized) under circumstances where there is a monopolistic steamship industry will be less than if there is competition.

However, if the elasticity of demand for shipping is variable and if its absolute value declines as output increases ($\omega < 0$), then with $0 < R < 1$, the profit-maximizing port will charge a higher price to competitive ships than to monopolists. With competitive steamships the addition to the port's profit-maximizing price is $p_s\omega/R$ against only $p_s\omega$ when steamships are monopolized (Equation (6.2)). For example, with $\omega = -1$ and $R = \frac{1}{2}$, p_p for competitive shipowners equals $2C_p' + C_s' + 2p_s$, but p_p for monopolistic shipowners equals $2C_p' + C_s' + p_s$. Consequently, the port's revenue need not be less under circumstances of a shipping monopoly.

The gains to national owners of cargo

The gain to cargo owners of reduced freight rates is measured by the quantity of cargo multiplied by the (small) reduction in the charge per ton of cargo; that is to say, $-X\Delta p_s$. This is the compensating variation of income associated with the price change Δp_s. This can be expressed in terms of ΔX by the transposition

$-X\frac{\Delta p_s}{\Delta X} \cdot \Delta X$. Taking the limit as ΔX becomes very small,

$$(8) \qquad \frac{-X\Delta p_s}{\Delta X} \cdot \Delta X = \frac{-Xdp_s}{dX} \cdot dX = \frac{p_s}{\epsilon} \cdot dX$$

defining $\epsilon < 0$.

This implies that the price (or freight rate) divided by the elasticity of demand will measure the marginal gain (loss) to nationals other than the port authority of a reduction (increase) in the freight rate associated with a small change in throughput.

Equalizing the marginal gain of traders with the marginal loss of the port

The optimum policy for a country as a whole is to pursue a policy of port pricing that will maximize total benefits to nationals. (The distribution of these benefits and costs between nationals and domestic authorities is ignored). This will occur when the marginal profit (loss) of the port is just equal to the marginal loss (gain) of the domestic traders.

THE COMPETITIVE CASE. The marginal profit is:

$$\frac{d\pi}{dX} = p_sR - C_s' - C_p' + p_s\omega \text{ (from Equation 7 above)}$$

assuming that $C'' = 0$. Thus the best policy would ensure that:

$$p_sR - C_s' - C_p' + p_s\omega = \frac{p_s}{\epsilon}$$

or that

$$p_s(1 + \omega) - C_s' - C_p' = 0.$$

Competition in the shipping industry assures that $p_p = p_s - C_s'$. Substituting this into the optimum policy relation:

$$(p_p + C_s')(1 + \omega) - C_s' - C_p' = 0$$

from which the port's profit maximizing price is:

$$p_p = \left[\frac{1}{1 + \omega}\right][C_p' - \omega C_s'].$$

With constant elasticity of demand curves ($\omega = 0$) it is then best for the port to charge marginal cost: $p_p = C_p'$. This result can be rationalized by the normal arguments. If the port charges above marginal cost, this will be reflected identically in the freight rates charged by the competitive firms in shipping, and so the traders will have to pay.

But if the elasticity of demand is variable and if it decreases arithmetically as output increases (so that $\omega < 0$), the optimum policy rule becomes more complicated. Moreover, it cannot be defined except for the range $0 > \omega > -1$. For values within that range the port will always charge a price above marginal cost. For example, with $\omega = -\frac{1}{2}$, $p_p = 2C_p' + C_s'$. Over the specified range, therefore, a declining elasticity of demand acts like a low elasticity of demand in that it lifts price above marginal cost.

THE MONOPOLISTIC CASE. Assume, as before, that the marginal cost of shipping is constant; hence $C_s'' = 0$.

The marginal condition for maximum national benefit is then obtained by setting the port's marginal profit (Equation (4)) equal to the marginal gain of traders:

$$\frac{d\pi}{dX} = p_s R\omega + p_p R + C_s' R - C_s' - C_p' = \frac{p_s}{\epsilon}.$$

From this the nationally optimal port price is derived:

$$(9) \qquad p_p{}^n = \frac{1}{R}\left[\frac{p_s}{\epsilon} + C_s'(1 - R) + C_p' - p_s R\omega\right]$$

where $|\epsilon| \geqq 1$ and $0 < R \leqq 1$.

First, note that as $R \to 1$, $p_p{}^n \to (C_p' - p_s\omega)$. In this special case there is thus no difference between the port's profit-maximizing price and the nationally optimal price (see, for instance, "The case where $|\epsilon|$ is not constant and decreases as X increases," above). If the demand curve for shipping has constant elasticity, the optimal price in either sense will be equal to marginal cost.

In all other circumstances, however, the port's unconstrained monopoly price will exceed the nationally optimal price. (The possibility of a positive elasticity of demand is excluded as being an oddity.) This can be verified by subtracting Equation (9) from Equation (6.2) to get:

$$(10) \qquad p_p - p_p{}^n = \frac{1}{R}\left[\frac{p_s}{\epsilon}\right] = \frac{p_s}{MR_s}\left[\frac{p_s}{\epsilon}\right]$$

where MR_s is the marginal revenue of the shipowners. An interpretation of this difference is suggested in Equation (13) of the main text of this chapter.

Last, the relation between the nationally optimal price and the marginal cost of the port must be examined. For this purpose Equation (3) is rearranged and a substitution is made for p_s. Thus an alternative formulation of the nationally optimal port price is obtained:

$$p_p{}^n = \frac{1}{1 + R^2 - R + R\omega}\left[(2R - R^2 - 1 - R\omega)\,C_s{}' + RC_p{}'\right],$$

where $1 + R^2 - R + R\omega \neq 0$.[32]

A solution for the optimal port price, $p_p{}^n$, for given ω and ϵ is shown in the following table:

ω	-1.5 $R = 1/3$	-2.0 $R = 1/2$	-10.0 $R = 9/10$
-0.5	$0.9\,C_p{}' - 0.7\,C_s{}'$	$C_p{}'$	$2\,C_p{}' + 0.1\ \ C_s{}'$
-1.0	$1.4\,C_p{}' - 0.5\,C_s{}'$	$2\,C_p{}'\ \ - C_s{}'$	$90\,C_p{}' + 89\ \ C_s{}'$
-2.0	negative	negative	negative
0	$0.6\,C_p{}' - 0.8\,C_s{}'$	$0.66\,C_p{}' + 0.33\,C_s{}'$	$C_p{}' + 0.01\,C_s{}'$
$+1.0$	$0.3\,C_p{}' - 0.7\,C_s{}'$	$0.4\ \ C_p{}' + 0.6\ \ C_s{}'$	$0.5\,C_p{}' - 0.5\ \ C_s{}'$

32. For purposes of comparison (see main text of Chapter 5), Equation 6.2 can be rearranged for the profit-maximizing port charge:

$$p_p = \frac{1}{\omega + R}\left[(1 - \omega - R)\,C_s{}' + C_p{}'\right] \qquad (R > \omega).$$

The formula given above must be used with considerable caution. It has been derived by considering the equality of marginal gain and marginal cost. But to ensure that the net benefit to the domestic residents is maximized, marginal cost must increase (or diminish less rapidly than additional benefits), and marginal gain must decrease (or decrease more rapidly than marginal cost). These are the second-order conditions for an equilibrium. In this Appendix it was not thought to be appropriate to explore formally the second-order conditions in this model; nor have the questions of existence and multiple equilibrium been pursued. In part, this reluctance is explained by the tedious and complex character of the exercise. But the main reason is that here the interest is in applications, and in applying this model to reality, it is likely to be quite obvious whether or not the equilibrium will be a maximum or a minimum.

The formula has an asymptote when $1 + R^2 - R + R\omega = 0$, and so, in the region of this equality, the optimum port price swings wildly from plus infinity to minus infinity. Such a result is, of course, absurd, yet it is by no means uncommon in calculations of this type.[33] The question remains how to interpret or perhaps to interpret away such absurdities.

These odd results arise primarily because port pricing is being asked to do more than it can deliver. The cost and competitive conditions of the shipping industry, port, and traders may be so out of joint that no conceivable juggling with port prices will correct them.[34] For example, it is clear that the above formula may produce a negative port price—shippers are paid to use the port. But on any common sense grounds, this is simply not feasible. And even if it were feasible, it is certain that other methods could be found which would solve better the problems of the cost and competitive condition of the economy.

---

33. For example, the reader will find that asymptotes of this kind appear in the formal statements of the UNIDO Guidelines (United Nations, Industrial Development Organization, *Guidelines for Project Evaluation* (New York, 1972)). Thus the shadow price of investment can be plus infinity or minus infinity according to the sign of the difference between the marginal rate of social time preference, and the product of the marginal saving rate and the marginal return on investment.

34. The analogue of this in the UNIDO Guidelines absurdities is that when the shadow price of investment approaches the asymptote, the instruction is to put all resources in investment and ignore the negative branch. But then we should all be dead very soon.

The range of applicability of the formula should be restricted to values which are neither massive multiples nor tiny fractions of the marginal cost of the port. In practice, it would be used to indicate the appropriate direction of deviations of price from marginal cost. If the indicated deviations are small—imagine that they suggest, for example, that a markup of marginal port cost by one-tenth of the marginal shipping cost (this is the result with $R = 0.9$ and $\omega = 0$)— then this is worth exploring in practice. But if the formula gives results which suggest that trivially low prices or very high prices should be charged, it is best to look elsewhere for instruments to correct the wrongs of the economy. And then port price should be fixed along the general line of marginal cost using the two-part tariff technique to ensure that cost is covered.

Chapter 6

Strategic Pricing

IN THE PRECEDING CHAPTER the use of port charge as an instrument to maximize the national gain from shipping was discussed. Much of the investigation was concerned with pricing port services to shipping monopolies. This attention to noncompetitive shipping is warranted by the large share of liner conferences in the trades of developing countries; some statistical evidence on this ill-documented subject is presented in Appendix A to this chapter. But the conclusions which were reached in the last chapter were based on two premises. The first was that the port authorities have to accept the competitive conditions in the country's ocean trades as unalterably given. This seems unduly restrictive; faced with monopolistic shipowners on certain routes, it is often possible to reduce the monopolist position in the country's shipping by a strategic use of pricing. The second premise was that changes in port charges will be reflected in freight charges; this may be plainly false.

Pricing to Promote Competition

It has been argued that shipping conferences would not transmit cost-saving price reductions or improvements in port services through the conference rate to that port because the conference tends to equalize freight rates for a number of ports in the same general area. For example, the same nominal freight rate is charged across the

Pacific for all the ports on the west coast of North America, and, as another example, Calcutta and Chittagong have the same rates for shipments from Europe. What then is the advantage to any port or its national users of improving its services since it is unlikely to secure any net benefits or competitive advantage over other ports in the region?

In fact the conference has many ways of responding to either changes in port charges or in the quality of port service. The obvious way is for the conference to rearrange its sailings so that the more expensive port is served less frequently or by less desirable services. Certain variations in the conditions may be imposed also.

More important, however, is the fact that conferences do introduce surreptitious variations in charges which do reflect the cost of port calls. In the case of Vancouver traffic that is routed through Seattle, the conference absorbs the additional cost of inland transport from Seattle to Vancouver. Thus conference vessels not only are saved from paying the higher port charges of Vancouver, but also, and more important, they avoid the cost of the additional ship time of a call at Vancouver. Essentially the conference cuts the rate for transit through Seattle.

The proposition that changes in port charges or services will not be reflected in freight rates is true in one important respect. The main constraint on conference pricing is the risk of entry of tramps and nonconference competition. This suggests that if the conference reduced its rates, it would attract little traffic since the overall elasticity of demand for ocean carriage is quite low. Thus there is a kink in the demand curve facing the conference.[1] This causes a discontinuity in the marginal revenue curve. Considerable variations can occur in the cost conditions of the conferences without any effect on the freight rate. In Figure 6.1 the demand curve facing the conference is given by the highly elastic section above its current freight rate, which is a little less than those of potential competitors, and it is relatively inelastic for ranges of freight rate below that value. In the region of X_0 the marginal revenue curve of the conference falls vertically. Thus for a considerable range of marginal costs, the level of output X_0 and the associated freight rate P_0 will continue to be the best ones for the conference. However, this argument merely ration-

1. See E. Bennathan and A. A. Walters, *The Economics of Ocean Freight Rates*, Praeger Special Studies in International Economics and Development (New York: Praeger, 1969).

FIGURE 6.1.   KINKED DEMAND CURVE AND CHANGES IN COST

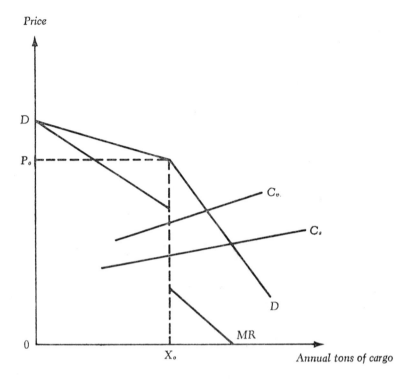

alizes the observation that changes in port cost do not appear to have a corresponding effect on the rate levied by the conference. It cannot explain why the conference maintains the same rate to ports where the cost of carriage and call differ considerably.

In principle an attempt may be made to incorporate the similarity of freight rates for different ports into the analysis by using the same type of reasoning. For example, let demand for transportation from London to two ports, say Vancouver and Seattle (or V and S) be the same as in Figure 6.1. If the cost of operating to Vancouver is higher than to Seattle, say C_v compared with C_s, then, provided there is not an enormous difference between them, the conference will be induced to equalize the two rates. This seems to explain the similarity of rates; but here appearances may be deceptive. The demand curve is drawn with respect to a given price charged by the competitors of the conference, and in particular the elastic branch of the kinked demand curve reflects this price. Under competitive conditions any variation in port charge will be reflected in the price of the tramps and bulk carriers or in the cost of using such chartered vessels relative to the liner freight rates. A reduction of port charges which is confined to the noncompetitive operators—and this may often just mean the liners since they tend to be cartelized—may indeed fail to show up in the freight rates. But if the reduced charges are extended also to competitive port users, it will cause the demand curve for the conference to move bodily downwards, so in principle, there would be an effect on the rate charged by the conference. In the extreme case, if P_0 is determined by the costs of competitors, which include the port charge, then a reduction in port charges will be reflected in an equal reduction in the value of P_0, and the price of the conference should fall correspondingly.

This result only follows if the port improvement or the reduction of port charges applies to all operations from the port at an equal amount per ton. Many port improvements, however, are not of this form. For example, the change from conventional handling to a container system will generally affect the port cost and charges only for general cargo carried in containers. The cost of bulk carrier and tramps and indeed of conventional liner operation will remain broadly the same. Under these conditions a reduction in costs and charges for port facilities (per ton) may well have no effect on the rate charged by the conference for container traffic or, indeed, for their conventionally handled traffic.

Therefore, if a container terminal is built, but no general improvement is made in port services for conventionally handled and bulk cargoes, then the reduced port charges for container traffic are unlikely to be reflected in the container tariffs. The cost curve will move down the vertical section of the marginal revenue curve in Figure 6.1, and the container tariff will be the same as the unchanged conventional tariff.[2] The traffic generally will be the same as it was before since the tariffs will not have changed. It is possible, however, that the reduction in cost is so great that it pays the conference to reduce its freight

2. In practice container operation may considerably improve the quality of service, so with unchanged tariffs there may be some implicit reduction in price. There are, however, many cases when the conference charges a container surcharge on general cargo, thus absorbing any benefit generated. With the kinked form of demand curve and the competitive conditions postulated, this is what is expected.

rate and to expand traffic. Given the normally low elasticity of demand for generated traffic, this is not a likely outcome except for competing ports.

There are, however, circumstances in which partial improvements in port facilities will lead to reductions in the rates charged by the beneficiaries. But the most important of these again depends on the state of competition or rather on the weakening of the market power which conferences and consortia seek to achieve. If competition develops between or within container consortia, the groups or the break-aways will lower their rate more or less in conformity with cost. The averaging of rates over a range of ports will cease by the same token.

Another realistic possibility is that the container terminal may be a new addition to the capacity of a port with congestion on its existing quays and sheds. Thus whether the port charges a congestion levy or whether the conference extracts one, the construction of the container berths will result in a reduction of the price (or a corresponding improvement in the quality of service) for conventional handling by nonconference vessels. If congestion falls equally on all vessels,[3] its disappearance will lower cost and the rate charged in the competitive sector of shipping. The reduced cost and so freight rate of competitive vessels would again modify the container consortium's charges.

Therefore, there are good economic reasons why the particular improvement of port facilities or the reduction of port charges will not necessarily result in any diminution of the freight rate charged by the conference or consortium. It is only by bringing down the competitor's price that the pricing policy of the conference or consortium will be affected, and this may be done only through general port improvements for conventional or bulk carriage which will, paradoxically, have some effect on the conference pricing.

It would be unwise, however, to conclude that the one way in which the country can be sure to collect the surplus from its improvement in port facilities is to lower port charges (or improve the service) for conventional or bulker vessels. Port charges are still only a small fraction of the total operating cost, except perhaps for coastal and short sea-route vessels; they are smaller, indeed, for conventional and bulk vessels than for mainline container vessels. The change in port charges may constitute a small fraction of the total cost of the con-

3. This is not always the case; see Chapter 5.

ference members. Conference tariffs are set by a committee procedure, and considerable cost is incurred in upsetting existing rates that, no doubt, were the product of long and protracted bargaining sessions. Conference rates tend to be sticky unless the conference happens to be fighting a vigorous attack by some outside vessels. The conference may absorb such cost reductions and even may suffer some small loss of traffic to its competitors to preserve the hard-won internal balance.

Discrimination and Counterdiscrimination

The most prominent feature of monopoly pricing in shipping is price discrimination, mainly by origin–destination and by the value of commodities. Discrimination is defined as differences in price, freight rate, or, for that matter, in port charge which cannot be attributed to differences in cost.[4] It is thus an emanation of monopoly, and the price strategy of the national port has to contend with it. Therefore, the possibilities have to be explored of countering discrimination directly by counterdiscrimination or indirectly by methods designed to weaken the price-discriminating power of the shipping cartel.

Discrimination by origin and by destination

Discrimination depends upon the ability of the seller to split his market into segments and to prevent resale from one customer to another. In liner conference tariffs, the same rates apply usually to a wide variety of ports. In the Far East Freight Conference, the same rates extend from the Arabian Gulf ports to the ports of Northern Europe, and there are nominally the same rates from Japan to Vancouver or Seattle. The conference finds it practicable to segment its market; for example, it is impossible for anyone to consign a shipment to the gulf ports from Singapore and then to send a shipment free of charge from the Gulf to Northern Europe on the argument that the ship space from Singapore to Bergen has been bought already. The conference would not allow such practices.

---

4. This differs from the common man's concept of discrimination where the idea applies to prices for services of a similar appearance whether or not those services cost the same to provide.

Discrimination can be practiced by the conference charging the same rate to destinations with widely different costs. The similarities of rates can be explained in part, and perhaps in large part, by the existence of alternative competitors to the carriage by the conference. For example, competition to the Gulf ports for general cargo is virtually nonexistent, whereas the European ports have large general cargo movements at competitive rates. Conferences can therefore recoup by large markups on Gulf traffic.

It would be quite fortuitous if the equalization practices of the conferences reflected exactly the appropriate discrimination according to their cost conditions, to the competition on that route, and to the elasticity of supply of traffic. There is, no doubt, a considerable pressure to simplify the tariff so that it has an air of nondiscriminatory fairness and differentials do not have to be defended. However, the situation in many countries where conferences have established strong positions clearly permits discrimination by origin, if only competition can be held sufficiently at bay. The temptation thus exists frequently, and there is ample evidence that it is also acted upon. It is not difficult to rationalize some of the observed forms of spatial price discrimination; in Appendix B the process and effects of this type of price discrimination are demonstrated in a stylized, yet not unrealistic, case. In the simplest case, the exporter's foreign-market price is assumed to be given and he will supply his goods—and thus demand shipping services—as long as that foreign price exceeds his cost, including transport cost. If exporters are located at different distances from the port, the conference with power to practice price discrimination will charge the highest rate to the nearest exporter and the lowest to the farthest exporter.[5] The abatement of price to distant shippers will be related to inland transport cost. In simple cases the rule would then be that the conference absorbs a particular percentage of inland transport cost down to the distant point where no more traffic is forthcoming because the freight rate and internal transport cost are too high. If, instead of thinking of shippers at different distances from a port, different ports are considered to be at a different distance from a main port, then it can be assumed also that the ships' cost will rise with distance. Rising cost will then naturally offset part of the rate reduction according to distance. The same principle of price dis-

---

5. In practice, the nearest exporter may have access to alternative means of shipping so that the farther exporter is charged more than the nearer one. But that is a case of price discrimination according to competitive conditions and not according to distance and therefore is a different matter.

crimination can also be transplanted into situations of regional productivity differences in export production. It will then lead the shipping monopoly to seek to absorb part of the productivity difference by charging lower rates to the less productive regions.[6]

It is clear that a discriminating conference will be able to earn more profits than a conference that is restrained from such discrimination; one, for example, that is required by law to carry all goods at the same rates, irrespective of their origin. It is also clear that the discrimination will result in a larger volume of exports through the conference ports than would have been the case with one price only.[7] However the populace of the country will be worse off with discrimination rather than without it. The conference will be appropriating their surplus. Indeed with the perfect discrimination assumed in this illustration, the conference will be expropriating all the surplus that arises from export demand.[8]

Expressed in terms of the effects on ports, the charging practices of liner cartels, including cartels of container operators, tend to absorb the relative advantages of location or port productivity. This policy is so generally accepted that container projects tend to take it for granted. The freight rates or through-transport rates that get accepted in the cost–benefit calculations of container projects are thus sometimes based not on ascertainable cost of a new service to and from a particular port but rather on the rates (possibly somewhat augmented to reflect the cost of the additional service) on the main nearby trunk routes. This is done with the firm expectation that the container lines will average out cost over the entire route.[9] But the use of such

6. All these variants are elaborated in Appendix B of this chapter.

7. This is true, however, only if the rigid assumptions of the model are adhered to. In particular, in the case of varying demand functions with distance the result may be a smaller output for export; but these cases are ignored.

8. It might be conjectured that if the conference were wholly owned in the country, then such discrimination would clearly improve the condition of the country generally. But even this argument is not correct. With a particular constraint, the discrimination is worse than single price solutions. But with other constraints, this result would not necessarily hold. Fortunately, however, these complications do not matter in this context since the country in question never has complete ownership or even any substantial fraction of the ownership of the steamship companies.

9. See Economist Intelligence Unit in association with Wallace Evans and Partners, Consulting Civil and Structural Engineers, *The Containerization of Thailand's Sea Trade* (prepared for the Government of Thailand, Ministry of Communications, 1973), p. 53.

administered prices may not always provide a safe ground for port investment that may not be profitable on the basis of competitive pricing or services.

The policy question for ports (if chosen as instruments of national policy) is whether they can recapture surpluses that have been annexed by ships. In the end this raises the question of counterdiscrimination. The alternatives are to discriminate against ships which absorb surpluses, to use opportunities for price discrimination to subsidize the use of shipping monopolies, or to seek to preempt the surpluses which ships extract from national shippers.

The first problem is to see whether it is feasible for the port authorities to discriminate and in what way they could discriminate. Variation in port charges often may be associated with variations in the price paid for inland transport. Both rail and port authorities are usually under the same authority, the Ministry of Transport, and it would not be too difficult to coordinate their charging practices. In some countries the railway authority is responsible for the port and can often discriminate against the road trucker. Thus, discrimination by the port authority is feasible, the question is whether it is desirable.

Discrimination among goods

Discrimination among goods is traditional in port economics largely because it is thought to enable the port to cover its cost and to charge low development levies for low-valued commodities. In principle the markup of charge above marginal cost should be proportional to the inverse of the total elasticity of demand. If the elasticity of demand is related in a significant way to the inverse of the value per ton or per volumetric quantity, the variation in the port levy with respect to the value of the commodity will extract revenue according to the ability to pay.

Since both the railways and the liner conference price according to ability to pay, it may be argued that the port authority should not add to such discrimination.[10] A particular objection is that the con-

---

10. In fact, however, where in-depth studies of the relationship between rail rates and cost have been attempted, the discrimination against high-valued commodities is often more apparent than real. In Gilbert Walker's phrase, "the cream lies at the bottom of the railway's bottle." The cream of the traffic, such as high-valued, high-rated commodities, costs so much more to move that the net revenue from them is lower than for low-rated commodities and is often negative. See Gilbert Walker, "Transport before and after 1953," Oxford Economic Papers, New Series, vol. 5, no. 1 (Oxford: Oxford University Press, March 1953).

ferences discriminate against the manufactured goods of developing countries being exported to both developed and other developing countries. Should not the port charges be adjusted so that they offset the discrimination of the conference?

It is clear that some of the variation in the conference rate could be offset, provided the conference and the port authorities did not pursue strategic bargaining. Any reduction in the port charge for high-valued goods may be passed on at least in part by the conference in the form of a rate reduction. But there is an important exception since the demand may have the characteristic kinked shape that would produce no response in rates over a variety of changed cost conditions. This is an important argument for the port not to attempt to counter directly the discrimination of the conference with respect to commodity. (There is, however, an argument for indirect discrimination which is discussed below.)

Granted that the port should not attempt to offset the discrimination of the conference, the question remains whether it should discriminate according to value of commodity at all; should it not price simply according to cost? If there are economies of scale in the port operation, then to recover total cost, it might be best to mark up all costs by a constant percentage. In particular if there is no way to price separately the port services to conference and nonconference vessels, then there may be a case for imposing a lower markup over cost on the high-rated commodities even though such cost reductions probably would not be reflected directly in the price of the conference. The lower port price for what is regarded as typically liner traffic may cause increased competition from nonconference liners and tramps. Thus the upper limit of the conference's pricing latitude will be brought down.

Discrimination against the conferences

The most important areas of discriminatory pricing to be considered by the port are in the field of differential ship dues. First the most obvious way is to levy different fees according to the type of ship used by liner operators, tramp owners, and bulkers. Again on the assumption that the best way to curb monopoly power is to encourage competitors (including nonconference liners), it would be best to discriminate in favor of bulk carriers or tramp vessels and to charge fees for the conference vessels so that the loss on the others is recouped. If the kinked demand curve theory is correct, then the increase in port charge for the conference will have little effect on raising the conference freight rate. On the other hand the competitive structure of the tramp industry will ensure that the lower port cost is reflected in the rate (or simply shows up in the charterer's accounts). The lower cost of shipping by chartered vessels should then provide more competitive conditions which, in their turn, will influence conference freight rate negotiations.

So far this discussion has been in terms of the charge varying according to the type of vessel used. This is probably the easiest form of discrimination to practice: there is a considerable variation in such charges levied at present with often little rhyme or reason to justify them. But it would be much more efficient to vary the port charge according to whether the vessel belonged to a conference or not. This charge would deliberately discriminate against the conference and avoid penalizing, and indeed would encourage, the nonconference competitors, whether they be liners, bulkers, or tramps. This would subject the conferences to a more effective competitive discipline.

The difficulty of discriminating port charges according to whether a vessel operates in conference or not is considerable. First, according to some port authorities, it is difficult to distinguish whether a vessel is controlled by a conference or not. No doubt differential charges would increase considerably such attempts to disguise conference liners. It seems possible, however, to decide whether a steamship company operates the conference tariff or not, and that is the critical issue. Secondly, it would tend to exacerbate the relationships between the conference on the one hand and the port authorities and government on the other since the discrimination is so obviously directed toward the conference as such. Such an especially high port levy may be rationalized, however, on the grounds that the conference enjoys special privileges of collusion, uncontrolled by government and that a price should be paid for this privilege (as indeed a price is exacted from the shippers and importers). However, those who have long enjoyed a free privilege are unlikely to appreciate the argument that they now ought to pay for it.

Finally, port pricing may be used to counteract in a limited way what are regarded as undesirable consequences of the organization of the liner industry. Thus, if conference organization causes an unnecessarily large number of sailings into port,[11] the port may allow

---

11. This can be the result of allocating sailing rights among the members of the conference, an adjunct or substitute for cargo quotas. Unless the allowed number of sailings is performed in a period, the rights are lost.

quantity discounts in the charges for moving general cargo. The simplest way to allow such discounts might be through raising those parts of the total ship payments in port that relate to the particular call while reducing the charge for working general cargo.

Where, on the other hand, conferences have rationalized the service (for instance, on the west coast of India), cargo tends to get shut out by vessels. In this situation, the policy should be the inverse of what is appropriate in a situation of an undesirably high ratio of ship calls to cargo worked. The rate for cargo working should then be raised relative to the cost of sailing into the port to encourage some excess capacity. The container ship might thus be allowed to sail into port and to take up a berth free of charge for a specified time, although a load is put on the charge for the actual movement of containers.

Appendix A. The Classes of Dry Cargo Vessels in the Ports of Developing Countries

Liners tend to predominate in the dry cargo trade of most developing countries. They clearly predominate in the distant voyage trades of Southeast Asian ports. Earlier studies showed that liners loaded over half of Singapore's cargo (dry plus vegetable oil and latex) and discharged almost two-thirds of all imports through the port. The traffic of Bangkok depended even more heavily on liners (Table 6.1). The situation has not changed substantially since these sample studies. More recently it was established at Chittagong that 90 percent of the vessels at the general cargo jetties (which handle bulk as well as break-bulk cargoes) were liners; only 10 percent were chartered vessels.[12]

Liners tend to be organized in conferences or rate-fixing agreements. Table 6.1 points to the dominance of conference liners in the imports of Singapore and in the imports and exports of Bangkok. The position of conferences is strongest on the long distance routes, as is illustrated by the share of conference carriers in the cargo tonnage on the main routes from and to Bangkok (Table 6.2).

12. Louis Berger International, Inc., "Feasibility Study, Port of Chittagong Expansion, Bangladesh," (prepared for the Asian Development Bank and Chittagong Port Trust), vol. II (December 1974). No similar statistics are available for Port Kelang.

TABLE 6.1. CLASSES OF VESSELS IN THE PORTS OF SINGAPORE AND BANGKOK, 1966 AND 1967

	Vessel calls		Cargo tonnage loaded and discharged	
	Number of vessel calls	Percentage of total vessel DWT	Percentage of total	
			Cargo loaded	Cargo discharge
Port of Singapore				
Liners	81	75	55	64
(Conference liners)	(58)	(70)	(36)	(54)
(Independents)	(23)	(5)	(19)	(10)
Tramps and other chartered vessels[a]	66	25	45	36
Total	147	100	100	100
Port of Bangkok				
Liners	110	84	80	88
(Conference liners)	(73)	(71)	(54)	(81)
(Independents)	(37)	(14)	(26)	(7)
Tramps and other chartered vessels	22	15	20	12
Controlled by conference	(7)	(6)	(9)	(4)
Total	132	100	100	100

a. Some of the vessels in this category performed the inward or the outward journey as liner on regular schedule.

Sources: D. J. Blake, E. Bennathan, and A. A. Walters, "Survey of Vessels in the Port of Singapore (Roads and Wharves) during One Week in September 1966" (Bristol, 1970; processed) and E. Bennathan and Direk Malakon, "Survey of Vessels in the Port of Bangkok (Klong Toi and Private Wharves) during Four Selected Weeks between November 1966 and August 1967" (Bangkok, 1970; processed).

Appendix B. A Simple Model of Origin–Destination Discrimination

A simple characterization of the process is to suppose that the conference carries the produce of farmers who live along a road going from the port to the interior.[13] Suppose that the conference can dis-

13. This is a slight adaptation of A. A. Walters, "A Development Model of Transport," *American Economic Review* (Papers and Proceedings), vol. 58, no. 2. (May 1968), pp. 360–377 and of A. A. Walters, *Economics of Road User Charges*, World Bank Staff Occasional Papers, no. 5 (Baltimore: Johns Hopkins Press, 1968), chapter IV.

TABLE 6.2.   THE SHARE OF CONFERENCE LINES IN THE CARGO
TONNAGE OF ROUTES INTO AND OUT OF BANGKOK, 1966 TO 1967

Route	Cargo tonnage[a] on conference carriers	
	Loaded (percent)	Discharged (percent)
Short-distance routes	0	6
Hong Kong	6	
Japan and Korea	93	90
Continental Europe and United Kingdom	74	100
Bay of Bengal	100	
U.S. Atlantic		100

a. Omitting all cargo flows with a tonnage less than 5 percent of the total Bangkok cargo flow counted in the survey.

Source: E. Bennathan and Direk Malakon, "Survey of Vessels in the Port of Bangkok (Klong Toi and Private Wharves) during Four Selected Weeks between November 1966 and August 1967."

criminate in its rates according to the origin of the goods. The farmer has to pay $t per unit for every mile of transport along the road, so that for m miles he pays $tm. Assume that one unit of quantity is the most that can be produced in a given mile and that all miles of country are homogeneous. The amount that the farmer will send for export (and correspondingly the amount that he will consume or spend in leisure) will depend upon the price that he must pay to deliver it at the foreign market. This is equal to the price which is levied by the conference for transport over the ocean, and since the conference can discriminate according to origin, the expression must be written as $P(m)$, the price for the m'th mile along the highway. Including the inland transport cost down the road, therefore, the cost per unit of sending the goods to the foreign market is: $P(m) + mt$ dollars. The farmers' demand for transport to the foreign market is therefore assumed to be a linear function of the price, that is to say,

$$(1) \qquad X(m) = a - b\,[P(m) + mt].$$

Cost of shipping and spatial discrimination

This, of course, is only the demand of the farmer situated m miles away from the port. Now suppose that the marginal cost of ocean transport for the conference is constant, c. The net revenue from the farmer at the m'th mile is then:

(2) $[P(m) - c] X(m) = [P(m) - c] [a - b(P(m) + mt)].$

The value of $P(m)$ at which this net revenue is maximized is then:

$$P(m) = 0.5b^{-1} (a - bmt + cb)$$

or:

(3) $$P(m) = 0.5 [(a/b) - mt + c].$$

This simply tells how the conference would price its services if it could discriminate according to the origin of the goods.

One interesting result is that the conference will reduce its rates as it gets farther and farther away from the port since it has to overcome the additional expense of the inland transport cost to generate additional traffic. The simple rule is that the conference will reduce its price by 50 percent of the overland transport cost. In the jargon of the conference or the container service, it will absorb 50 percent of the inland transport cost. Of course, the conference will not continue to absorb 50 percent of the transport cost as the farms become more and more distant. There is a limit, and that will occur when no traffic is offered because the freight rate and internal road transport cost are too high, and this is clearly when:

(4) $X(m_{max}) = a - (b/2) [(a/b) - mt + c + 2mt] = 0$

that is to say,

$$a - (a/2) + (bmt/2) - (bc/2) - bmt = 0$$

(5) $$m_{max} = (a - bc)/bt.$$

This gives the maximum distance down the road that the conference will find it profitable to collect traffic as a function of the conference's cost (c) and the cost per mile of road transport (t).

Variations in cost

One interesting aspect of this analysis concerns the variation of conference ship cost with the origin of the traffic. The model simply has one port and cannot reproduce the variation in port and traffic conditions which are characteristic of operations. Suppose that there is a continuous port operation along the road—as though the ship can travel up the highway and collect traffic at each point. Although seemingly absurd, this assumption does capture the essential feature of the conference collecting traffic at different ports at varying cost.

The marginal cost of collecting a small unit of cargo $c(m)$ may be an increasing function of the distance from what may be called the main port. The solution is now taken as:

$$(6) \qquad P(m) = (a/2b) - (mt/2) + (c(m)/2).$$

Thus the increasing cost of ports as m increases offsets part of the tendency to reduce freight rates for the more distant locations. (To maintain the fiction the collection points at point m are assumed to be associated with additional transport costs of mt to get the goods to the port at m.)

It is conceivable (if unlikely) that the function $c(m)$ is of the form: $c(m) = tm$. Then the conference would not vary the price according to the port. There would still be discrimination since prices do not vary according to cost; they are constant. This would provide an alternative rationalization for the constancy of freight rates over the region. Alternatively the cost of ports could be classified according to the amount of traffic that passes through them—marginal cost diminishing as the quantity of traffic increases. This assumption would give similar results.

The model of the single port and its hinterland may be developed further, and incidentally made more realistic, by supposing that there are several such ports serving hinterlands, each through its road; each differs, however, in its productivity. This will be reflected in the parameters a and perhaps also b of the model. The highly productive hinterlands may be considered to have large values of the parameter a, and relatively low-productivity areas will have low a's and stop. The result will then be that monopolistic shipowners would charge high freight rates for the high-productivity areas. If the volume of traffic from such areas is higher than from poor areas and if shipping and port operations are subject to economies of scale, there will be a reaction on the cost of collecting the cargo $[c(m)]$ which will counteract, through the cost relation, the ship's price discrimination against the high productivity area.

Movements in cost, however, may be relatively unimportant in determining the conference tariffs as was pointed out earlier in this chapter. Only when traffic becomes attractive to tramps, bulkers, and other nonconference carriers will the conference's markup over cost be limited.

Chapter 7

Competition among Ports

IN ANALYZING PORTS it is often convenient to assume that there is little or no competition for their services. But in practice this is rarely true.

Inland Competition

The most straightforward case of competition among ports is where two or more of them share a continuous hinterland. The ports thus compete for the business of importers or exporters who could route their goods through any one of the ports and could switch from one to the other. Ports in a situation of inland competition will, therefore, keep their prices for identical services closely in line with each other.

A clear example is the competition between Port Kelang and Singapore: the Malaysian trader may ship his goods across the causeway and use the facilities of Singapore instead of shipping through Kelang. Congestion at one port should quickly lead to vessels being diverted to the other, absorbing, if necessary, the additional cost of inland transport to a particular location.[1] In the opinion of traders

1. Congestion in Kelang in 1961 thus led to the diversion of vessels to Singapore from where cargoes for Malaysia were carried by Malaysian railways at subsidized rates to the consignee's nearest siding.

at Kelang, vessels and cargo would find it profitable to switch to Singapore if delays at Kelang mount to 2 days and if a surcharge was imposed on the port. Even where the quality of facilities differs much more than between Singapore and Port Kelang and where inland access is much more differentiated, congestion regularly leads to substitution between ports. The 1976–77 congestion in Middle Eastern ports offers many examples of this. Another case is the diversion of cargoes from the port of Chittagong to the anchorage of Chalna in Bangladesh across the traditional line of division according to geographical catchment areas and to the handling requirements of cargoes. Developments of transport infrastructure in Bangladesh lead to similar results.[2]

Even where a particular country has a feasible and seemingly efficient port located outside its borders, the issue is, in principle, simple. Traders should ship through that port where the cost is less, allowing as always for any service differential between the two ports. If port pricing and internal transport pricing policy (for example, from Malaysian farms or factories to the port) are based on marginal cost, there will be an efficient allocation of cargo and traffic.

The total overall cost will depend on whether the commodity is shipped by conference vessel or by competitive shipping. First consider the conference service: the price of a shipping service is the same whether the goods are carried from Singapore or from Kelang. It seems as though the cost of the ocean carriage would be the same, but this is not the case. By virtue of its size, Singapore has many more frequent and varied services. Consequently, by shipping through Singapore, the goods probably will not have to wait so long for a ship, and the trader will save on inventory and wastage costs.

An example of this is timber shipments from West Malaysia. The difference in the frequency of services is such that the average waiting time of one timber shipper was estimated to be about 4 to 5 weeks for Kelang against 1 to 2 weeks for Singapore. Even a delay as small as 3 weeks involves considerable inventory cost and, when interest rates are high and liquidity is scarce, may cause considerable cash flow problems.

Such differences in the quality of service are not offset easily by

2. The opening of the Ghasiakhali canal has made Dacca equidistant from Chittagong and Chalna anchorage. Moreover, if the Pusur River channel to Chalna is dredged as has been proposed, traffic at Chittagong may be reduced by 15 to 20 percent, which is roughly the output of two berths.

port charges.[3] Charges at the usual levels are frequently small beer compared with the cost of internal transport. In Malaysia, for example, internal transport cost will be at least US$0.10 a ton-mile even under the most favorable conditions, for bulk commodities such as timber. Thus even a differentiation in port charges of US$1 is only likely to shift the boundary of equal cost access by 10 miles. Improvement in domestic transport, such as building better roads, is likely to tip the balance in favor of the port with the relative advantages, given the prices ruling. Thus the improvement of the highways through Johore and up to Kuala Lumpur has made Singapore more attractive as a port outlet.

As a result Malaysia has tried to discourage Malaysian traffic from using Singapore and to induce traders to use Kelang and other Malaysian ports. Undoubtedly, one method has been to keep the port charges low for Kelang. Second, the Malaysian authorities have not streamlined the customs exit and entry procedures on the Johore causeway that connects Singapore to Malaysia. They have, so to say, introduced an impedance to discourage the use of Singapore. Third, the rates of Malaysian railways discriminate in favor of the domestic ports and against Singapore.

Very similar practices are found in the competition between Vancouver and Seattle. Traffic originating in the province of Ontario will receive a special "crow's nest pass" rate if it is sent through the Canadian railways to Vancouver, rather than by the U.S. railways to Seattle. And there is an absorption practice that has the same discriminatory effect. The absorption of inland transport cost—or rather of differences between transport cost to different destinations—is a common practice of container carriers. It discriminates both against a particular port (by reducing the inland transport charge for carriage from another port) and against shippers located nearer to the favored port.

The cost of protecting the national port is usually borne by the

---

3. For example, wharfage plus stevedorage plus labor charges at Kelang to move the timber direct from a road vehicle to ship or lighter came to M$13.30 per metric ton in 1973; the similar set of payments—in neither case exhaustive for the shipment of timber—came in Singapore to perhaps S$8.75 per ton. In neither case did such rates apply to all the timber shipped: much of it goes over private jetties into junks, and then overside mid-river onto the ship. The port tariff at Kelang was increased in 1975 by about 30 percent. See Port of Singapore Authority, *PSA Tariff 1973* (Singapore, 1973) and Port Swettenham Authority, *Scale of Rates, Dues, and Charges, By-laws, 1966*, incorporating amendments up to April 18, 1974.

country's residents. An interesting example of this is once again the export of Malaysian timber through Singapore, most of which is exported over private jetties. The total ocean transport cost of timber delivered in Europe comprises 31 to 40 percent of the c.i.f. value; internal trucking cost accounts on average for another 20 percent. Port charges at the loading end only are about 3 to 5 percent of total cost.[4] But with transport cost absorbing over 50 percent of the c.i.f. price, the port charge is quite a large proportion of the remainder. Allowing for labor and other expenses, the ratio of port cost to residual income may be approximately 1:4 to 1:3. This illustrates the sensitivity of timber exports to the port charge, all other things being equal.

Transshipment Competition

The more complex form of interport competition involves transshipment and multiport use. A commodity shipped from the United States to Surabaya may be shipped direct from New York to Surabaya or may be transported to Singapore and then transshipped to Surabaya. In this sense, Singapore competes with Surabaya. But Singapore may also be competing with an alternative transshipment port, such as Hong Kong. In such a case of pure transshipment competition, the interest of Indonesia (assuming that it cannot hope to get the cargo direct to its ports) is simply to obtain the most competitively low rate, no matter where the goods are transshipped. For Hong Kong and Singapore, however, the transshipment business is a matter of competitive contention. If Singapore is to secure the business in this example, her transshipment rates will have to be set sufficiently low in relation to both Surabaya import rates and Hong Kong transshipment rates.

When equidistant ports compete for transshipments to a third port, then port charges become the decisive factor in the outcome of the competition. Equidistance of alternative transshipment ports and the equality of all the other determinants of transit cost are not, of course, the usual situation. Hong Kong is thus farther from Indonesia than is Singapore, so that the size of vessels and the economic volume of cargo has to be greater for transshipment through Hong Kong.

4. Some timber is exported over the quays in conference vessels as well as in nonconference tramps. Little or no timber is exported in containers, although they are being used for plywood and other regular lengths.

Much of the transshipment business from Singapore to Indonesia and East Malaysia, on the other hand, is being done by small coasters carrying modest loads. But their location relative to high density traffic flows eliminates many ports from a particular race. For those that remain, the relative volume of transshipment trade will be determined largely by port charges, including labor rates. A market exists that is potentially larger—and sometimes much larger—than the market for their home traffic. If there is competition between transshipment ports within the same region (such as Singapore and Hong Kong) or between the transshipment port and well developed ports in the country of destination (for example, Singapore and Djakarta or Port Kelang), then the transshipment demand will have relatively high elasticity.

In Figure 7.1 the home demand for the port's services and transshipment demand are drawn side by side, each linearized. The total

FIGURE 7.1.   DEMAND FOR THE SERVICES OF A REGIONAL TRANSSHIPMENT PORT: "SMALL" HOME TRAFFIC AND "LARGE" TRANSSHIPMENT MARKET

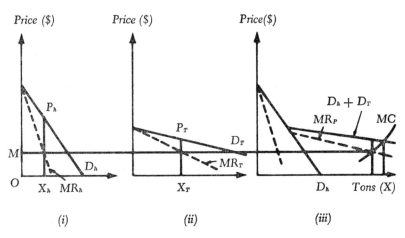

(i)   (ii)   (iii)

Home traffic demand   Transshipment demand   Total demand

Note: D_h = home demand; D_T = transshipment demand; $D_h + D_T$ = total demand; $X = X_h + X_T$; OM = marginal cost for X tons of traffic annually; P_h = profit- maximizing price for home traffic; P_T = profit-maximizing price for transshipment traffic.

market consists of the limited home market with relatively low demand elasticity (i) and the relatively large and elastic demand for transshipments (ii). After the separate demand curves have been added up horizontally, a total demand curve with a convex kink results (iii). If the port maximizes profits, it would set prices for each of the two submarkets according to the rule: marginal cost (for the total output) equal to marginal revenue for the submarket.

The principle of discrimination in favor of transshipment cargoes exists in most port tariffs, although not on the scale found in major transshipment ports like Hong Kong or Singapore. In Table 7.1, the

TABLE 7.1. PORT OF SINGAPORE AUTHORITY TARIFF, 1973:
TRANSSHIPMENT DIFFERENTIAL PER TON OF CONVENTIONAL
CARGO FOR A HYPOTHETICAL VESSEL

	Normal import/ export cargo (S$ per ton)	Trans- shipment cargo (S$ per ton)	Reshipment cargo (S$ per ton)
Charges Account Vessel (assume vessel of 6,000 GRT discharging/loading 3,000 tons)			
1. Port dues	0.30	0.30	0.30
2. Pilotage, tugs, berthing/ unberthing labor, garbage removal	0.43	0.43	0.43
3. Dockage and stand-by charge	3.00	3.00	3.00
4. Stevedorage	4.75	4.25	4.75
5. Total of above for two vessels	16.96	15.96	16.96
Charges Account Shipper/Consignee			
6. a. Receiving, storing, reshipping: 1 ton	0	3.00	3.00
b. Wharf handling charges: 2 tons	4.00	0	0
7. a. Storage (up to 4 weeks)	0	0	0
b. Storage: 7 days for imports; up to 3 days for exports	8.80	0	1.00[a]
8. Total of above	12.80	3.00	4.00
Grand total	29.76	18.96	20.96

Note: S$ per ton in and out.
a. S$0.10 per day for first 4 weeks; say, 10 days = S$1.00.

Singapore charges per ton of conventional cargo for a hypothetical shipping operation are compared, distinguishing normal cargo (exported from or imported into Singapore), transshipment cargo, and reshipment cargo.[5] Charge per ton (on the basis of roughly similar services and thus omitting many items that would in practice be required for one or the other type of operation) are 36 percent lower for transshipment cargoes and 29 percent lower for reshipment cargoes than for normal import or export cargoes.[6]

If marginal cost in the Port of Singapore was known, the perceived differences in the elasticities of demand for port services that are implicit in the transshipment differentials could be determined readily. As it is, the value of marginal cost must be guessed. It may either be taken as approximately equal to handling charges for transshipment cargo (items 2, 4, and 6a of Table 7.1) or as exceeding handling charges by the remaining charges levied on the onward carrier per ton of transshipment cargo (items 1 and 3).

The justification for the latter alternative is that each ton of transshipment cargo received by the port will cause an income under the heads of port dues and dockage at the time of the outward movement; handling charges for transshipment cargo might, therefore, have been set below marginal cost to that extent. Both alternatives suffer from the implicit assumption that the marginal cost of storage was in fact zero, and this seems implausible for 1973 and parts of 1974.

Applying the standard formula,[7] the elasticities of demand calculated under the former assumption are (in absolute value) 1.7 for home traffic; 2.4 for reshipment, and 2.9 for transshipment traffic.

---

5. The main difference between transshipment and reshipment cargo is that the former must be moving on a through bill of lading. Transshipment must, therefore, be arranged before the cargo leaves its original port of shipment. Reshipment cargoes are imported usually by local merchants who leave the goods in the port until they have arranged a sale to a buyer in another port, often after dividing up the original consignment.

6. The value of the advantages obtained by transshipment and reshipment cargoes is most probably rather greater than these average margins because operators regard storage terms—4 weeks free for transshipment and S$0.10 per day for reshipment—as perhaps the major advantages. Reshipment cargoes can be stored at low cost while a buyer is being found, and a long period of free storage for transshipment cargoes allows shipping companies to use the lowest-cost method of on-carriage without any offset to the possible savings.

7. Elasticity of demand (submarket) = price (submarket)/[price (submarket) − marginal cost (total)].

Under the alternative latter assumption they become 2.1 for Singapore traffic; 3.9 for reshipment, and 5.7 for transshipment traffic.[8]

These results, although based on much guesswork, are not markedly inconsistent with prior expectations. They are the estimates that are revealed by the behavior of the port authorities in setting tariffs. Naturally they reflect the possibility that, if Singapore changes its tariff, competitive ports will also change theirs. If competitors did not react, the elasticity of demand would be considerably larger than these estimated values.[9]

Of course, Singapore is not typical of ports in the developing countries. It is in close inland competition with various Malaysian ports, and this should account for the size of the implicit elasticity of demand for home cargo services—not far from 2 and thus higher than would be expected in ports such as Bombay that have a substantially captive hinterland. Furthermore, the size of its transshipment and entrepot business is unusual in the developing world. Thus, its demand elasticities may seem to be atypical and of little interest for preparing systems of port tariffs for other countries. However, this is not so. The entrepot and transshipment business of the world's, and particularly the developing countries', ports is likely to increase dramatically over the next decade or so. This is not because of the growth of conventional transshipment cargo; indeed this is expected to decline relatively. The real impetus for concentration and transshipment comes from the economies of containerization, which are discussed next.

8. The latter assumption yields a higher elasticity of demand for transshipment services because it comes closer to the assertion that transshipment traffic gets charged marginal cost, which, if introduced into the calculation, would make elasticity of demand infinitely large.

9. The demand for port services for Singapore (home) trade should not be very inelastic. So much of what appears to be home trade is really transit or entrepot trade; the port of Singapore is in inland competition with the ports of peninsular Malaysia and even southern Thai ports. In terms of recorded foreign trade values for 1974, 41 percent of all exports and 18 percent of the total imports were entrepot trade, and in terms of the balance of payments, the gross income from "other transportations and services, n.i.e." amounted to 29 percent of merchandise exports. Reshipment trade, again, may have an appreciably lower elasticity of demand than transshipment (as indeed reflected in the PSA rates). It seems to be a profitable branch of Singapore commerce. The gross reward of reshippers is reported to be 1 to 2 percent of the invoiced value. The net return on capital used will be determined by turnover, and if this is seventeen times the working capital, the return would be 20 to 25 percent annually.

The Effect of Containerization

Conventional transshipment has been losing ground, certainly relative to the home trade of the chief transshipment ports and possibly even in terms of absolute tonnages.[10] The reason is not just the more rapid growth of the home trade, but also the development of port facilities in traditional countries of destination and the accompanying political or administrative measures to foster direct shipments at the expense of indirect shipments. The growth of national merchant marines reinforces this trend. National lines gain admission to conferences on the basis of deals which tend to militate against transshipment. The conferences themselves discourage free transshipment, if only by ensuring that the freight rate for indirect shipment is not below that for direct shipment.[11] The object is to keep cargo under conference control and to channel any savings which transshipment might offer to the conference carriers.

But these tendencies are being reversed by the advent of container shipping. Main line services are spreading more widely than was expected some years ago, but they, nevertheless, continue to be restricted to narrow routes; distribution and collection farther afield is left to feeder services.[12] The main container ship is highly capital intensive and, therefore, depends on fast voyage turnaround. This implies a shortened conventional liner itinerary and a reduced number of port calls. The growth of large container companies and consortia permits a high degree of rationalization of container ship movements except during rate wars.

The competitive aspects of port containerization manifest themselves in the investments of many ports in national container projects and in the associated competition, actual or potential, between established or aspiring transshipment ports and national ports in the same region. Furthermore, it is reflected in the lively competition between the transshipment ports. The catchment areas for container trans-

---

10. Singapore entrepot trade—not transshipment trade—has declined from 59 percent of the value of total trade in 1965 to 28 percent in 1974.

11. Compare B. M. Deakin, *Shipping Conferences*, University of Cambridge, Department of Applied Economics Occasional Papers no. 37 (Cambridge: Cambridge University Press, 1973), p. 55.

12. See Appendix A.

shipment are wide: Singapore thus transships for ports in the Bay of Bengal, and Singapore and Hong Kong are themselves feeder ports for Japan.

Container port managers are thus anxious to keep their prices below those of others, cautiously allowing for quality differences.[13] The intensity of competition for the container transshipment business is reflected clearly in port tariffs. In Singapore, transshipment containers thus are paying 43 to 52 percent less than normal import or export containers—a significantly greater proportional difference than the 36 percent allowed for conventional transshipment cargoes.[14] Containerization has also raised the competition between ports for mainline container services as distinct from feeder service.

With the advent of containerization, the elasticity of demand for port services thus will have increased. It should have increased most for transshipment ports competing with others in the same region because port prices should then have the greatest scope for influencing port use.

Competitive transshipment differences imply discrimination. Container handling rates in Kelang result in charges to national exporters or importers which are between 36 percent and 100 percent above those charges on transshipment operations; and the mean percentage excess is even higher than that in Singapore. (See Appendix B, Table 7.5.) Therefore, the real size and the effects of this discrimination must be evaluated.

First, the case when the port authority is required to break even is examined. Realistically, average cost may be assumed to be declining and operations well below the capacity level. Thus in Figure 7.2, the marginal cost (MC) is constant, and average cost (AC) falls continuously over the whole of the relevant range of throughput. A useful caricature is the case when the demand for domestic containers is very inelastic and the demand for transshipment highly competitive. Then such competition will drive the price of transshipment down to the competitor's price. However, the port authority will levy average

13. The actual relation between the prices of different ports, some of them common user ports and others containing mainly private terminals, is difficult to establish; the very meaning of equality depends on the operations methods and requirements of users; Singapore handling rates thus are thought to be well below those of Hong Kong or Taiwan, but its storage rates are higher.

14. These figures relate to 1973. See Appendix B.

FIGURE 7.2.   AVERAGE COST AND TRANSSHIPMENT PRICING
IN CONTAINERS

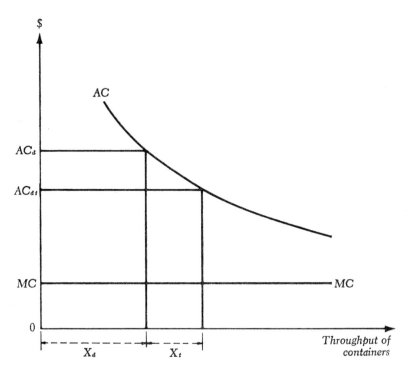

cost for domestic traffic (AC_d).[15] With X_d and X_t as the numbers
of domestic and transshipment containers, respectively, it is clear that
the average cost of domestic containers AC_d exceeds the average costs
of total traffic AC_{dt}. The larger the amount of transshipment traffic
for a given number of domestic containers (X_d), the higher the domestic charge (AC_d) relative to the average cost of all traffic (AC_{dt}).

In this model, provided that the quantity of domestic containers
is fixed, the difference between the tariffs is the same whatever the
throughput of transshipment containers. Similarly, if the degree of
discrimination is defined in terms of deviations of price from marginal

---

15. However, no two-part tariff is levied; it is assumed that a one-price system
is in operation. It would be easy, however, to extend the argument to multipart
pricing systems as can be seen in Chapter 8.

cost, then the amount of discrimination remains the same—again for any level of transshipment, provided that the quantity of domestic containers remains the same.[16]

In a port of given size, price discrimination may be the only way for the port to cover cost. Nondiscriminatory pricing, such as marginal cost pricing, may then only be possible in a port of different size. Price policy is thus not separable from the issue of investment. The model in Figure 7.2 can be developed further. In Figure 7.3, national demand for container port services is relatively limited and inelastic, with the demand curve NN'. Aggregate demand, however, including transshipment, is NKD. Let marginal cost be constant until a certain level of capacity is used. Consider the special situation where the smallest feasible berth could cover its cost by charging either a price P_a = average cost or P_m which is the profit-maximizing price. P_a is less than P_m and will be charged if the port is under orders to cover cost at the lowest price level. If it is decided to equip the port for trading in the wider regional market, the port will work with higher fixed cost and, it is assumed, lower marginal cost (MC_2) over the relevant range. It is easy to imagine the situation in which average cost for the larger scale (AC_2) lies continuously above the total demand curve NKD. If the port is then instructed to break even, it will be forced to exercise its monopoly power over home trade by moving from average cost pricing toward profit-maximizing pricing combined with price discrimination. The price charged to national shippers will accordingly be lifted from P_a to or toward P_m' depending on whether the port is allowed to make profits, is merely enjoined to break even, or to minimize losses.

Annual throughput increases in this case from OX_2 tons to OX_3, but service to nationals shrinks from OX_2 to OX_1. The less elastic is national demand for the port's services, the smaller will be the change in quantity demanded. In the limit, the quantity $(OX_2 - OX_1)$ will be zero, and the sole effect of the increase in the charge to nationals will be to reduce their income. The result may thus be to transfer revenue from exporters or importers to the port. But if the enlarged

16. Although this is the appropriate definition of discrimination for economic analysis, it is probably not the one espoused most readily by traders and men of commerce. They may tolerate readily a low-priced occasional transshipment container, but domestic traders are likely to complain energetically when transshipment becomes important and when nationals are precluded from enjoying the reduced charges to the low average cost occasioned by such success.

FIGURE 7.3.   NATIONAL PORT VERSUS REGIONAL PORT

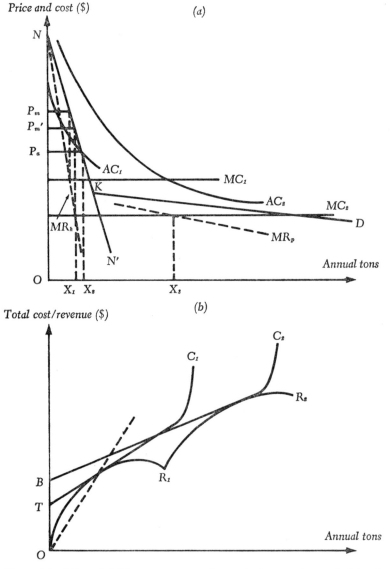

Note: (a) AC_1 and MC_1 = average and marginal costs (respectively) of a national port; AC_2 and MC_2 = average and marginal costs (respectively) of a regional port; $N\,N'$ = national demand; NKD = regional demand. (b) C_1 = total cost of national port; C_2 = total cost of a regional port; R_1 = total revenue of a national port; R_2 = total revenue of a regional port.

port merely covers cost or if its net profit does not increase by the full amount of the loss of national shippers' revenue, the redistribution of income benefits nonnationals. The most obvious beneficiaries in this case would be the shipping lines—some of them nationals but the great bulk nonnational. The cost conditions leading to this result were discussed already in Chapter 3, but the demand conditions which face the aspiring regional port are peculiar (Figure 7.3b).[17]

No regional port of importance—let alone one aspiring to that position anew—has any reason to expect the demand for its services to be stable. The chief reason for this uncertainty is competition of other regional ports. In addition, however, the decision of container consortia whether to ship directly to a particular port or to transship will be based largely on criteria of the relative volumes of cargo emanating from different ports. Feeder operations cause additional handling cost. The main ship will, therefore, go where there is most cargo available for direct loading or unloading, leaving other ports to feeder services. The balance of cargo on offer is bound to change over time, and the carrier's responses will not be very sensitive to differences in port rates. The development of regional port services thus is attended by risks which flow both from the great development cost and from the economics of container carriers and their potential monopoly power. Whether the matter is considered from the point of view of the port or of the national shippers—two components of the economy—competitive container port building looks risky even for well established transshipment ports. Some implications of this are explored below.

Economic Causes and Implications

Declining average cost of port operation suggests that the port may find it possible and profitable to discriminate in its tariffs. Discounts may be offered for distant locations in its catchment area. It is possible, however, that other agencies may operate discriminatory pricing systems; for example, conferences tend to absorb internal transport costs or port costs to get traffic that would otherwise have gone to

17. Compare, Joan Robinson, *The Economics of Imperfect Competition* (London: Macmillan and Co., Limited, 1933). Chapter 15 contains a curve of this type.

another port served by a noncolluding conference or by other non-conference vessels.

As port size increases, the element of fixed cost becomes more important, the degree of indivisibility becomes larger, and so marginal cost tends to become smaller relative to average cost for normal operating conditions. The large port is under great pressure to fill up available capacity, especially when marginal cost moves close to zero. As the technology of ports switches from labor-intensive to capital-intensive forms, the potential for port competition increases considerably.

An example of this form of competition is the location of the main terminal for the container services (usually operated by consortia) between the United States and Europe, and the Far East. Both Singapore and Hong Kong are natural locations for main terminals. The container consortia will choose between them on the basis of prices and the other services that are available. For this entrepot port status, therefore, there is enormously keen competition. The natural geographical advantages might be imagined to yield overwhelming cost differentials, but in practice, both in the Far East and on the western seaboard of the North American continent, that does not seem to be the case.

The critical question is what differential in port pricing, assuming a given and equal level of service in Hong Kong and in Singapore, would cause a shift from the one—at present this is Hong Kong—to the other? The changes in relative port prices which will lead to such a switch cannot, however, be regarded as taking place bit by bit since any shifts would occur in lumps, and in practice, they would be large lumps. For example, the transfer of the large SL7 ships of Sealand would mean a loss of about one-seventh of Hong King's container operation. Similarly, once it has been decided to build oil refining capacity in a port with ships as main customers in response to the relative cost situation that is also determined by port charges, the development and its competitive impact are not easily reversible.

Unfortunately, an accurate impression of the consequences of changing the port charges cannot be obtained unless an exhaustive modeling of the whole system is carried out—a task far beyond the aims of this study. The impressions gathered from interviews can only be reported here. Port authorities and container operators in Singapore thus agreed that there are considerable opportunities for switching services between Singapore and Hong Kong and for demoting one of the contenders to the status of a feeder port. As a rough order of magnitude, Singapore thought that if the container charge were doubled, the port would lose virtually all its container vessel traffic, assuming that no other ports changed their charges. The effect of clean slate decisions and decisions by consortia already using the port must also be distinguished carefully. The former are likely to be much more sensitive to movements in relative price than the latter. In sum, however, the demand elasticity for container operations seems undoubtedly greater than two (in absolute value) for ports such as Singapore, Hong Kong, and Seattle, which at present have substantial main terminal container services.[18]

It follows that if the elasticity is (absolute) 2, if there is constant marginal cost up to the capacity of the terminal, and if the demand is such that the facility is being operated well below its capacity, then the charges that are levied by the profit-maximizing port will be twice the marginal cost. In fact, the calculations for Singapore suggest that container charges are probably higher than this. One conceivable explanation of the apparent inconsistency is that the port is not a profit-maximizing agency and so does not follow optimum pricing policies—but in the case of Singapore, this seems implausible. The most obvious explanation is that the calculation of marginal cost does not consider the probability of congestion that, even when the berths are used only 25 percent of the time, does nevertheless occur and involves cost to container consortia in the small but finite probability of delay.[19]

The existing situation between Singapore and Hong Kong reflects the great importance of size and the service quality differential. Although the Singapore tariff for containers is only a little more than

18. In the earlier experiment with the Singapore transshipment tariff a value of minus 2 for the elasticity of demand for conventional home traffic was accepted as reasonable. The implicit values of the elasticity of demand for conventional transshipment and reshipment cargo (some 20 percent of total conventional port traffic) were higher than this. The aggregate elasticity of demand for conventional cargo services would thus also be higher than (absolute) 2.

19. There are two alternative explanations: (a) Singapore is expecting a secular growth in container traffic primarily because it has switched from more conventional methods (which perhaps may capture some traffic from Hong Kong) and because it expects capacity to be filled even at existing prices in the near future. In that case, the cost of reducing the price now and then raising it again later may be greater than the loss of interim underuse; (b) the port authority is expecting inflation, and so by maintaining the same nominal price, they are, in fact, reducing the relative price.

one-half of the Hong Kong tariff, it seems that Singapore has not made significant inroads into Hong Kong's existing main terminal container traffic so far. It is, of course, somewhat early to draw conclusions since the first full year of operation was only 1973. The cost of breaking into the mainline container terminal market is large.

This suggests another reason for the fact that Singapore has not launched into a fully fledged rate war against Hong Kong—Hong Kong may retaliate by cutting its rates also. Although the elasticity of demand may be above 2 if Hong Kong maintained the same rates, the threat of a substantial traffic loss would induce Hong Kong to cut its tariff schedule. The perceived elasticity of demand for Singapore may thus be considerably less than 2, thus justifying the higher markup above marginal cost. This rate-war reason seems to be important to port authorities.

The effects of interport competition are not restricted to the two main terminal ports. Competition has effects throughout the whole port complex of a region. Low container rates through Singapore will be instrumental in keeping down the container tariffs through Kelang, Bangkok, Djkarta, and other ports in the region. The effects of competition emerge clearly from a comparison of the container tariffs of Singapore and Port Kelang (Appendix B, Table 7.5).

The direct inducement is to engage in feeder services to the main transshipment centers rather than to set up small container ports for direct small ship or low frequency container service direct to Europe and to the United States. The economies of scale in container operation make feeder service operation efficient. Not surprisingly, the competitive solution is best for all parties. The smaller ports would not have to operate inefficient and costly (probably subsidized) container services, ports such as Singapore would operate at minimum cost, and there would be the maximum efficient container penetration of conventional traffic. Unfortunately, this ideal is unlikely to be achieved. In part, this is because countries are unwilling to have their traffic handled by a port in a country that could conceivably become unfriendly and so discriminate against it. But there is no sense in which, should a confrontation occur, a country could be denied container operations; they would merely have to pay more for it. In general, countries probably retain expensive container services in the belief that they provide jobs which would otherwise migrate abroad, even though such jobs may have to be subsidized, and the subsidy may exceed the value added when that is calculated at world prices rather than in terms of domestic cost.

To attempt to maintain port monopolies in the face of increased competition by administrative measures may be worse than subsidized port competition. Boycott arrangements are particularly expensive, and it is doubtful whether they achieve many of their aims. The most common protective devices, apart from discriminating charges, are discriminatory regulations (barriers of red tape). Whether these attempts to limit the development of port competition are at all successful cannot be ascertained at present. However, it is worth summarizing the consequences of the increased competition that is realized.

The first consequence is that ports will have considerably reduced monopoly power and will find it harder to make a profit or to cover their cost, at least for container services where there is considerable excess capacity and where marginal cost is low relative to average cost. The switch from conventional to container methods increases markedly the average competitiveness of ports.

The second effect is that the erosion of port monopoly power has been associated with some increase in the monopoly power of the steamship owners, primarily through the consolidation of container consortia. The consortia can play one port off against another, and full-fledged container services are very expensive to produce since they require massive injections of capital.[20]

The methods by which ocean carriers service a particular port are largely under their control, and in the case of container shipping, almost wholly so. The carriers' demand for the facilities of a particular port may, therefore, turn out to be rather unstable. This will be least true of those well established ports in which container operators set up their own terminals. But there are many other ports in which container operators will only undertake minor investments, if any. The decision whether to serve such a port by feeder or by main service will be taken on considerations of the relative cost of feeder service and of diverting the main line vessel.

The lesson seems to be, first, that many ports may much overestimate the virtue of full-fledged container projects to attract and secure regular use by mainline vessel rather than by feeder. The probabilities are difficult to estimate because so much of the information lies out-

20. Nevertheless, on the Pacific conference, the behavior of nonconference vessels—mainly Russian owned—has provided considerable competition during the slack trade period of the summer of 1975. But such competition has created an even more ruthless search for cheaper port facilities.

side the country itself, and some of it consists of the intentions of container lines which they would not, under all normal circumstances, find it wise to disclose fully. Second, mainline service to a port brings with it a certain amount of transshipment business. But for all but a few ports, the demand for transshipment services should be even more unstable than demand for mainline container vessel berths. Not only does a port's transshipment business depend on the carrier's decision on how another port is to be serviced, but transshipment itself is also subject to intense competition between ports.

This leads, finally, to port pricing. It may seem natural for each port to offer some price reductions for transshipments. It is clear, however, that ports should not plan to use monopolistic price discrimination against national shippers except if it would result in lower charges to the national shippers than would be possible without price discrimination.[21] Tactics may occasionally require discrimination that would produce such a result. Port investment projects, however, should not countenance it. It may, of course, be claimed that the large port offers a better service to the national shipper than the small one: a greater frequency of direct service and a better choice of vessels. The greater price demanded of the national shipper, it might then be argued, would be more than compensated for by the improved quality. There is no denying that the larger port offers a service of greater value to shippers. Nevertheless, investment projects which can be shown to yield a net benefit only on that argument should be very suspect; at least in the case of existing ports with facilities of normal quality. Price discrimination against national shippers can benefit not the port but the carriers who, if they are conferences, may not even pass on their gain to shippers in the same region. The port should never risk becoming the instrument by which national exporters and importers subsidize the international shipping industry.

Appendix A. Container Services: Mainline and Feeder

Container services, unlike conventional break-bulk services, comprise both mainline and feeder operations. Operators tend to concentrate their main container ships on the routes between the main cargo

---

21. In the example analyzed in Figure 7.3 *above*, the opposite result was observed. If the port had been a profit maximizer rather than an average-cost pricer, price discrimination and the enlarged port service would have lowered the price that shippers have to pay for port services.

ports to minimize the turnaround time between the chief terminal ports of the service. The scope of feeder operations in the Far East is documented in Table 7.2 which summarizes the late 1975 position on the U.S./Far East route. Southeast Asia's two main container ports—Hong Kong, which handled 726,000 TEU in 1974, and Singapore, which handled 153,000 TEU—are also the chief transshipment ports for South and Southeast Asia. They are served by both mainline and feeder services. Malaysia, which handled 37,000 TEU in 1974 with Port Kelang as its only container terminal able to take main line vessels of the second and third generation, receives direct calls but is served mainly by feeders. Bangkok depended entirely on feeders until the opening of full-scale facilities in 1976.

TABLE 7.2. U.S./FAR EAST CONTAINER SHIP OPERATORS: DIRECT AND FEEDER SERVICES, OCTOBER 1975

Operator	Frequency of calls per month	End points	Direct call	Feeder
American President Lines	4	California, Japan, Pacific NW, U.S. Atlantic	Hong Kong, Malaysia, Korea, Singapore, Taiwan	Philippines
Evergreen Line	1	U.S. Atlantic	Hong Kong, Korea, Taiwan	
Fesco Pacific Line	3	California, Japan, USSR		Hong Kong
Japan Line, K-Line, Mitsui–OSK Line, NYK Line, Showa Line, U.S. Line	4	Japan, Pacific NW		Hong Kong
Japan Line, K-Line, Mitsui–OSK, YS Line	6	California, Japan		Hong Kong, Korea
NYK Line, Showa Line	4	California, Japan		
K-Line	3	California, Japan, Pacific NW		Hong Kong, Korea, Philippines, Taiwan

(*Table continues on the following page*)

TABLE 7.2 (*continued*)

Operator	Frequency of calls per month	End points	Direct call	Feeder
Japan Line, K-Line, Mitsui–OSK Line, NYK Line, YS Line	4	Canada, Japan, U.S. Atlantic		Hong Kong, Korea, Philippines, Taiwan
Maersk Line	4	California, Canada (via NY), Japan, U.S. Atlantic	Hong Kong, Singapore, Taiwan	Indonesia, Malaysia, Philippines, Thailand
Orient Overseas Container Line	3	Japan, Pacific NW	Hong Kong	Korea, Philippines, Singapore
Orient Overseas Container Line	4	California, Japan	Hong Kong	Korea, Philippines, Singapore
Orient Overseas Container Line	2	Canada, Japan, U.S. Atlantic	Hong Kong	Philippines, Taiwan
Phoenix Container Liners	2	California, Japan, Pacific NW	Hong Kong	Hong Kong, Korea, Malaysia, Philippines, Singapore, Taiwan
Sea–Land Service	4	California, Japan, Pacific NW	Hong Kong	Korea, Philippines, Singapore, Taiwan, Thailand, Vancouver
Seatrain Lines	2	California, Japan		
Seaway Express Lines	4	Atlantic, California, Japan, Panama	Guam, Hawaii, Hong Kong, Korea, Taiwan	China, Malaysia, Philippines, Singapore, Thailand
Zim Container Service	2	California, Canada, Japan, U.S. Atlantic	Hong Kong, Korea, Taiwan	Philippines

Source: *Containerization International* (London), vol. 9, no. 11 (November 1975), p. 25.

Feeder operations add two handling operations to those required by direct call. Cost comparisons between movement by feeder service and by the mainline ship making a diversion from its main route normally show the cost per container to be higher for the feeder service, except where the distance is relatively great or the numbers of containers small. A containerization study for Thailand,[22] for example, produced the estimates for methods of container transport given in Table 7.3.

TABLE 7.3. Shipping Freight Cost per Ton, Europe–Bangkok on the Europe–Japan Route, 1972

Type of vessel	Cost (US$)
Main vessel (2000 × 20 feet; load factor: 0.75; 11 tons per container) Europe and Japan	31.70
Additional cost of diversion to Thai deep water port, averaged over 1,000 TEU (= 11,000 metric tons): 500 discharged and 500 loaded at Thai port	4.40
Feeder vessel (500 × 20 feet) Additional cost of carrying 500 units from Singapore to Bangkok and 500 units from Bangkok to Singapore, from and to main vessel	12.40

Another recent study compares the cost of moving containers by feeder service or by diverting a container ship with a capacity of 2,500 TEU. It finds that for 750 miles the cost of the feeder service exceeds that of the direct call when there are more than 300 containers.[23] The least that can be concluded from these calculations is that great constancy should not be expected in the optimal methods of serving individual ports. The growth of container traffic in a particular port might well unsettle the pattern and lead to direct calls replacing feeder services. In any case the decision will be highly sensitive to the level of port charges in the transshipment port. Fifty-five percent of the cost of feeder services from Singapore to Bangkok thus consists of handling charges. From the figures in the containerization study quoted earlier, it is found that a 10 percent increase in Singapore port

22. Economist Intelligence Unit in association with Wallace Evans and Partners, Consulting Civil and Structural Engineers, *The Containerization of Thailand's Sea Trade* (prepared for the Government of Thailand, Ministry of Communications, 1973), pp. 56–58.

23. E. T. Laing, "The Costs of Deep Sea General Cargo Shipping," Marine Transport Centre (University of Liverpool, June 1974; processed), pp. 43 et seq.

cost would reduce by 5 percent the number of containers for which feeders—and thus the use of the port of Singapore—would provide a cheaper service than direct calls.[24] Containerization has thus increased the elasticity of demand for port services with respect to port charges and port costs.

Appendix B. Container Transshipment Differentials in the Port Tariffs of Port Kelang and Singapore

In Table 7.4 the Singapore tariff rates of 1973 have been combined into the cost per container of a hypothetical container transport operation. This illustration assumes a particular and typical ship size, a rather fast rate of working, and a particular rate of use of port storage. All cost items are omitted that are irrelevant to the comparison. The calculation of the total price for this hypothetical basket of services shows that the FCL transshipment container pays 52 percent and the LCL transshipment container 43 percent less than the corresponding normal import or export container. This differential is thus much greater than that for conventional transshipment cargoes (36 percent).[25]

Port Kelang and Singapore compete in many ways. Port Kelang seeks to attract main vessels instead of feeders and wants to take over container transshipments to Penang and ports in East Malaysia. Several instruments of policy are being used to this end; inland competi-

24. See Daniel, Mann, Johnson, and Mendenhall; Louis Berger, *Development of the Ports of Sattahip and Da Nang and of Route 9* (study conducted on behalf of the Southeast Asian Coordinating Committee for Transportation and Communications at the request of the Governments of Laos, South Vietnam, and Thailand. Contract AIR/SA/IR-197 (Regional)). (Los Angeles: March 1973).

25. No direct comparison is possible between the prices in Tables 7.1 and 7.4. The nature of operations, including the size of vessel and use of storage, are different in the two hypothetical cases. Furthermore, Table 7.1 is based on the price for a complete transshipment operation—in and out—and a corresponding double operation with a normal shipment. In Table 7.4, merely one-half of a transshipment operation is compared with one normal cargo operation—in or out. After adjustments of this last difference, the hypothetical cases yield about the same price per ton (assuming 11 tons = one 20-foot container) for a normal conventional shipment and for a containered FCL shipment (S$14.88 and S$14.90, respectively); but for the FCL container transshipment, there is a markedly lower charge than for the conventional transshipment: S$7.09/ton against S$9.48/ton. The charge for the LCL transshipment is higher than for the conventional transshipment.

TABLE 7.4.   PORT OF SINGAPORE AUTHORITY TARIFF: TRANSSHIPMENT DIFFERENTIAL PER CONTAINER AND PER TON OF CONTAINERED CARGO FOR A HYPOTHETICAL VESSEL, 9,000 GRT, 1973

Containership using container quay crane; conventional ship using ship's derrick. Using port equipment and ship's chassis	FCL		LCL[a]	
	Normal import/ export (S$)	Trans- shipment (S$)	Normal import/ export (S$)	Trans- shipment (S$)
Charges Account Vessel (assume vessel of 9,000 GRT, discharging/loading 545 20-foot containers, staying 1 day, one-half of which is for unloading)				
Port dues	2.48	2.48	2.48	2.48
Pilotage, tugs, berthing, labor, garbage removal	2.58	2.58	2.58	2.58
Dockage and standby charge	2.90	2.90	2.90	2.90
Total of above: 1 vessel	7.96	7.96	7.96	7.96
Stevedorage, including wharf-age	140.00	70.00	180.00	110.00
Storage:				
a) Transshipment		0		0
b) Home: free period + 4 days empty	16.00		16.00	
Grand total	163.96	77.96	203.96	117.96
Per ton (1 container = 11 tons)	14.90	7.09	18.54	10.72

Note: S$ per container or per ton in or out.

a. The service to LCL transshipment containers consists of receiving the transshipment container from first carrier, removal to CFS and unstuffing, then stuffing the same cargo into another transshipment container and reshipping on a second carrier. For normal shipments, the LCL tariff is applicable (a) when a unit of loaded container is discharged from the ship, moved to the marshalling yard for storage and subsequently removed to the CFS, the contents unstuffed and the empty container moved to the marshalling yard or (b) when a unit of empty container is stuffed at the CFS and the reverse operations to (a) are performed.

tion with Singapore for containerable commodities such as rubber and plywood has led to the erection of informal impediments in the frontier procedures and the use of government influence, and port rates for normal and transshipment containers have been set close to those of Singapore. Kelang port rates for the handling of normal FCL containers—of importance in the import trade and in rubber exports—were thus apparently held below the Singapore rate in 1974 (Table 7.5).

TABLE 7.5. TRANSSHIPMENT DIFFERENTIALS FOR CONTAINERS: PORT KELANG (1974 AND PROPOSED 1975) AND PORT OF SINGAPORE (1972 AND 1973)

Container tariff: Stevedorage including wharfage per 20-foot-long container	Containership using container quay crane or conventional ship using ship's derrick (Wholly using port equipment)				Containership using ship's container crane (Wholly using port equipment)			
	Port Kelang		P.S.A.		Port Kelang		P.S.A.	
	1974	1975	1972	1973	1974	1975	1972	1973
FCL container								
Normal (S$)	140	190	140	150	120	170	120	130
Transshipment (one operation) (S$)	110	140	100	80	90	120	100	60
Normal/transshipment	(1.27)	(1.36)	(1.4)	(1.88)	(1.33)	(1.42)	(1.2)	(2.2)
LCL container								
Normal (S$)	260	330	180	200	240	310	160	180
Transshipment								
1. Receiving from first carrier, removal to CSF and un-stuffing (S$)	140	180	130	120	120	160	130	100

Normal/(transshipment 1)	(1.86)	(1.83)	(1.38)	(1.67)	(2.0)	(1.94)	(1.23)	(1.8)
2. Stuffing same transshipment container with export/transshipment cargo and reshipping in second carrier (S$)	260[a]	330[a]	—	200[b]	240[a]	310[a]	—[b]	180[c]
Empty FCL								
Receiving (S$)	140	180	140	150	120	160	120	130
Stuffing with break-bulk transshipment cargo and reshipping (S$)	140	180	—[b]	200[c]	120	160	—[b]	180[c]
Stuffing with break-bulk transshipment and Malaysian export cargo and reshipping (S$)	260[a]	330[a]	—[b]	200[c]	240[a]	310[a]	—[b]	180[c]

a. A rebate of S$4 per ton is given for every ton of transshipment cargo moved in a container.

b. The break-bulk cargo shall be charged according to the transshipment/reshipment rates by tonnage for one operation only and the container, including stuffing or unstuffing, shall be charged according to Tariff Item 56. This transshipment/reshipment rate will not apply to Singapore cargo.

c. A rebate of S$3 will be given for every ton of transshipment cargo moved in a container.

Sources: Port of Singapore Authority, PSA *Tariff 1973* and Port Swettenham Authority, *Scale of Rates, Dues, and Charges, By-laws 1966* and *By-laws 1975.*

Second, competition expresses itself in the transshipment differentials and in the way they are being charged. Port Kelang thus offers a larger rebate for transshipment cargo to be stuffed into containers together with national cargo, and between 1974 and 1975 the differential in favor of FCL transshipments was raised. For LCL transshipments, which involve a great deal of labor in stuffing or unstuffing containers, the percentage differential adopted by Port Kelang was substantially greater than in the Singapore tariff. The absolute Singapore rate for this type of service is probably too low relative to Singapore cost but is being kept so low to win the business from private container freight stations. Kelang rates for this service are absolutely higher, but the size of the percentage differential indicates the importance of LCL trade in Malaysia as in most other developing countries. The table further points to the sharp increases in the Singapore transshipment differentials both absolutely and relative to normal rates; in 1973 rates for transshipment were lowered, but those for normal container handling were raised.

Chapter 8

Multipart Tariffs

THE MAIN FEATURES of port cost functions are a large fixed cost and a relatively low variable cost up to the point where congestion really becomes felt. These features are even more marked for the new methods of cargo handling such as containerization. The main expenses are the heavy charges for financing the substantial capital required, and these are the same however much the port is used.

One of the main tasks of an efficient pricing system is to ensure that use is extended where the cost is less than the revenue to be obtained. Thus the price for using the facilities should be suitably low—and probably not much above the marginal cost of use. On the other hand, to the user of the facilities the total value per unit will be considerably larger than the marginal cost. This value to the user can be extracted, at least in part, by levying a charge that is completely unrelated to the extent to which the facility is used by him.

In the near future this form of charging should become more prevalent since certain kinds of port facilities, particularly container terminals, are being overbuilt in the developing world. Since the marginal cost will be very low, it is important to make full use of installed capital. It would be inefficient to waste this large capacity.

General Problems of Design

In principle, charges should be designed so that one part (the fixed charge) pays at least for the fixed cost of the facilities and one part (the variable charge) is levied according to the use of the facilities and measures the marginal cost. The variety of fixed and variable charges can be multiplied according to the number of specified services.

The main difficulty with two-part tariffs is that often there is no specific piece of plant associated with the supply of a service to a particular customer. Port services are unlike, for example, electricity services in the sense that the port does not install an end-distribution plant and a generating plant to supply all customers on demand, and many of the steamship owners will call only very occasionally at a port and will not use these services regularly. Although in the developing world, generally the greater part of traffic is handled by conference liners on a regular call basis, charges must be designed that allow for the casual port call and the one-off visit.[1]

The obvious approach is to give the steamship owner the option of paying for services on a two-part tariff basis or on an all-in charge basis. But it will follow that the two-part tariff must produce a charge per call which is less than the charge for a casual call by a tramp, otherwise the two-part tariffs would be ineffective. This arrangement will confer an advantage on the shipowners who call in regularly at the port as against the casual caller. However, this differentiation may do no more than reflect the cost advantages to a port of knowing that it has a regular subscription-list clientele. With regular calls it is easier to plan a quay occupation schedule to avoid waste and waiting. There is, therefore, good reason to arrange charges such that the regular subscription-list clients have lower overall charges than the casual visitor. Alternatively, the service may be differentiated by negotiating booked quay space at the times specified and agreed so that the steamship owner is assured that there will be no waiting, whereas the casual visitor will have to chance incurring considerable waiting cost. In this case the nominal subscription-list charge may be considerably larger than the casual tariff, but the difference is more than overcome by the differential quality of the service provided.

The possibility of covering cost without simultaneously restricting the use of facilities forms the main traditional case for a two-part tariff. But the method possesses further advantages. The flat charge of the two-part tariff can be used discriminatively to implement poli-

---

1. The casual caller is likely to be a tramp or bulk carrier and thus provides the very important competitive constraint on conference pricing.

cies on welfare or income distribution, once again without major effects on the use of the things that are thus priced. The flat charge can thus be varied between different classes of vessels (for example, between liners and tramps or between cartellized and independent liners insofar as they can be distinguished) or between different classes of the port's customers. Changes in an all-in charge, on the other hand, can be undertaken to affect either the use of resources or the distribution of income between different groups of buyers but not usually both at the same time.

Possible Designs of Multipart Tariffs

The main problems in designing systems of two-part tariffs is to relate the elements of the charge to some easily observed measure that, at the same time, reflects the cost. Principles must be compromised by practical possibilities.

Lease-a-quay (LAQ)

Probably the most extreme form of two-part tariff is in the lease-a-quay (LAQ) system. The port authority simply would build the facilities and then rent them out to either a single user or to a consortium on an annual basis or on a longer term lease with reversionary clauses. Normally the rent would be quite independent of the extent to which the facility is used, although there may be a clause in the contract to allow for use intensity. Such LAQ arrangements are normally associated with the exclusive use of the quay by the steamship companies' staff and equipment, and the steamship company would look after its own quayside services.

A charge will be made for any nonquay services supplied by the port authority. If the nonquay facilities are not congested and do not involve resources—perhaps the most obvious example is the channel—then any such charge should be included in the lease arrangements for the quay. If, on the other hand, the services do involve the use of resources, then they can be charged according to the principles in Chapters 5 and 6. Perhaps the most obvious examples are the use of tugs, storage outside the quay area, and special port equipment.

The most important advantage of this arrangement is that the steamship owner may adjust his use of the port facilities to minimize his cost. If, for example, the quay would otherwise lie unused, he will regard the marginal cost of using the quay as zero, and so he will be induced to use the service as a free good. Similarly he will not be deterred from shipping goods through the port because of any goods levy over and above the marginal cost of the carriage.

The second advantage of such an arrangement is that it may use the incentive of private profit to enhance efficiency. Port authorities are not generally under the same compelling pressure as firms in a competitive environment to seek the least-cost method of delivering the services. Ports tend to be either less efficient labor managers than private employers or else more vulnerable to political or organized pressure.[2] The leasing arrangement thus makes possible an amicable combination of public ownership and private efficiency.[3]

The main problem with the LAQ system is that it only can be applied in a few situations in developing countries. The most obvious cases are specialized commodity or trade quays, such as for timber (as in Malaysia, for example), cement, grain (Chittagong), or bulk foodstuffs or oil. In many cases the quay is restricted to one user or consortium. Ownership conditions may vary considerably; some buy a freehold interest in the port and build their own quay and facilities. In principle the port exercises no control over the quay and its use, although, in practice, the port will often exact a small fee per ton as in the Singapore oil facilities. Such an annual payment will be capitalized as a negative value in the contract, and the port will gain nothing except some insurance that it will share in an unexpected increase in trade with the obvious corollary that it will suffer from unforeseen declines.[4]

LAQ schemes also operate between a port and shippers. Petroleum facilities leased to oil companies are perhaps the most prominent examples, but there are many other instances of jetties or other parts

---

2. In Singapore, for example, conventional vessels tend to turn around faster in the roads than in port. This discrepancy is attributed to the fact that cargo operations in the roads are by shippers' labor and that shippers control their labor more effectively than the port, which pays labor by the tonnage of cargo worked.

3. A corollary of this is that the port authority must recognize that the steam-ship owner may earn substantial profits from his port operations.

4. The fact that the governments of developing countries with more or less substantial monopoly ports do have great power over firms that have sunk their costs in the facilities is excluded from consideration. Withdrawal would be extremely costly.

of ports being let to private or public sector shippers. In La Goulette, for example, the bulk grain facilities were leased to the government monopoly in charge of cereal marketing.

The LAQ system also has been used extensively for container quays and terminals, but virtually all the examples are in developed countries. Probably the most notable are the Sea–Land operations at New Jersey, Seattle, and Hong Kong. These require an enormous flow of traffic—far greater than appears in the countries of the developing world. Most of the large ports in the developing world will require only two container berths at most. It would usually be unfeasible—and even if feasible, undesirable—to reserve one berth entirely for one container firm.

The main objection to an LAQ system in developing countries is that it would surrender some of the monopoly power of the port to foreign steamship owners. Consider, for example, the most likely arrangement in the port of a developing country that offers a quay for rent on, say, a 5-year contract. If that rental is advantageous to the lessee, it will be so only because he manages to secure a large enough part of the market for shipping services to assure intensive use of the quay. This can be achieved by eliminating competition either by mutual agreement or by aggressive practices. The single-user berth will ensure that the steamship owner has more power to exclude potential competitors. Even if the contract specifies that the lessee may sublet the berth to other users, this will not generally limit his power since control is still vested in the single firm. It is possible to stipulate in the contract that the lessee be required to offer the berth to third-party steamship owners for specified fractions of the time at specified prices. But there are obvious difficulties in securing a suitable form of agreement and of enforcing it.

The monopoly power of the shipowner might be thought to be limited by the fact that the lease was offered for sale on a competitive bid basis. But this is not so. First the bidding is unlikely to be competitive since it would be easy to organize collusion, at least in liner traffic (including container ship traffic) on the pattern of the existing conference. Furthermore, approaches by potential lessees come at long intervals and have to be treated one at a time and occasionally in the knowledge that if no agreement is reached, the company may set up facilities in another port: the potential lessee frequently succeeds in making the potential lessors compete with one another.

But even if it were possible to arrange competitive bidding, this merely would ensure that the successful bidder did not secure monopoly profits from the berth. He would be induced to pursue monopolistic policies to earn the surplus necessary to pay for the lease. However, one of the basic objectives of the LAQ system will be achieved since the lessee will regard the payment of the lease as a fixed cost, and he will be induced to seek traffic provided that the marginal revenue covers the very low marginal cost up to capacity. The structure of charges will induce him to expand output well beyond what he would produce under the single charge or single fee system. The LAQ system, therefore, is particularly useful when there are commodities, such as timber, which move in sufficient quantity that a country may require several of these quays and jetties which would compete with one another or with overside loading.

In the container field and perhaps in other specialized unitized cargo handling systems, the opportunities for the LAQ approach are limited by the small size of the market. It is likely, however, that the potential for LAQ will grow partly because of the growth in world trade and the increasing use of containerization but also partly because of the concentration of port facilities. The example of Hong Kong and Singapore is of interest here. Hong Kong and Singapore compete for the role of main terminal for the large container vessels; the offer of an LAQ arrangement is, undoubtedly, an important bargaining counter in securing the traffic. With the annual growth of international trade at 5 or 6 percent, other countries will find that their ports, when suitably concentrated, may be able to offer LAQ container arrangements. Therefore, LAQ arrangements have limited applicability in developing countries, but their potential importance is likely to grow.

Leasing arrangements are quite frequently contracted for facilities other than quays and berths such as special cranes that the particular shipowner requires. In cases of this kind the customer usually pays for and installs the equipment, leasing only the site and general services from the port. But the shipowner will try to put such equipment on his ship if at all possible. This enables him to use the equipment at any port and avoids the hostages to fortune and political change involved in locating costly facilities on the premises of some foreign port. Shipowners tend more and more to install, for example, suitable cranes on their vessels. This is noticeable, for example, in Keppel Wharf at Singapore, where the ship normally is unloaded and loaded by the local port labor force using the ship's gear.

In general, the need for flexibility in patterns of operation and the desire to give few hostages to fortune or politics inhibits the lease-a-facility system. Except for certain specialized and specific pieces of equipment it is unlikely to provide a model arrangement for pricing in developing countries.

Annual fee to enter (AFTE)

Another way to introduce two-part tariffs is to provide an annual fee to enter the port. Once a steamship owner had paid his annual subscription, he could enter the port for, perhaps, a low nominal fee, or if the port has considerable overcapacity, the visiting fee could be made virtually zero. This sort of charging arrangement is particularly important when the particular facilities are uncongested.

The AFTE case is best made with respect to the charge usually levied for dredging the port. The most common basis for this charge is one of the traditional indicators of vessel size. The trend of expert opinion, however, is to relate this charge to the ship's draft, and draft, of course, is also correlated with the size or capacity of the vessel. Given the depth of channel, however, cost does not vary with ship size, so there should be no difference in the dredging charge.[5] Large vessels drawing a deep draft should not be penalized in favor of small vessels. However, it is commonly suggested that since the channel was dredged deeper especially for the larger vessels, somehow their willingness to pay for the additional dredging should be tested. And there is no better test of willingness than to see if, when actually charged for the additional dredging, they continue to use the channel and do not bypass the port. But if it is to be at all useful, the willingness-to-pay criterion is required before the decision is made to dredge. Evidence after the fact is of little value except for analogous decisions in related ports. In any case, the correct criterion of willingness to pay should not be formulated in terms of a payment for each use of the channel; the users will normally prefer to pay AFTE annually for unlimited use of the channel.[6] Commutation of user fees generally will be a much more efficient way both to measure the

5. See also A. A. Walters, "Marginal Cost Pricing in Ports," *The Logistics and Transportation Review*, vol. 12, no. 3 (1975).

6. This point has been argued and developed in A. A. Walters, *Economics of Road User Charges*, World Bank Staff Occasional Papers, no. 5 (Baltimore: Johns Hopkins Press, 1968).

willingness to pay and to use the channel.[7] But still such commutation fees will, in any case, usually provide a rationalization after the channel exists, although in a limited number of cases where there is a single dominant user, the contracts can be entered into before the construction is undertaken.

Several questions have to be settled at the outset when designing two-part tariffs of the AFTE type. The first is whether the charge should be levied only on the shipping firm (covering a specific list of vessels) or whether it should also be paid by a wider group such as a conference or container consortium in respect of all their members. In one sense, this issue does not matter provided that the ships that are entitled to use the specified port services are listed and defined precisely in the agreement. Nevertheless, the more vessels admitted under the aegis of the AFTE, the greater the advantage to the constituent firms or conference.

The second question is how to calculate the standing charge. One natural approach is to levy the standing charge on the basis of the previous years' history. This is the way that such charges were fixed on the railways in Britain, and there is considerable administrative experience in arranging what were called agreed charges. The AFTE must be fixed so that it is advantageous to the shipowner since it cannot be made obligatory without seriously discouraging occasional calls. Furthermore, it should not be revised yearly on the basis of last year's traffic, because then it would merely amount to a discount on actual traffic but paid with a delay of one year. Contractually it might be best to revise it every 3 years on the basis of (say) 6 months picked at random throughout the year, duly allowing for any seasonal variation. The AFTE as a charge per ship, nevertheless, should decline as the number of visits of ships increases.

This suggests an alternative way to introduce a modified form of the AFTE. Ships may receive a discount according to the number of visits they make; alternatively, the port authorities may offer to sell packages of ten visits during the year. Since quantity

---

7. The annual fee will not deter the steamship owner from using the channel. This is appropriate since the cost to the port is virtually zero, and so he will be able to extract the maximum services from the facility. This will in turn induce him to make a maximum annual bid for the right to use the channel, and so this will better measure his willingness to pay. In practice, such commutation fees must be combined with a system of daily fees.

discounts are not at all uncommon in shipping arrangements, this would be easier to administer than the strict AFTE method. Even so, there are problems: should the quantity discounts be specific to a particular ship, to a particular firm, or to a conference? The transferability of the right to a discount must be limited in one way or another, otherwise there would be a secondary market in port rights; this would simply let the single price system in through the back door. If the quantity discount were made available to the conference as an entity, there would be some considerable additional advantage given to a firm that belonged to a conference. This could be offset by a conference registration fee which would then entitle the conference to the greater quantity discounts.

There are certain disadvantages to such AFTE arrangements. Perhaps the most serious is that the scheme is likely to confer some advantage on the large user. It might also be thought that the regular user will gain: the liner services on which the trade of developing countries tends to depend so heavily against the tramp operator who has a small share of the trades. In practice, this will often be true, but not always so. In the case of chartered vessels—tramps or bulk carriers—the large charterer who plans to bring vessels reasonably regularly to the port can then easily become the contractor under the AFTE scheme; in a later section the scheme is extended to him. Essentially, therefore, the scheme is biased towards the large user; although in practice often also in favor of the liner company and within that class it is biased towards the large operators rather than the less frequent or occasional callers. The liner conferences will thus be certain gainers. Throughout this study, it has been stressed that the main safeguard for a developing country is the vigorous competition of nonconference vessels. And any discrimination against such nonconference vessels would add in some measure to the monopoly power of the conference. If, for some reason, this cannot be offset by restructuring the charges to redress the handicap suffered by the nonconference type of vessels, then such AFTE arrangements may not be worthwhile. Furthermore, such quantity discounts will encourage the conference to make additional calls at the port. Although this will give additional frequency of service, the conference may take the opportunity to exploit its additional monopoly power farther, perhaps using the usual rationalization that costs have increased.

The other main disadvantage of the AFTE is the administrative complexity. The only variant, without quite daunting administrative difficulties, is the quantity discount system where an owner buys a block of services (say, ten port entries) and cannot transfer them.

To illustrate the working of a quantity discount AFTE system, figures from the port of Singapore can be used. The ship charges for a 6,000-ton GRT vessel entering Singapore in 1975 were about S$6,000 (US$3,000). This is only about half of the total charge, amounting to, say S$17,000 for a cargo of 3,000 tons discharged. The quantity discount arrangement would charge for the first visit at S$9,000, for the second S$8,000, and so on down to say a S$3,000 minimum. This system would involve an increase of the total charges of about 19 percent for the casual one-off caller and substantially reduced charges for more than seven calls each year.

The cost of port operations for the one-off casual tramp caller, which unloaded 3,000 tons, would increase from about S$5.50 to S$6.50 per ton—a rise of roughly US$0.50. And this would be reflected partly in the tramp's cost and freight rates; only partly because tramp services would be expected to reorganize somewhat to avoid such high charges, by using larger vessels or by accumulating bigger loads. Although this might appear to be a small amount per ton, it might cause a significant reduction in tramp competition against the conferences and illustrates the point made above. On the other hand, however, the regular bulk carriers will benefit even more than the conventional conference vessels from the quantity discount arrangements.[8] Consequently more competition would be expected from this growing sector as a consequence of the change of pricing policy. Whether the cheaper bulk carriage will offset the conference's advantage must be a matter for practical judgment in particular cases.

In order to introduce a policy of quantity discounts, the following guidelines are suggested. First, the charges should be calculated so that the port revenues are increased, and certainly every precaution should be taken to see that they are not reduced. In the illustrative argument for Singapore, it seems likely that the change suggested would result in a considerable increase in revenue, but more analysis is needed to make certain of this.

Second, the system should only be introduced if persistent excess capacity for some time—say, more than 1 year—is likely. In many ports of the world this is liable to be the case. In the Singapore example, with excess capacity, the charge of S$3,000 for the marginal vessel

8. Stevedoring charges are a much smaller fraction of total port cost per ton with bulkers than with conventional vessels.

is probably still considerably above the marginal cost of dockage and standby.[9]

Third, the quantity discount system is probably most useful when the business of the port is dominated by a handful of conferences, as in the case of Bangkok. This is the usual situation in developing countries; in this respect, Singapore is an exception. Then suitable quantity discount schedules may be agreed on with the whole conference.[10]

Container charges

The most important application of the two-part tariff and the quantity discount is in container operation. This results from a combination of factors. The first factor is that there is considerable over-investment in container facilities, particularly in developing countries. It is remarkable, but perhaps not surprising, that the ports of Kelang and Singapore were not making any profits on their container installations. The state of Kelang's container accounts is not astonishing, but it is surprising that even as large and as vigorous a port authority as that of Singapore with all the geographical advantages of her location could not make an adequate return on capital invested.[11]

The second factor is associated with this unprofitability; there is considerable competition between ports for container vessels and services. Ports with existing container installations have little bargaining power, as is demonstrated by the competition between Singapore and Hong Kong.

The third factor is that unit cost declines rapidly for any use substantially below capacity. As shown in Chapter 3, the marginal cost is very low compared with average cost. For example the marginal cost of handling a container may be only $1 to $2 compared with an average variable cost of $6 to $10. These are often associated with port charges of $30 to $60 for handling a container.

The rationalization of such a markup over cost is that, because of

9. Singapore is one of the ports where there is now little or no excess conventional capacity, but the building of Pasir Panyang as well as the extension of other facilities is likely to create some in the near future.

10. In those circumstances also it often appears that the frequency of service is a most important variable for traders. The quantity discount system would encourage greater frequency of sailings and so improve the service.

11. This is taken to be a true statement of the situation even for the period before the recession of 1975.

the faster turnaround of container vessels, the container carrier, often a consortium, enjoys a considerable reduction in his cost. The sizable markup is explained as a way to recoup some of the advantages of container operation for the port. The container operator will still be willing to offer a service provided that the cost is less than the conventional alternative. If the port authority is not too greedy in raising handling cost, the port and the operator will share the benefits.

But port authorities discourage the development of containerization by such a high markup. This may be of little consequence. Containerization may be so advantageous that it is worthwhile paying the higher handling charge for virtually all cargoes; this approximates to the case in Seattle where all general cargo is now containerized. But in many ports this is not so; conventional operation is often important and continues as the dominant form of handling alongside some containerized cargoes on certain routes. The port handling charge is an important factor in determining whether or not to containerize cargo.

The most compelling considerations, however, are the very large economies of scale in container operation. As the number of containers increases, there are dramatic reductions in the average handling cost primarily because of the more intensive use of equipment. It is important not to inhibit in any way the realization of these economies and so to encourage the containerization of marginal cargoes. Once container facilities are installed, the charges for container handling should be kept low enough to realize the economies of scale.

This suggests that the charging system should have a low variable charge for handling, which is consistent with the low marginal cost implied by the economies of scale, and a fixed charge for the use of the port facilities by the consortium. The contract of the port with the container consortium would specify the annual rent for the right to operate a container service to the port.[12] The two-part tariff will encourage the container firm to bid vigorously for additional traffic and to realize the economies of scale inherent in container operation. The fixed rental charge, however, will ensure that the country or port will share in the advantages of containerization. If there is considerable competition among container firms for the privilege of supplying a port with containerized service—and there is evidence of this on

12. This payment is in addition to the real cost of renting any of the normal facilities of a port that a container firm may require.

certain routes—then the port authorities can extract much of the additional profit of container operation by this method of charging.

This argument applies to specialized container facilities where normally the ship carries only containers. There is no inherent reason, however, why the same system should not apply to the part-container ship which is more common in the developing world. The fixed rental charge could be based on the capacity of the ships to carry containers, whether they are carried or not. Then this would encourage the containerization of traffic, again assuming there is excess capacity in the port's container facilities.

Shippers' license to use the port (LUP)

The port's charges to shippers could, in principle, be based also on a variant of the AFTE scheme. The most obvious application would be to those shippers—often a well-defined group—who normally import or export their cargoes on chartered vessels and who, therefore, exercise control over most of the shipping operation in port. The prices of the various services available in the port to shippers who have paid the standing charge could then be set as close as possible to marginal cost. There also are less obvious extensions of the principle to shippers who use the port regularly. A nontransferable license to use the port (LUP) could thus be sold to shippers, entitling the holder to use the port's resources at prices equal to incremental variable cost. Once again the administrative problems are sufficiently grave to make it worthwhile only where sizable excess capacity exists.

The disadvantages of the LUP proposal for shippers are similar to those of the AFTE proposal for ships. In order not to discourage occasional shippers, it may be necessary to offer shippers the choice between regular charges and special charges available only to those who choose the two-part tariff. If shippers are to be attracted to the LUP system, it would have to incorporate a quantity discount which might be based on a shipper's total payments to the port for a past period or, in the case of a new shipper, on a typical annual payment made to the port by shippers of small or medium size shipping similar commodities. As in the case of the AFTE scheme, apart from indexing for changes in the general price level, the flat or standing charge should be revised only infrequently.

If a quantity discount is built into the scheme, then, like AFTE, it may cause a bias in favor of large size and thus of concentration and monopoly. But this may be regarded as less of a problem in the case of two-part tariffs applied to shippers, especially in those countries where foreign trade is already largely monopolized by public corporations. The difficulty of preventing resale of the LUP, however, is at least as great as it is under AFTE. Resale might be preventable where import and export licensing is being practiced but only at the expense of additional bureaucratic activity. In the absence of such licensing, LUP could be confined to shipping agents, but again only at the expense of fostering concentration.

The difficulties of the scheme are clear; unless it can be policed adequately to prevent major evasion, its object will be frustrated. The disadvantage in the form of a stimulus to concentration may also be serious. But the advantages of two-part tariff can be great, and these or alternative schemes merit close study and experiment.

Port Charges as a Percentage Levy

One of the main conclusions from the discussion of the two-part tariff is that it is difficult to apply to conventional vessels. There are many problems of how to design the fixed charge so that unfortunate side effects are avoided. Perhaps the most important side effect is that such multipart charges would favor conference vessels. Although special schemes of charges might be introduced to avoid such discrimination, there are great administrative complications, and it is doubtful whether they would be worthwhile.

As an alternative there is a simple method of charging that would retain at least some of the desirable effects of the two-part tariff and that avoids many of its pitfalls. This is to convert part (and in some cases even all) of the port charges into a percentage levy on the freight charge; the port charge would be fixed at a constant fraction of the freight charge. Thus the vessel calling at a port would make available to the port authority (as they do now to the customs) the manifest of the goods to be unloaded or loaded, except that the ship's agent would be required to leave the manifest, including the data on freight charges, intact. The levy of the port authority would then be calculated at (say) 10 percent of the total of the freight receipts.

There are many consequences of the fractional freight charge. First, the conference and other vessels will be encouraged to make more frequent visits with smaller loads. It has been argued that conferences make too many sailings under normal port charging, thus this system of charges may encourage this particular inefficiency.

There are, however, good reasons for thinking that any such inefficiency will be small because of the tendency to encourage rate cutting. In ports where the number of sailings seems excessive relative to the average cargo tonnage, a disincentive can be built into the percentage levy in the form of a discount based on the cargo tonnage per vessel. The fraction of the freight charge might thus decline from, say, 10 to 8½ percent as the quantity of cargo per vessel increased from 1,000 to 7,000 tons. Insofar as the largest loads will contain a relatively large element of homogeneous cargo, which is cheaper to handle per unit than heterogeneous consignments, the discount will reflect the pattern of cost.

Second, one of the main advantages of a fractional freight charge is that the steamship owners will be encouraged to reduce rates if, at the same time, one of their main costs—port cost—is reduced in equal proportion. The port charge will decline along with the price as the throughput of a shipping firm is expanded by price cutting. The big difference between the fractional freight charge and the ordinary quantity discount is that the latter awards the discount for all increases in quantity, whereas the fractional freight charge gives discounts only if the steamship owner reduces the freight rate. Thus it avoids all the administratively complex problems of deciding what is the appropriate quantity measure and of policing such agreements to avoid resale or other forms of masquerade.

Third, the fractional freight charge does discriminate against long-haul traffic. But such traffic is more likely to be cartelized than the short-haul voyages. In terms of ability to pay the long-haul voyages have greater potential. In addition, there is discrimination according to the value of the commodity as well as to the cost of carriage. Again this would vary port charges according to ability to pay.[13] It would also be possible to favor transshipment cargo, which is normally shown separately on the manifest. Insofar as the elasticity of demand for port services by transshipment cargo is considerably greater than domestic cargo, this may be considered a sensible way to raise revenue and to maximize the profit of the port.[14]

13. Some discrimination in favor of exports might be expected also. For example, the charge for exports may be considerably less than the import fractional charge. Although there is no reason to suppose that by rigging charges in this way the foreigner will pay more than the domestic resident, governments are often misled into bad policies by deceptive appearances.

14. See Chapter 7.

Fourth, the fractional freight charge would vary with oscillations in freight rates. When there is a slump, the freight, and so also the port charge, would fall; under boom conditions the port charge would rise. Broadly speaking this automatic movement of charges with the cycle is a good thing. Under slump conditions there is likely to be excess capacity, and the marginal cost is likely to be very low. The port charge would not be expected to vary nicely to reflect the marginal cost of port operations over the cycle, but it is about the best that can be done.

Fifth, secularly the charge would tend to adjust automatically to any inflation of the general world price level. Freight rates, and particularly conference rates, have generally risen with bunker, labor, and ship prices. The fractional charge would reflect these variations. Of course by the same token as in the argument above, the freight rates may not reflect exactly the inflation in the cost of the port, but the deviation is likely to be small.

Sixth, characteristically this fractional freight charge moves away from charges fixed according to cost, and this undoubtedly has disadvantages. Where cost deviates greatly from normal, it is probably best to arrange for special port charges. The obvious example of this is the congestion charge. All port levies would be negotiated subject to the overriding right of the port to impose a congestion charge on specific facilities. Similarly the port should levy charges for the use of storage space or quay space beyond the period specified in the fractional charge tariff. The different vulnerability of different items of port services to congestion may serve as the criterion for selecting those port charges that are to be compounded in the percentage levy. But the exclusion of conventional items of port charges from such a scheme diminishes its simplicity. A major question in the detailed design of a percentage levy is the extent to which the services of port labor are to be covered by the fractional charge. This is a particular concern for liners since the terms of carriage include a part of shore handling in the freight charge. The nature of the best compromise will vary from case to case, depending on the standardization of labor operations, on the labor intensity of cargo operations, and on the extent to which the port's labor is casual or a fixed force.

Seventh, the simplicity of the fractional charging system is its greatest asset. It requires neither a knowledge of all costs nor a detailed specification of port operations. With all its disadvantages it possesses built-in flexibility. Furthermore it is easily understood and, congestion apart, everyone will know how the charges are going to vary for some time ahead. There will be no sudden jumps in charges to catch up with inflation, and the adjustment should be smooth.

There are many problems about the appropriate way to introduce such a charging system. Probably the most acceptable way is to calculate charges, preferably just after one of the periodic increases, on the basis of the traditional tariffs and then to offer the steamship companies the same total freight payment (less a small discount as an inducement) calculated as the fractional freight charge. The second question is whether there should be some minimum payment per ship. It seems feasible to design the tariff so that each ship pays a minimum of, say, $400 per visit to the berth. Arrangements already exist in Bangkok, Singapore, and Kelang for charging ships that merely put into harbor.[15]

There may be many other, perhaps undesirable, side effects of such a system of fractional charging. First, it may encourage cargo to be sent to neighboring ports and transshipped on a short feeder route to its destination port where the fractional freight rate charging operates. There might be some artificial distortion of the pattern of ocean transport. (However, as in the case of Singapore, Kelang, and Indonesian ports, governments often discriminate, on what seem to be doubtful arguments, in favor of direct services; the short-sea-route bias would offset this.) Second, it might lead to incorrect recording of the freight charges to secure a lower port charge. It is difficult to see how this would upset the port's charges, however, since characteristically the conference liner would be tempted to show charges greater than those that are actually paid; any chiseling would not be revealed in the manifest, which would record the agreed conference freight rate. The chiseling conference member will have an incentive to report the high rate and to pay the higher port charge. Third, the charge may be difficult to apply to certain tramp vessels that may be on charter hire and where no specific freight rate is charged for identified cargo. The problem is not likely to be important in the case of an arm's-length charter, where the charter party includes the rate and is as

15. There are, however, good reasons for keeping such charges very low when there is no risk of congestion. The nationals will benefit from the purchases of bunkers, stores, and services made by the ship, and the corresponding increase in the surpluses of nationals is a pure gain.

easy or as difficult to inspect as the liners' freight revenue. But where importer and exporter are closely related (and all the more where one of them owns the ship), the problem of transfer pricing is likely to arise. The rate may have been chosen at the convenience of the accounting system. The natural procedure is then to charge the conference freight rate or alternative tramp rates to calculate port charges; but there are many other alternatives that might be used.

Last, in this review of practical questions, different percentages will have to be fixed for freight charges covering different ranges of service. Conventional port-to-port service on liner terms is standardized as regards the services to be rendered by the shipowner to the shipper, and this makes conventional liner traffic a good candidate for the fractional scheme. By contrast, a great variety of terms can be found in charter contracts and in container carriage. Containers may be stuffed and stripped in the port, at freight stations outside the port, or at shippers' premises. Container traffic is thus characterized by additional labor services and at least some inland transport on the shipowners' account. The administratively feasible solution to these problems will depend much on local circumstances.

Concluding Comments

From all this discussion it emerges that no simple scheme can be applied to all port charges. Cost, in the sense in which it has been defined, provides only the floor on which a tariff system should be erected. The outline of this system must depend on judgment of the extent of competition and of the opportunities for generating or killing traffic and trade. However, such systems will be difficult to devise and complex in their form. This is the rationale for seeking some simple rule-of-thumb such as the fractional-freight-charge method.

In practical cases of existing port tariffs inconsistencies, absurd differentials, and gross discrimination exist based on political favor rather than on the economic advantage. This suggests that even using the basic principles of cost and comparability, there is ample room for tariff reform. A start can be made easily. There is no need to wait for the formulation of any of the methods of charging outlined above. Yet even when the tariff reform program has just begun with the elimination of absurdities, the various systems do provide a framework to give direction and an objective for designing new tariffs. As with all reform proposals, the best must never be allowed to emerge as the enemy of the good.

Chapter 9

Port Pricing in Practice

THE ULTIMATE TEST of the usefulness of principles is whether they are practicable; and this test cannot be performed in the confines of this study. Not only would it demand the simulation of a complete system based on a realistic case study, but in addition the cost of change and its optimal phasing would have to be assessed. A test of practicability obviously should be the next step after the consideration of principles, but it remains a separate task.

However, the meaning of at least some of the propositions in this study can be clarified by applying them to concrete examples. The cases were selected from the port tariffs and procedures of four South and Southeast Asian ports: Singapore, Kelang, Bangkok, and Chittagong.[1]

---

1. Port of Singapore Authority, *PSA Tariff 1973* (Singapore, 1973). *Port Swettenham Authority, Scale of Rates, Dues and Charges By-Laws, 1966*, incorporating all amendments up to April 18, 1974 and *By-laws, 1975* (proposed amendments of charges). Port Authority of Thailand, *Tariff of Port Charges, Port of Bangkok*, 2d and 4th ed. (Klong Toi, Bangkok, 1966 and 1974). Coopers and Lybrand Associates Limited, *Report on the Tariff Review*, (prepared for the Port Authority of Thailand) (London, January 8, 1975). W. D. Scott and Co. Pty. Ltd., *Final Report: Port Operations Consultancy Services* (prepared for the Port Authority of Thailand, Port of Bangkok, Klong Toi, Bangkok. Sydney, June 1973; processed). Chittagong Port Trust, *Schedule of Charges on Goods and Vessels* (corrected up to notification no. CAO-IV(98)/7534, January 29, 1975). *Bangladesh Gazette* (Chittagong, 1975). Government of Pakistan, Ministry of Communications (Railway Division), *General Rules and Schedules for Working*

The Port of Singapore is large by international standards with much transshipment and transit business and a marked excess of inbound cargo (Table 9.1). Port Kelang competes with Singapore for Malaysian traffic and differs from the other ports in that it handles somewhat more exports than imports. Bangkok, the chief civilian port of a country larger than Malaysia, is a river port with a pronounced excess of imports and a past history of shed congestion. Chittagong, a river port that had the lowest number of calls and cargo tonnage among the four ports in 1974, is predominantly an import port with great problems of cargo clearing and a history of severe shed congestion.

Comparisons between the tariff policies or the tariffs and the charges are not made because of the dissimilarities between the tariffs and the economic and technical situation of the ports. Their pricing rules will merely be used as realistic examples, and not surprisingly, those rules which appear on the surface to conflict with the propositions in this study will be given the most attention.

The Base of Port Charges

For ports operating in competitive conditions, the base of their charges is the single most important consideration in the design of the tariff. A wrong choice in this matter will distort the use of the port by setting up a bias in favor of relatively costly methods of using the port.

Channel dues and berth hire

The first example is the base of channel or port dues (the entry fee to the port) and of berth hire. A very common base for both is the ship's net registered tonnage (NRT); Bangkok uses this measure for its channel dues and wharf rates (dockage), and Chittagong uses it

---

of the Chittagong Port (Railway) Jetties (in force from January 1, 1959), Gazette of Pakistan (Karachi, December 15, 1958, with amendments). Louis Berger International Inc., "Feasibility Study, Port of Chittagong Expansion, Bangladesh," (study prepared for Asian Development Bank), vol. II (December 1974). Economist Intelligence Unit in association with Scott Wilson Kirkpatrick and Partners, Bangladesh Transport Survey, Final report (prepared for the Government of the Peoples' Republic of Bangladesh under assignment by the Overseas Development Administration of the Foreign and Commonwealth Office) Part 9, Management and Financial Studies (London, November 1974).

TABLE 9.1.   FOUR PORTS IN DEVELOPING ASIA: INDICATORS
OF OUTPUT, 1974

	Number of vessels	Imports (million tons)	Exports (million tons)	Total cargo (million tons)
Port of Singapore				
Ship calls[a] (over 75 NRT)	19,629			
Cargo handled (freight tons)		37.7	22.8	60.5
Dry		(9.1)	(5.7)	(14.8)
Oil in bulk		(28.6)	(17.1)	(45.7)
Port Kelang				
Ship calls	3,170			
Foreign going and container ships and tankers	(2,524)			
Cargo handled (long tons)		2.7	2.9	5.6
Dry cargo		(2.0)	(2.2)	(4.2)
Over authority's facilities		(2.4)	(1.9)	(4.3)
Port of Bangkok (provisional)				
Ship calls	4,330			
Cargo handled (measurement tons) (authority's installations)		8.6	2.4	10.0
Dry		(3.5)	(2.4)	(5.9)
Petroleum		(5.1)		(5.1)
Port of Chittagong (July 1974–June 1975)				
Ship calls	749			
Cargo handled excluding bulk oil		4.2	0.3	4.5
		(3.0)		(3.3)

a. One-half of arrivals and departures of vessels.

Sources: Port of Singapore: Port of Singapore Authority, *Report and Accounts for the Year Ended 31 December 1974* (Singapore, 1975), pp. 52–56. Port Kelang: Kelang Port Authority, *Annual Report 1974* (Kelang, 1975), pp. 33–45. Port of Bangkok: Port Authority of Thailand, Port Operations Department, *Port Operations Statistics 1974* (Bangkok, 1975), and information supplied by Ministry of Communications, Royal Thai Government, Bangkok. Port of Chittagong: Chittagong Port Trust, *Statement of Cargo Handled at Chittagong Port during the Period from July 1974 to June 1975* (processed), pp. 1–4 and *Budget estimates of income and expenditure for 1975–76 with revised estimates for 1974–75* (Chittagong, 1975), pp. 1–2.

for port dues. But the NRT of ships can be varied enormously by quite small changes in ship design and in dead weight tonnage without affecting the port's cost of servicing the ship. NRT is thus altogether unsuitable as a base for port charges. A popular alternative is gross weight tonnage. Singapore uses it as the base of port and light dues and of dockage, and Kelang uses it to determine the minimum wharfage for ships alongside the wharf.[2] GRT is less open to abuse than NRT, but the correlation with cost is again not at all high; nor is there a good correlation with cargo carrying capacity.

None of these ports use length of ship as the basis for entry fees or berth hire. This seems an unequivocal and easily ascertainable measure, clearly related to the cost of providing quay length or maneuvering basins, but it is rarely used by ports.[3] A ship's draft might be thought to be another reasonably efficient basis for port dues or berth hire, but there are measurement problems, and a ship's actual draft may vary widely from its maximum.[4]

Fundamental issues in fixing the base

The choice of base for channel dues as discussed so far hinges on the avoidable cost of port services. Whichever characteristic of a ship best indicates variations in port cost caused by different ships should be chosen. The choice of base for berth hire can be examined in the same light. In particular there is the question whether the charge for using a berth should vary with measurable characteristics of the vessels, such as NRT or DWT or draft, or whether the port should fix a different rent for different berths. The latter solution has been adopted at Hong Kong and at Chittagong where it has caused objections by shipowners and consultants.[5] If the cost of servicing ships differs more between a port's berths than within any berth, then berth hire should, of course, differentiate between berths, whatever else it may be doing in addition; and the simplest system may be to set different prices for different berths.

---

2. At Kelang, wharfage is the equivalent of cargo dues in other ports.

3. Haifa and Ecuador are ports that charge berth hire by length.

4. In Rotterdam, the prevailing method of charging is by the actual draft or the depth of the water in the dock. This has the disadvantage that the port may be tempted to direct a small draft ship into a deep water dock.

5. Louis Berger International Inc., "Feasibility Study, Port of Chittagong Expansion, Bangladesh."

But what if the port's costs do not vary with a ship's NRT, DWT, or draft, or according to which berth the ship occupies? As discussed in the earlier chapters of this study, the cost to be reflected in prices is short-run marginal cost. The case can be dealt with easily where marginal cost as reflected in the port's accounts does not differ between different berths but where berths differ significantly in the convenience of using them. Some of them will then fill up regularly at times of high demand before the others are taken up. The scarcity rent generated by the convenient berths should then be appropriated by the port through differential pricing of berths, just as expounded in Chapter 4. Whenever one ship would be willing to bid against another for the use of a berth at a particular time or where one ship would be willing to bribe another into letting it use a particular berth, the port would be justified in appropriating this surplus if it can do so without incurring a cost greater than the prospective gain.

That leaves other cases where there is neither excess demand for a particular berth nor any noticeable difference in the port's private short-run marginal cost of operating different berths. (For simplicity assume these costs to be zero across all the port's berths.[6]) This case may describe very well the situation envisaged by tariff makers in many ports. To deal with this case the discussion in later sections of this chapter must be anticipated. First, insofar as cost is concerned, there is no argument in the case for charging different amounts for different berths or for different NRT or DWT. The use of each berth produces the same variation in port cost. Second, with positive fixed cost and zero marginal cost for operating the berths, what charge should be levied for the use of berths and channel; should they differ as between users and, if so, what should determine the differences? If the port is not perfectly competitive, it could of course raise some of its charges above marginal cost without driving ships away. In that case it should load fixed costs onto those charges which ships could not avoid if they wish to enter the port at all; in other words, the port should avoid any distortion in the use of its resources. The port may then decide to levy these loaded charges according to the ship's ability to pay, and this ability can often be correlated with certain technical characteristics of the vessel or with the length of its voyage. But as pointed out in Chapter 6, a mere exploitation of the ability to pay

6. This situation is not difficult to imagine for a port which does not levy inclusive charges but prices different operations such as labor, cranes, berthing services separately.

may not be the optimal policy for a port in this situation. A concrete example is a berth that is particularly suited for loading or discharging bulk cargoes. Vessels taking bulk cargoes—bulk carriers or just tramps —tend to operate more competitively than general cargo vessels. If the policy is to encourage competition among the vessels serving the country's trade, lower rates should be charged for the berths suitable for bulk trades than for the standard general cargo berths.

Further consideration of the base: the case of handling charges

The normal basis for cargo handling charges is the unit of cargo, for example, tons. But if the ship causes delays to cargo movement— perhaps because it is not designed for cargo handling at the average rate of the port—the optimal basis of the rate would be time rather than tonnage. Charges based on tonnage are indeed sometimes combined with penalties for slow movement.[7] But labor charges based solely on time, for example, rates for labor and clerks charged to ships at Kelang, have all the disadvantages of cost-plus pricing except if the party which pays the charge can also control the labor operations.[8]

Port traffic managers agree readily that tariffs should be designed to attract certain types of vessels into their wharves—particularly vessels which allow a fast movement of cargo. Port and berth dues should thus act as an incentive for quick turnaround. As the port's ability to clear ships increases, it can strengthen this incentive. But a distinct incentive is required for the optimal use of distinct services; if the port's labor force or wharf equipment complementary with labor are fixed factors of production, tariffs should encourage their efficient use. This consideration argues for basing labor charges on both the quantity of output and the rate of output. Naturally such a system is less convenient than a charge based on a single criterion; it would require a multiplicity of scales (for example, charges for 10, 15, or 20 tons per hour at rates which rise in lesser proportion than the tonnage). It is true that in many ports or wharves the average ship can move cargo faster than the port can; this accounts presumably for shipowners and shippers everywhere preferring to employ their own labor whenever the rules permit. But there is nothing in this situation

7. This is the rule in Pasir Panjang (Singapore) which serves coasters and lighters.

8. Port Swettenham Authority, *Scale of Rates, Dues, and Charges, By-laws, 1966*, incorporating amendments up to April 18, 1974.

that should argue against labor charges being graduated by the rate of working; the scheme would never work to the disadvantage of the more modern ship. The counterarguments are just the administrative inconvenience of the scheme and the possibility that it might enlarge the scope for undesirable practices by labor or by those who control it. An alternative method is to set minimum rates of working below which the vessel incurs penalties or is banished from the wharf.[9] This suffers from the weakness that it provides a discontinuous incentive, unlike, for instance, a charge for space occupied by cargo. A superior alternative is the Port of Singapore's dockage remission coefficient. The dockage charge within the main conventional harbor at Singapore (Keppel Harbor) is thus abated according to the total cargo loaded or discharged per unit of time.[10]

Marginal-Cost Pricing: Charging for the Use of the Uncongested Channel

Dredging cost is often one of the most important costs of maintaining a port, sometimes as much as one quarter of total port cost. There are two main issues connected with dredging. First there is usually a choice in the depth to which the channel is dredged—the deeper the water, the larger the ship that can use it and usually the lower the cost of shipping. Second, there is the problem of choosing a method of financing the additional dredging cost; obviously some charge on ships should be made, but there are many possible choices of dredging levy. In practice channel dues are often levied according to the NRT or GRT of the ship; thus the larger ships pay the higher dues. But NRT and GRT are only related indirectly and inaccurately to the allegedly significant factor in the use of the channel. The draft required by a ship is thought to be the best measure by which to levy channel dues. The deeper the water required by the vessel, the more it should contribute to the total dredging cost of the channel.

9. In the Pasir Panjang wharf at Singapore, coasters incur a penalty if they work at less than 15 tons per hour per hook. At Chittagong, the authority may order a vessel off the jetty if it is working less than 400 tons per day.

10. Port of Singapore Authority, PSA Tariff 1973, Item No. 13. The abatement is made in accordance with a dockage remission coefficient, which varies directly with the amount of cargo and inversely with time alongside and the GRT. Remission is given when the coefficient exceeds a minimum value.

The criterion for the best channel depth does depend upon the charging practices actually used to finance the expenditure on dredging. Furthermore the dredging may be considered a good thing by the world as a whole, but for the national interest, the issue is simply whether the net benefit accrues to residents, including the port authority. If the dredging is primarily to permit bulk carriers to use the port, then the lower cost of the bulkers generally will be passed on to the shippers; and for most developing countries, as argued above, these would be in the form of increased export prices and reduced import prices. Similarly any dredging charge would be shifted virtually intact to domestic nationals. This simplifies the incidence analysis greatly. But there are many ways to levy the dredging charge that have markedly different effects on the vessel composition of the service to the port.

It is normal practice for economists and management consultants to advise that the vessels requiring the deepest draft of the channel should pay for the additional cost of dredging. For example, if the channel is dredged to clear 40-foot vessels yet only (say) twenty vessels drawing 40 feet of water pass through the channel in a year, whereas all the others draw only 30 feet, then the twenty vessels should bear the cost of dredging the channel from 30 feet to 40 feet. This is thought to be some sort of principle of marginal cost pricing; those vessels that cause the cost pay.[11]

While such debates have substance for issues of equity and ability to pay, they are irrelevant for marginal cost pricing. Once a channel is dredged, or once it is decided to maintain a channel at a certain depth, then, unless the channel is congested, the marginal cost of the passage of a vessel, of whatever draft, is virtually zero. It is true that the wash from the larger or deeper or faster vessels may create conditions that require more frequent dredging to maintain the channel, but the evidence suggests that such additional dredging is minor

11. Ian Heggie, "Charging for Port Facilities," *Journal of Transport Economics and Policy*, vol. VIII, no. 1 (1972), pp. 15–16. This method of charging was also thought best by the U.K. Docks and Harbour Authorities Association. The principle seems to have been accepted also by the consultants advising on the tariff of the Port Authority of Thailand (Coopers and Lybrand Associates Limited, *Report on the Tariff Review*, Appendix G3). Such studies often point out the difficulties with levying charges according to actual draft. This value is difficult to interpret and to measure. And even though maximum draft figures are available from Lloyds, their relevance might be reasonably disputed when a vessel uses a port only half laden.

compared with the amount that is required to remove natural silting. Thus a useful approximation is that the passage of an additional ship of any draft less than the maximum of the channel will generate no additional costs.[12]

There are two important reasons for not penalizing the large ship by heavy channel dues. First, the large ship will exploit the economies of scale of ship size, and second, the large ship—particularly the bulk carrier—is operated on a competitive basis and provides a threat and a discipline to the conference operators. The first point is particularly important. It seems silly to dredge a deep channel only to charge such high fees for the very vessels that the channel was designed to accommodate that some are deterred from using the port. Charges must be designed not to discourage use, so that the port and population of the country may share in the economies of the large ship that the construction of the deeper channel has made possible. The second point is of considerable importance for countries such as Thailand or Canada that ship exports in bulk. The conference operators are to a large extent disciplined in their pricing policies by the competitive behavior of tramps and bulkers, and this competition is particularly important in the export trades of countries that ship large quantities of low-valued goods. Any discouragement to the competitors of the conference will encourage the conference to maintain high tariffs. Furthermore, it will provide an additional coherence to the conference structure and will discourage chiseling, the usual process by which conferences break down.

Marginal-Cost Pricing and Congestion Pricing: The Case of Storage Charges

Transit sheds are a major focus of port congestion. Thus the form and size of storage charges are particularly important elements of port tariffs. All the four ports allow a certain amount of free time, but the length of this free period varies: Singapore allows 3 days for imports and exports; Kelang also allows 3 days but computes them more generously and excludes holidays; Bangkok allows 3 days for imports but only 1 day for exports; and Chittagong allows imports 4 free days,

12. Pilot, tugboat, and other ancillary costs are excluded.

holidays excluded, but 15 days, excluding holidays, for exports. Some of these differences probably result from the situation of the ports. Chittagong is predominantly an import port, located quite far from the chief internal markets. At Bangkok, many of the exports are deposited first in private warehouses where they could stay in principle until the ship arrives without encumbering the port's facilities.[13] But storage absorbs resources. If practically all cargo always stays in port for at least X days, there would be a patent inconvenience if a separate charge were to be made for the unavoidable stay, and the cost should be recovered from a general charge. But this is clearly not the case: some cargo never enters the sheds. Therefore there is no good reason other than tradition of allowing free storage time after the vessel has concluded discharging operations.[14]

Port tariffs further differ in the size of the charge and in the progression of the charges with time elapsed. Singapore and Kelang levy relatively high charges expressly to clear their sheds. The time progression of the scales, however, shows great contrasts. The schedules in the tariffs of Singapore and Kelang thus contain daily rates which rise rapidly over the first 14 days and are then succeeded by a lower rate for any successive week. For example, for the Kelang Port Authority (1975), storage charges on imports in transit sheds and covered yard storage sheds, levied from the common landing date, excluding port holidays are:

	M$ per day per ton
4th day or part thereof	1.60
8th day	3.80
14th day	9.80
3rd and subsequent weeks, per week or part thereof	7.50

Storage rates in the tariffs of Bangkok and Chittagong, by contrast, escalate steadily to a level which then is maintained. For example,

13. A similar consideration accounts for an exception made in the allowance of free storage time at Kelang: only 1 day is allowed to goods loaded from private godowns.

14. We agree in this matter with the views expressed in United Nations, Conference on Trade and Development, Secretariat. *Port Pricing*, (TD/B/C.4/1110/Rev. 1) (New York, 1975), paragraphs 155 and 156.

for the Port Authority of Thailand (1974), charges for inward cargoes stored within or outside transit sheds are:

	Bht per day per ton
1st week	4.00
3rd week	6.00
8th week	11.00
9th and subsequent weeks	12.00

No generally valid rules can be established for the form of the storage tariff except that it should be consistent with the port's cost of storing goods. It seems to be generally accepted that port warehouse storage should be charged according to cost. There is no reason why transit sheds should be treated differently. If ships and cargo arrive at random, there is no reason why the daily charge should vary with the days of storage. On the other hand, if there is a regular flow of cargo arrival, marginal cost of storage rises with time, and there might be a case for escalating the daily rates; and so there would be if expected cost rises with length of storage. The most difficult scheme to rationalize is that practiced by Singapore and by Port Kelang. Rapidly escalating daily rates are appropriate in some circumstances as has been pointed out. The subsequent abatement of the daily charge, however, amounts to a quantity discount for space-days in the transit sheds. The argument that quick removal causes the largest cost to the shipper is true but irrelevant; what matters is the port's cost, not the shipper's, and that will be constant or rising each day the sheds are occupied.[15]

Loading Port Charges

A port that expects normally to operate with unexhausted economies of scale faces the problem of how to cover cost. If all prices are set at the level of marginal cost, there will be a deficit. If competition for port services is not perfect, the port may levy charges at a level that will cover fixed cost or at least that will contribute something towards it. The problem may be attacked by a multipart tariff such

15. Compare the discussion of the point in Coopers and Lybrand Associates Limited, *Report on the Tariff Review*, D.3 and following. Their reasoning is difficult to follow.

as discussed in Chapter 8, but this is the exception in conventional ports. The second best solution is to load some of its charges, and the problem is then to design the tariff (select charges for loading) so as not to discourage use of the port's facilities.

Port tariffs therefore contain general charges and specific charges. The general charges are unrelated to the use of specific services and act as a sort of cover charge which ships must pay if they wish to use the port at all. River or channel dues and cargo dues are the main examples of general charges. Specific charges are levied for services that cause an avoidable cost. Crane charges represent the class of specific charges.

Ports differ in their use of this form of tiered tariff. In Kelang the distinction is defined least clearly; the port, for example, levies no separate berth hire charge but merges it in the charge for wharf labor.[16] Bangkok, on the other hand, charges separately for the use of the wharf and uses a tapering scale: the initial payment of wharf rate entitles the vessel to stay for 72 hours, but additional time at the wharf is charged for at a lower rate per day.[17] This seems an attractive idea and corresponds to the method of charging for telephone calls in some countries: a high rate per minute for the first 3 minutes and less for additional minutes. But the rate is still tied to time: instead of buying a right to use the port or the wharf, the vessel buys time at the wharf. This method only seems safe if there are no grounds for expecting congestion, and that is not really the case of Bangkok. Moreover, the implicit quantity discount for time at the wharf works against ships equipped or organized for fast cargo working, against cargoes that tend to move fast and thus of bulked cargoes, and therefore against competitive vessels which should perhaps be given an incentive by the port tariff.[18]

The purpose of distinguishing between general and specific charges

16. Port Swettenham Authority, *Scale of Rates, Dues, and Charges, By-laws 1966*, Item 25.

17. Port Authority of Thailand, *Tariff of Port Charges, Port of Bangkok*, 4th ed. (Klong Toi, Bangkok, 1974), p. 5. A vessel of 4,000 NRT will thus pay Bht4,400 for the first 3 days and Bht1,200 for the fourth day (or Bht8,000 for 6 days).

18. These charges apply only to the wharves at Klong Toi. Bulk imports are discharged largely at private wharves within the port area. This point may, therefore, not be relevant to the case of Bangkok so much as to the general method which the tariff illustrates.

is to price certain underused facilities more nearly at marginal cost while still adhering to the normal rule that, as far as possible, cost should be covered for the port as a whole. Underused facilities can thus be priced at average cost for the capacity actually used; the cost of the unused part (say, forklifts or manhours) is treated as overhead cost and is transferred to the general charge. Whether this policy succeeds in its twin aims of improving the use of all the port's facilities and of raising its revenues will depend on whether the tariff makers have foreseen correctly all the possibilities of substitution. For instance, if the port has more equipment than is demanded even at peak times, the cost of the excess may be loaded on to port dues.[19] But if port dues are only payable on cargo worked across the wharf, ships can avoid the higher charge by discharging into lighters for direct delivery to the consignees. The one sure result would be to lower further the use of shore equipment. Alternatively, if port dues are levied on all cargo worked in the port's territory but at different rates for cargo discharged over the jetty or midstream, the pattern of vessel operations may again be altered to minimize the cost of discharging.

Basically similar questions about the effects of loading up port charges are raised by an example from the history of the Port of Bangkok tariff. Bangkok charged wharfage at the same rate per ton, irrespective of whether the cargo was discharged over the wharf (landside) or overside into lighters with the vessel standing in either case alongside the wharf. In 1973 the wharfage or cargo dues on cargo discharged overside were raised, on the recommendation of a consultant who had pointed out that by charging the same rate the port was losing revenue. This was happening because shore labor and equipment had to stand idle while the vessel discharged some of its cargo landside and another part overside and because cargo discharged landside also paid handling charges and often incurred storage charges as well.[20] But if a vessel discharging into lighters immobilizes shore labor and equipment, it should have paid for them at marginal cost. If more revenue was required, the charge for using the port or the wharf should have been raised for everyone, leaving it to the vessel to decide whether to discharge overside or over the wharf. It is at least

19. Coopers and Lybrand Associates Limited, *Report on the Tariff Review.*

20. W. D. Scott and Co. Pty. Ltd. *Final Report: Port Operations Consultancy Services.* Prepared for the Port Authority of Thailand, Port of Bangkok, Klong Toi, Bangkok. Sydney, June 1973. Processed, pp. 14–18.

possible that the recommendation would lead to an uneconomic substitution; this would have occurred if an increase in the amount of
cargo discharged over the wharf had raised the port's avoidable cost.

Price Discrimination in Port Tariffs[21]

Ports, as pointed out in Chapter 5, cannot control the way in which
the burden of their charges is distributed ultimately between ships
and shippers. This at least is the situation under competition. The
situation may seem to be different whenever liner conferences appear
to average out increases in the cost associated with a particular port
over the freight rates charged to all the ports within a certain range.
There are grounds, however, for believing that this equalizing practice
is only effective in the short run; in the longer run the relation between the shipping companies' cost and price in a particular port
should not be affected by this particular cartel policy.[22]

Price discrimination in the more normal sense, on the other hand,
is available readily to any port which does not operate under conditions of perfect competition. Ports exercise this power to discriminate
in various ways and in pursuit of many different objects—of fairness[23]
or national policy or port profits. Transshipment differentials are
made on commercial considerations (see Chapter 7), but the reduced
charges to ships engaged in local (near-distance or coastal) trades
contain an element of national policy.[24] Apart from transshipment
charges, however, the most interesting instances of differentiation are
between export and import cargoes and between different commodities. Price discrimination at Singapore is confined wholly to transshipment cargo. The examples are taken therefore from the port
tariffs of Bangkok, Chittagong, and Kelang.

21. Price discrimination was discussed in Chapters 6 and 7. The term is used
here in its technical sense of services produced at the same cost being sold at
different prices.

22. See Chapter 6, above.

23. An example is provided by the Chittagong port tariff which abates storage
charges for cargo held up in the port through delays caused by customs or for
other reasons that are not the shipper's fault. See Chittagong Port Trust, *Schedule
of Charges on Goods and Vessels*, section 9.

24. Instances of this treatment are found in the ports tariffs of Chittagong and
Port Kelang.

Exports versus imports

The three ports offer a variety of concessions to export traffic. At Bangkok, landing charges on inward cargoes and quay dues on outward cargoes are difficult to compare because they vary according to commodities. The ranges of these class rates are:

Landing (inward cargo)   Bht15–31.25 per cubic meter
Quay due (outward cargo)   Bht1.15–1.25 per cubic meter

Handling charges for export cargoes are levied at half the rate of imports. The free storage time for exports is just 1 day against 3 days for imports, but the storage rent for the first week after free time is Bht11.25 per cubic meter of export goods against Bht21 per cubic meter for imports.

At Chittagong, landing and shipping charges strongly favor exports. Summary comparisons are difficult because of differentiation by commodity. The residual class charges are:

Landing charge (goods charged freight by weight
in parcels less than 35 cwt)   Tk6.20 per ton
Shipping charge (all other goods, freight charged
by weight, parcel not exceeding 35 cwt)   Tk3.38 per ton

River dues (the equivalent of wharfage) are charged at Tk4.50 per ton on goods arriving from foreign ports and at Tk2.25 per ton on goods shipped abroad; raw jute is charged only Tk2.00 per ton. Free storage time is 4 days for imports and 15 days for exports, but storage rent for comparable classes is charged on imports at seven times the rate on exports. The port furthermore possesses punitive powers to charge four times the scheduled rent on imports but only three times the scheduled rate on exports.

At Kelang, free storage time is 3 days for imports but 7 days for exports; storage charges for imports are a multiple of those for exports. For example,

Imports
first 4 days after free time   M$1.60 per ton per day
tenth day after free time   M$5.80 per ton per day
Exports
first 14 days after free time   M$0.70 per ton per day

In some of these instances lower charges to exports may correspond to lower costs; imports and exports will often require different amounts or types of services because they tend to be presented to the port in different ways. Similarly, port resources are saved if ships can be dispatched quickly, and this depends on the presence of the export cargo when the ship is ready for loading. But cost differences cannot account for all these differences in charges, whether in terms of the type of charge (for example, river dues) or of the size of the difference (for example, handling or storage charges). To some extent the port is charging what the traffic will bear: exports tend on the whole to have a lower c.i.f. value per ton than the import cargoes of developing countries. But it is clear from investigations in the various ports that discrimination in favor of export cargo is meant to promote exports. At Chittagong it thus appears that while landing charges for several classes of commodities are always well above the labor rates paid by the port for shore handling, this is not so for all export commodities.[25] But it does not seem to be in the best national interest to channel aid to exporters through the ports, irrespective of whether the port has to recover cost or is allowed to operate at a deficit. If the provision of export subsidies is thus diffused, the control over the use of national resources is weakened. If states at the same time levy taxes on exports (for example, the Thai rice premium and the taxes on rubber in Malaysia and on raw jute in Bangladesh), the situation becomes distinctly confused.

Discrimination among commodities

Liner freight rates are differentiated according to commodities; in addition many rates are based on weight or volume, whichever will yield the larger revenue to the ship.[26] Commodity differentiation in freight tariffs exists also in the traditional railway tariffs and is im-

25. This conclusion emerges from comparing Chittagong Port Trust, *Schedule of Charges on Goods and Vessels*, with the Chittagong Port Trust, *Rate Schedule for Shore Handling Work for the Calendar Year 1975* (Chittagong, 1975, processed). The schedule lists the rates payable by the port to the shore-handling contractors—the stevedoring firms which have been selected by the ship and are employed thereupon by the port to undertake the shore handling.

26. If the freight rate is given as $5 W/M ($W = 1$ ton and $M = 40$ cubic feet) and if 1 ton of the commodity occupies 60 cubic feet, the shipper will pay $7.50 per ton to the ship.

bedded also in many port tariffs. Chittagong and especially Bangkok thus vary charges according to the class of the commodity.[27]

At Chittagong raw jute bears a lower river due than other export cargoes. Landing and shipping charges contain further differences between commodities, and some of the differences are patently unrelated to cost differences. Storage rent is differentiated similarly according to commodities. For example, rent on export cargo for cotton, hemp, and fiber, is Tk0.10 per bale per day; for jute manufactures is Tk0.15 per bale per day; and for tea is Tk1.50 per chest per week.

At Bangkok, landing charges (imports) and quay dues (exports) as well as handling charges are based on an elaborate commodity classification.[28] Landing charges consist of four class rates, ranging from Bht15 per cubic meter to Bht31.25 per cubic meter, and of seven special classes. The classification appears to have been based largely on the value of goods. For example, landing charge for antiseptics is the Class 2 rate and for perfumery and cosmetics is the higher Class 3 rate. The ranking of commodities in the classification for applying handling charges is not the same as for landing charges or quay dues.

The rates based on commodities reflect certain differences in the cost of handling and of port liability. Above all, however, they appear to reproduce rather than to counteract the ocean liner practice of charging what the traffic will bear. They reflect the value of the commodity within the limits imposed by competition from other ports or by other modes of transport. Container port tariffs normally do not discriminate according to value of commodity even though discrimination still persists in the freight rates of many container operators. If port charges for conventional break bulk cargo discriminate according to the value of commodities while containers are charged at a flat rate, the port encourages wittingly or unwittingly the containerization of high-value cargoes. In these cases, the shippers' decisions whether to containerize will not be based on the true cost.

27. In the Port Kelang tariff, the export shipping charge (payable by the cargo owner) for dry rubber is M\$5.00 per ton against M\$5.50 for other export goods. See Port Swettenham Authority, *Scale of Rates, Dues, and Charges By-laws*, 1975. Item 40.

28. The tariff recently proposed by Coopers and Lybrand Associates Limited does not differentiate between commodities.

Allocation of Resources by Rule

All port managers allocate some of the port's resources by rule rather than by pricing. In many cases this is sensible since allocation by pricing involves cost: the administrative cost of levying a charge and the cost of changing prices as the demand and supply situation in the port changes. Nonprice allocation thus will be economical in temporary situations of excess demand. For example, cranes and other heavy lift equipment then may get shared out equally between users. It would not be sensible to try to auction them off at such times. But there are other and more permanent problems of allocation that ports tend to solve by nonprice methods but where the advantages of allocation by rule are less obvious. Allocation by rule is resorted to when there are conflicting demands for scarce resources. This confers a benefit on the recipient of the resource and results in a loss for the one whose request is denied. Two conclusions follow. First, the beneficiary of the rule gains from being given access to a scarce resource without having to pay for it. The owner of the scarce resource (the port) does not obtain the benefit; if it did it could either use the revenue to expand the facility or to reduce charges elsewhere in the port. Second, there is no certainty that the gain obtained by the beneficiary exceeds the loss to the one who was ruled out. Whether the revenue position of the port or of ships and shippers is considered, the outcome of allocation by rule thus is not normally very satisfactory. Allocation by rule—in small things as in big—can create unwholesome temptations. If prices were used instead of rules, the gains from the scarce resource would be obtained by the port, and the resource would be allocated to that user who places the greatest value on it.

Among the various instances of nonprice allocation practiced by ports, berth allocation seems a possible candidate for the introduction of pricing. In the allocation of berths the rule first-come-first-served is widely practiced, but there are many exceptions. In Bangkok and Chittagong, for example, import vessels tend to get preference over others, such as vessels arriving in ballast for loading. At Kelang, the North Port tends to give preference to container mother ships and secondly to ships carrying more than seventy-five containers. In the South Port, ocean berth preference is given apparently to liquid carriers.[29] A recent feasibility study which proposed the construction of new timber wharves also recommended that bulk timber carriers should be given priority at these wharves. The recommendation was based on the argument that time is more costly for these specialized carriers than for general carriers and that delays to timber carriers would lead to the greater increase in freight rates. Container terminals have similar priority rules: the largest vessels get served first.

These few examples point to various reasons for berth preference. Ships thus are given preference in the berths most suitable for servicing them, which means either that the port's cost of servicing them in that berth is lower than elsewhere or that the ship's cost is minimized. Alternatively, preference is given to the ship for which delay would be most expensive.[30] In yet other circumstances, the experienced port manager will give preference to the vessel that will discharge and load fastest, holding off the slower vessels.

Berth allocation is a continuing activity, and differences in the layout and equipment of berths are fixed features of the port. The use of price to take some of the strain of allocation by rule therefore may be particularly appropriate. The cases cited contain their own prescriptions; where the ship is indifferent between different berths but the port is not, lower the relative price of this berth to this type of ship. Where a type of ship prefers one particular berth, raise the relative price of that berth.

It is not always easy to price a resource so as to obviate the need for regular allocation by rule. If the price is set too high, the resource will be underused; if too low, the price cannot perform the allocation. While port prices need not perhaps be fixed as rigidly as they tend to be—and certainly not for such long periods—frequent changes are costly, and auctioning is impracticable. If the need for allocation by rule can be reduced somewhat by pricing, there is reason enough to be satisfied.[31]

29. Berths 4 and 5 are pumping berths.
30. That is the full import ship at Chittagong or the large container ship at Singapore or Kelang.
31. Even so, some facilities in some ports will have to continue to be allocated by rule because of sharp, frequent, and irregular fluctuations in demand which leave them alternately standing idle and in excess demand.

Glossary

Port and Shipping Terms

All-in charges: Single charge for all services.

Alongside: With the vessel standing at the quay or jetty, the cargo is moved from ship direct to surface of quay (or in inverse direction). Opposite: **overside.**

Berth: Section of quay (pier, wharf, or jetty) notionally designed to accommodate one vessel and including a section of the surface over which labor, equipment, and cargo move to and from the vessel. By transference, in shipowner's language, service to a port.

Berthing fee (or charge): A charge levied by certain ports on the vessel to pay for the use of the berth (and not always payable, or fully payable, if the ship stays mid-stream).

Break-bulk (cargo): Cargo packed in separate packages (lots or consignments) or individual pieces of cargo, loaded, stowed, and unloaded individually; as distinct from bulk cargo.

Bulk carriers; bulker: Ship designed to carry bulk, nonliquid cargo.

CFS: Container freight station.

Channel: Passage of water leading to the port that is normally dredged and policed by the port authority.

Channel dues: Charge levied (on the vessel) for using the channel.

Charter rate: Payment by charterer (such as cargo owner) to shipowner for the charter of the vessel. It is determined by market conditions and terms of charter.

c.i.f.: Cost + insurance + freight. This corresponds in principle to the landed price of shipments before tax.

Coaster: Ship that plies between coastal ports on the same coast or archipelago or in interisland trades.

Conference (liner or steamship conference): A combination (technically, a cartel) of shipping companies (or owners) which sets common liner freight rates on a particular route and which regulates the provision of services.

Conservancy authority: Regulates navigation in channels and port. It is also charged with the maintenance of banks and dredging and generally with the safety of vessels using the river, channel, or port, and occasionally also with the provision and maintenance of navigational aids.

Cranage: A port charge levied for the use of cranes. It is paid by ship or cargo owner or by both parties in certain proportions according to the customs of the port.

cwt: Hundred weight, 112 lbs.

Decasualization of dock labor: Policy implemented in various countries to depart from the system of casual (daily hired) dock labor toward a regularly employed labor force that is subject to the usual terms of employment and job security. In several countries, dock labor under this system is employed not by the port but by a separate body (dock labor board).

DWT: Dead weight tonnage. The weight in long tons that a vessel can carry when fully laden.

FCL: Full container load; a container that is delivered to the shipping company full of the consignor's cargo. The meaning changes according to who uses the term; ports may describe containers as FCL if they leave the port's area without having been unstuffed (or stripped).

Feeder (service): Transport of containers which are first carried by the main line container vessel to a port of transshipment, unloaded, and then loaded on a smaller vessel for feeding to a further port. Feeder service implies transshipment.

f.o.b.: Free on board. In the case of ocean carriage it means the value of the goods (including the value of packing) when placed on board the vessel. It includes such charges as the shipper had to pay to the port but excludes cargo insurance (and freight) and corresponds only approximately to market value in the exporting country.

Freight tons: A heterogeneous unit for counting cargo or traffic in liner shipping. It is based on the rules by which freight rates are assessed. For cargo paid by weight tons, the weight ton (long, short, or metric) is a freight ton. For cargo paid for by measurement tons (for example, 40 cubic feet), the measurement ton is the freight ton.

General cargo: Cargo, not homogeneous in bulk, which consists of individual units or packages (parcels).

GRT: Gross register tonnage, a measure of the total space of a vessel in terms of 100 cubic feet (equivalent tons) including mid-deck, between deck, and the closed-in spaces above the upper deck, less certain exemptions. The GRT of most of the world's ships is recorded in Lloyds Register. See also, **NRT** and **DWT**.

Hook: Loading and discharging point along a vessel; the hook is lowered by ship's derrick or crane to receive the net holding the cargo. Hence, hook hours, the base of a measure of port output (cargo tons moved per hook hour).

Landing charges: A charge levied by certain ports on the cargo-owner for receiving and handling imports. The corresponding charge for exports is called **shipping charge**.

Lash: Lighter aboard ship. This is a technique of water transport by which cargo is loaded on barges which are in turn taken up by an ocean vessel which transports them and ultimately releases them to carry the cargo into port.

LCL: Less than container load; cargo destined for shipment in a container that is delivered by the consignor for consolidation with other cargo and insertion in a container by the shipping company at a container freight station.

Measurement ton: A unit of quantity of cargo based on its cubic measurement (for example, 40 cubic foot or 1 cubic meter).

n.i.e.: Not indicated elsewhere. This term is applied to goods or services in port tariffs.

NRT: Net register tonnage, the **GRT** minus the spaces that are non-earning—machinery, permanent bunkers, water ballast, and crew quarters. Over the range 0 to 6,000 **NRT** there is a reasonably good correlation between **NRT** and **DWT: DWT** = 2.5 **NRT**.

One-off visit: A nonroutine or nonschedule call at a port.

Overside: Cargo being loaded or unloaded from ship into barges standing along the vessel. Opposite: **alongside**.

Palet (palette): Tray or other solid base on which cargo is loaded for loading or unloading; a form of **unitized** cargo (paletized). Palet ships are designed to carry cargo piled on palets.

Port dues: A charge levied by certain ports on the vessel or cargo.

Quay charges (rent): A port charge levied on the vessel for the use of the quay.

Roads (Singapore): Water passages or stopping places in the port's area for vessels working cargo overside or waiting for berth.

Roll-on/roll-off: Cargo carried in wheeled containers or wheeled trailers aboard and moving on to the ship and off it on wheels, usually over ramps.

Ship measurements: Measures of cubic capacity, in tons of 100 cubic feet; see **GRT, NRT,** and **DWT**.

Shipping charges: See **landing charges**.

Stevedore: Labor employed to load and unload cargo and, by transference, the organizer of this work. In many ports, stevedores only work aboard ships for the account of vessel or cargo-owner, and work ashore is done by the port's labor.

TEU: Twenty-foot equivalent unit. Standard unit for counting (equivalent) containers of various dimensions: 20 x 8 x 8 feet; in other words, a 20-foot equivalent container.

Trampers (Tramps): Nonsheduled, nonconference vessels.

Transit shed: A shed in the port area, usually in customs-bonded area, which is positioned behind the berth to receive cargo unloaded from vessel or for loading. Distinct from warehouse.

Unitized cargo: Cargo packed in units for easy presentation to vessel and port; for example, containered cargo and paletized cargo.

Wharfage: A charge levied by some ports on the cargo owner for the use of the port surface over which the cargo moves.

Domestic Currency Rates per Unit of Special Drawing Rights

	1971	1973	1975	1977
Bangladesh (Tk)	8.068	9.891	17.373	17.486
Thailand (Bht)	22.721	24.579	23.882	24.780
Malaysia (M$)	3.133	2.958	3.030	2.873
Singapore (S$)	3.149	2.999	2.914	2.841
India (Rp)	7.833	9.808	10.462	9.971
United Kingdom (£)[a]	2.351	1.926	1.729	1.569
United States ($)	1.086	1.206	1.224	1.162

Note: Special drawing rights (SDRs) are defined in terms of a weighted average of the sixteen most important currencies in world trade.

a. In SDR per £ sterling.

References

The word *processed* indicates works that are reproduced by mimeograph, Xerox, or another manner other than conventional typesetting and printing.

All India Shippers Council. *Fourth Annual Report for the Year 1970.* New Delhi, 1971.

Bennathan, E., and Direk Malakon. "Survey of Vessels in the Port of Bangkok (Klong Toi and Private Wharves) during Four Selected Weeks between November 1966 and August 1967." Bangkok, 1970. Processed.

Bennathan, E., and A. A. Walters. *The Economics of Ocean Freight Rates.* Praeger Special Studies in International Economics and Development. New York: Praeger, 1969.

Bennathan, E., A. A. Walters, and others. *The Cost of Ocean Transport in the Foreign Trade of Asia.* Processed.

Blake, D. J., E. Bennathan, and A. A. Walters. "Survey of Vessels in the Port of Singapore (Roads and Wharves) during One Week in September 1966." Bristol, 1970. Processed.

Canadian Transport Commission, Systems Analysis Branch, *The Container Study in Summary.* Report 70. Principal authors, P. M. Bunting and L. M. O'Connell. Ottawa, November 1973.

Chittagong Port Trust. *Budget Estimates of Income and Expenditure for 1975–1976 with Revised Estimates for 1974–1975.* Chittagong, 1975.

Chittagong Port Trust. *Rate Schedule for Shore Handling Work for the Calendar Year 1975.* Chittagong, 1975. Processed.

Chittagong Port Trust. *Schedule of Charges on Goods and Vessels*. Corrected up to notification no. CAO-IV(98)/7534, January 29, 1975. *Bangladesh Gazette*. Chittagong, 1975.

Chittagong Port Trust. *Statement of Cargo Handled at Chittagong Port during the Period from July 1974 to June 1975*. Processed.

Coase, R. H. "The Economics of the Lighthouse." *Journal of Law and Economics*, vol. 18, no. 1 (April 1975), pp. 25–31.

Containerization International (London), vol. 9, no. 11 (November 1975), p. 25.

Coode and Partners, Economist Intelligence Unit, and L. E. Taylor. *Port Swettenham Improvement Scheme. 1968 Pre-Investment Feasibility Study*. Prepared for the Honourable Minister of Transport, Government of Malaysia. London, 1968.

Coopers and Lybrand Associates Limited in association with Sir Bruce White, Wolfe Barry and Partners, and Shankland Cox Partnership. "Lembaga Pelabohan Kelang. Port Development Feasibility Study." Final Report, 2 vols. August 1974.

Coopers and Lybrand Associates Limited. *Report on the Tariff Review*. Prepared for the Port Authority of Thailand. London, January 8, 1975.

Dally, H. K. "Containers—a Note on Berth Throughputs and Terminal Handling." *National Ports Council Bulletin* (London), no. 4 (April 1973), pp. 60–65.

Daniel, Mann, Johnson, and Mendenhall; Louis Berger. *Development of the Ports of Sattahip and Da Nang and of Route 9*. Study conducted on behalf of the Southeast Asian Coordinating Committee for Transportation and Communications at the request of the Governments of Laos, South Vietnam, and Thailand. Contract AIR/SA/IR-197 (Regional). Los Angeles, March 1973.

Deakin, B. M. *Shipping Conferences*. University of Cambridge, Department of Applied Economics Occasional Papers no. 37. Cambridge: Cambridge University Press, 1973.

Deakin, B. M. "Shipping Conferences: Some Economic Aspects of International Regulation." *Maritime Studies and Management*, vol. 2, no. 1 (July 1974), pp. 5–31.

Directorate of Transport Research, Ministry of Shipping and Transport, Government of India. *Port Transport Statistics of India*. New Delhi, March 1971.

Economist Intelligence Unit Limited in association with Scott Wilson Kirkpatrick and Partners. *Bangladesh Transport Survey*. Final report. Prepared for the Government of the Peoples Republic of Bangladesh under assignment by the Overseas Development Administration of the Foreign and Commonwealth Office. Part 9, Management and Financial Studies. London, November 1974.

Economist Intelligence Unit in association with Wallace Evans and Partners, Consulting Civil and Structural Engineers. *The Containerization of Thailand's Sea Trade.* Prepared for the Government of Thailand, Ministry of Communications, 1973.

Fellner, W. "Prices and Wages under Bilateral Monopoly." *Quarterly Journal of Economics,* vol. 61 (August 1947), pp. 503–32.

Government of Pakistan, Ministry of Communications (Railway Division). *General Rules and Schedules for Working of the Chittagong Port (Railway) Jetties* (in force January 1, 1959). *Gazette of Pakistan.* Karachi, December 15, 1958.

Heaver, Trevor D. "The Routing of Canadian Container Traffic through Vancouver and Seattle." Study prepared for the Western Transportation Advisory Council and the Centre for Transportation Studies of the University of British Columbia. Vancouver, B.C.: WESTAC, January 1975.

Heggie, Ian. "Charging for Port Facilities." *Journal of Transport Economics and Policy,* vol. 8, no. 1 (1972), pp. 15–16.

Houthakker, H. S., and S. P. Magee. "Income and Price Elasticities in World Trade." *The Review of Economics and Statistics,* vol. 51, no. 2 (May 1969), pp. 111–25.

Israel Shipping Research Institute, Freight Research Division. *Information Paper,* no. 30 (November–December 1973); no. 31 (January 1974); no. 32 (February 1974); no. 33 (March 1974); and no. 46 (April 1975). Haifa: Israel Shipping Research Institute.

Kelang Port Authority. *Annual Report 1974.* Kelang, 1975.

Laing, E. T. "The Costs of Deep Sea General Cargo Shipping." Marine Transport Center, University of Liverpool, June 1974. Processed.

Louis Berger International, Inc. "Feasibility Study, Port of Chittagong Expansion, Bangladesh." Study prepared for the Asian Development Bank and Chittagong Port Trust. 2 vols. December 1974. Processed.

Martinez, Miguel. "Distribution of Benefits of Port Improvements: Case Study of the Port of La Goulette (Tunisia)." Study prepared for the World Bank, 1976. Processed.

McCaul, James R., Robert B. Zubaly, and Edward V. Lewis. "Increasing the Productivity of U.S. Shipping." Paper read at the Spring Meeting, Williamsburg, Va., May 24–27, 1972, no. 3. New York: the Society of Naval Architects and Marine Engineers, 1972.

Organization for Economic Cooperation and Development (OECD). "Ocean Freight Rates as Part of Total Transport Costs." Paris, 1968.

Plumlee, Carl H. "Optimum Size Seaport." *Journal of the Waterways and Harbors Division.* Proceedings of the American Society of Civil Engineers. vol. 92, no. WW3 (August 1966), pp. 1–24.

Port Authority of Thailand. Port Operations Department. *Port Operations Statistics 1974.* Bangkok, 1975.

Port Authority of Thailand. *Tariff of Port Charges, Port of Bangkok.* 2d ed. (1966); 4th ed. (1974). Klong Toi, Bangkok.

Port of Singapore Authority. *PSA Tariff 1973.* Singapore, 1973.

Port of Singapore Authority. *Report and Accounts for the Year Ended 31 December, 1974.* Singapore, 1975.

Port Swettenham Authority. *Scale of Rates, Dues, and Charges, By-laws, 1966,* incorporating amendments up to April 18, 1974 and *By-laws 1975,* incorporating changes applied in 1975 and proposed for 1976.

Producers Boards' Shipping Utilization Committee, New Zealand. *New Zealand's Overseas Trade: Report on Shipping, Ports, Transport, and Other Services.* Wellington and London, February 1964.

Ray, Anandarup, and James W. Loudon. "Central American Ports Study." World Bank Economic Staff Working Paper, no. 117. Washington, D.C.: World Bank, October 1971.

Robinson, Joan. *The Economics of Imperfect Competition.* London: Macmillan, 1933.

Scott, W. D., and Co. Pty. Ltd. *Final Report: Port Operations Consultancy Services.* Prepared for the Port Authority of Thailand, Port of Bangkok, Klong Toi, Bangkok. Sydney, June 1973. Processed.

Shoup, D. *Ports and Economic Development.* Washington, D.C.: Brookings Institution, 1967.

United Nations, Conference on Trade and Development, Secretariat. *Port Pricing.* (TD/B/C.4/1110/Rev. 1). New York, 1975.

United Nations, Conference on Trade and Development. *United Nations Conference of Plenipotentiaries on a Code of Conduct for Liner Conferences.* vols. 1 and 2. New York, 1975.

United Nations, Economic and Social Council, Economic Commission for Latin America, ECLA/OAS Joint Transport Programme. *Maritime Freight Rates in the Foreign Trade of Latin America.* part I (E/CN.12/812/Rev. 1) and part II (E/CN.12/812/Add. 1). New York, 1970. Processed.

United Nations Industrial Development Organization. *Guidelines for Project Evaluation.* New York, 1972.

United States Congress, Subcommittee on Federal Procurement and Regulation of the Joint Economic Committee. *Discriminatory Ocean Freight Rates and the Balance of Payments.* Hearing. 89th Cong., 1st sess., June 30, 1965. Washington, D.C.: U.S. Government Printing Office, 1965.

Vanags, A. H. "Flag Discrimination: an Economic Analysis." *Advances in Maritime Economics,* ed. R. O. Goss. Cambridge: Cambridge University Press, 1977.

Vanags, A. H. "Maritime Congestion." *Advances in Maritime Economics,* ed. R. O. Goss. Cambridge: Cambridge University Press, 1977.

Walker, Gilbert. "Transport Policy before and after 1953." *Oxford Economic Papers,* New Series, vol. 5, no. 1 (March 1953), pp. 1–33.

Walters, A. A. "A Development Model of Transport." *American Economic Review,* Papers and Proceedings, vol. 58, no. 2 (May 1968), pp. 360–77.

Walters, A. A. *Economics of Road User Charges.* World Bank Staff Occasional Papers, no. 5. Baltimore: Johns Hopkins Press, 1968.

Walters, A. A. "Marginal Cost Pricing in Ports." *The Logistics and Transportation Review,* vol. 12, no. 3 (1975).

Walters, A. A. Review of *Advances in Maritime Economics. Journal of Political Economy* (April 1979).

Walters, A. A. "The Theory and Measurement of the Private and Social Costs of Highway Congestion." *Econometrica,* vol. 29 (1961). Reprinted in *Readings in Economics of Transport,* ed. Dennis Munby. Harmondsworth: Penguin, 1969.

Index

Aden, 86
AFTE. *See* Annual fee to enter
All-in charges: defined, 215
All India Shippers' Council, 95n
Anglo-Saxon doctrine: defined, 3–4
Annual fee to enter (AFTE): for bulkers, 11; for charter vessels, 11, 185–86; congestion and, 183; dredging cost defrayed by, 11, 183; for liner conferences, 11, 184–87; for one-off caller, 11, 184, 186; quantity discount system for, 11, 184–87; ship size and, 183; for tramps, 185–86. *See also* Channel dues

Bangkok, 98n, 166, 196–97; discrimination in tariffs at, 209–10, 212–13; feeder lines and, 169, 171; fractional freight charge at, 193; labor for moving cargo at, 15; liner conferences and, 73, 145–46; port tariffs at, 88; quantity discount system for, 187; storage charges at, 204–05; tiered tariff at, 207–08
Basrah (Iraq)), 89n
Bennathan, Esra, 29n, 79n, 86n, 94n, 135n
Berthing fee: defined, 215
Berths: congestion in, 82–85, 86n, 87; container throughput and condition of, 20, 55, 57, 87; cost according to type, 20, 55–57; defined, 215; feeder service and, 20; NRT ship capacity

and, 12–13; port size and, 51; pricing base for, 12–13, 22, 199–201; tramps and, 201; turnaround time in, 201. *See also* Quays
Bombay, 90, 157
Break-bulk cargo: defined, 215. *See also* Cargo
Bulk carriers: AFTE for, 11; channel dues for, 13, 203–04; defined, 215; discrimination against, 10, 137, 143–44, 201; freight rates of, 91–93; LAQ and, 11; liner conferences and, 79, 137. *See also* Charter vessels; Tramps

Calcutta, 86, 135
Cargo: break-bulk, 16, 22, 145, 215; bulk, 145, 201; dry bulk, 16, 145; unitized, 16, 29. *See also* Container vessels
Cargo handling: competitive port model for, 16–25; congestion indicator and, 82–83, 85, 87, 89; container services and, 15, 22, 163, 171–76, 194; for feeder lines, 163; port size and, 51; pricing of, 22–23, 201–02; turnaround time for, 13. *See also* Labor
Cartels. *See* Shipowners (monopolist)
Chalna (Bangladesh), 86, 151
Channel dues: based on GRT, 199; based on NRT, 12, 197, 199–200, 202; for bulkers, 13, 203–04; defined, 216; dredging cost defrayed by, 202–

225